Since its inception, *Nokoko*, the journal of Carleton University's Institute of African Studies, set out to build theory about Africa in which the continent, its people and diaspora, are the priority. The work has always been international, grounded in the politics of solidarity and empathy. Now *Daraja Press* has collected selected articles from its first five issues in book form. A wide range of contributors, representing different generations and Africans and Canadians, present fresh and novel takes on range of topics and subjects, including gender, migration, political economy, economic governance, and social movements, among others. The result is a series of accessible and well-argued contributions on urgent political questions. Particularly poignant is that one of the editors, Pius Adesamni, tragically died in a plane crash as they were finalizing the book. (The afterword by fellow editor Blair Rutherford contains a tribute to Adesanmi's genius.) The book is a worthy testament to the journal's contribution to decolonizing African scholarship as well as to Adesanmi's extraordinary life and intellectual contributions.
**Sean Jacobs**, Founder and Editor of *Africa is a Country* and Associate Professor of International Affairs at The New School.

Scholarly and genuinely compassionate, Africa Matters deploys cross-pollinated methodologies to imaginatively present both the positive and the challenging realities of quotidian lives in Africa. The book's significance lies beyond pointing attention to what we must know, but to how knowledge supplies the path to critical dialogue and mature interventionist strategies to affirm both the value of life itself, as well as suggesting how productive collective lives can energize actions with transformational effects.
**Toyin Falola,** The Jacob and Frances Sanger Mossiker Chair in the Humanities, University of Texas at Austin

# Africa Matters

# Africa Matters

Cultural politics, political economies,
& grammars of protest

Edited by

Pius Adesanmi and Blair Rutherford

**Daraja Press**

OTTAWA

Published by Daraja Press
https://darajapress.com

© 2019 Institute of African Studies, Carleton University, Ottawa, Ontario, Canada
All rights reserved

ISBN 9781988832319 (softcover)
ISBN 9781988832326 (ebook)

Cover design: Kate McDonnell

**Publisher's comments**: Apart from the Introduction and Afterword, the text of the chapters here were originally published in *Nokoko*, the journal of the Institute of African Studies, Carleton University, Ottawa, Ontario, Canada. We have taken the liberty of making corrections to the original versions, and in some cases undertaking light editing of tenses where appropriate to reflect that this version was published in 2019. Our thanks to Emma Bider for proof corrections.

**Library and Archives Canada Cataloguing in Publication**
Title: Africa matters : cultural politics, political economies and grammar of protest / edited by Pius Adesanmi & Blair Rutherford.
Other titles: Africa matters (2019)
Names: Adesanmi, Pius, editor. | Rutherford, Blair A. (Blair Allan), 1965- editor.
Identifiers: Canadiana (print) 20190082763 | Canadiana (ebook) 2019008281X | ISBN 9781988832319 (softcover) | ISBN 9781988832326 (ebook)
Subjects: LCSH: Africa—Social conditions—21st century. | LCSH: Africa—Politics and government—21st century. | LCSH: Africa—Economic conditions—21st century.
Classification: LCC DT14 .A47 2019 | DDC 960.3/3—dc23

# Contents

Introduction: On the matter of African matters     1
Blair Rutherford and Pius Adesanmi

Two cities: Guangzhou / Lagos     13
    Wendy Thompson Taiwo

Catherine Acholonu (1951- 2014): The female writer as a goddess     37
    Nduka Otiono

Filming home, plurality of identity, belonging and homing in transnational African cinema     57
    Suvi Lensu

'Spare Tires', 'Second Fiddle' and 'Prostitutes'? Interrogating discourses about women and politics in Nigeria     79
    Grace Adeniyi-Ogunyankin

The South African Reserve Bank and the telling of monetary stories     99
    Elizabeth Cobbett

The neoliberal turn in the SADC: Regional integration and disintegration     119
    Jessica Evans

Indian hair, the after-temple-life: Class, gender and race representations of the African American woman in the human hair industry     137
    Nadège Compaore

The role of radio and mobile phones in conflict situations: The case of the 2008 Zimbabwe elections and xenophobic attacks in Cape Town     155
    Wallace Chuma

The story of Cape Town's two marches: Personal reflections on going home     171
    Stephanie Urdang

| | |
|---|---|
| Beyond an epistemology of bread, butter, culture and power: Mapping the African feminist movement<br>    Sinmi Akin-Aina | 177 |
| Setting the agenda for our leaders from under a tree: The People's Parliament in Nairobi<br>    Wangui Kimari and Jacob Rasmussen | 193 |
| Politics across boundaries: Pan-Africanism: Seeds for African unity<br>    Gacheke Gachihi | 211 |
| Afterword: Incorporeal words: The tragic passing of Pius Adesanmi<br>    Blair Rutherford | 213 |
| About the contributors | 217 |
| About the Institute of African Studies | 221 |
| Nokoko podcasts | 223 |

# Introduction: On the matter of African matters

Blair Rutherford and Pius Adesanmi

In the opening shots of the 2019 documentary *Système K*, the camera follows a middle-aged dreadlocked man meandering through the crowded and often decrepit streets of Kinshasa. At one point, he bends down, digs around the debris on the ground and pulls out a discarded bullet case, which he keeps. Shortly afterwards the camera shows him entering through a metal gate into a courtyard full of arresting sculptures of two or so metres high male and female bodies lined up against a wall, constructed out of old bullet cases and rusty cutlery. We soon find out that this *bricoleur* is Freddy Tsimba, one of the few Kinshasa artists profiled in this film who has "made it," in terms of finding an actual market for some of his work beyond the Democratic Republic of Congo.[1] But in the film his sculptures join that of other innovative creators, including performance artists whose bodies become the jarring work – bedecked in astronaut outfits made from scraps ("a Congolese man in space, Kinshasa space"), rolling in the filth and puddles of the roads, hotwax dripping down on one or blood on another which he pours over himself as he stands unsteadily in an old bathtub fastened with wheels being dragged over the potholed roads by a small group of men, and so on – in the streets of a *quartier* of Kinshasa, trying to disturb the numbness of many riding in the *fula fula* ("quick quick," commuter-taxi minibuses and trucks), commercial trucks, private autos or weaving through crowds of pedestrians. In Kinshasa—an urbanscape whose "constant energy and movement," entangled in a series of "invisible cities" which resist "objectification, colonization … and constantly out of focus" (de Boek and Plissart 2004: 8)—the boundary between art and quotidian life, one of the artist adds, is quite porous for simply trying to survive in this city of more than ten million with limited public investments is like creating art itself.

While recognizing that many of us involved in this book are like Renaud Barret, the Kinshasa-based French film director of *Système K,* and are in relatively privileged positions in our various communities around the world, we nonetheless all have striven in varied ways and forms to both show how wider projects, forces, and processes affecting and shaping African geographies, livelihoods, and imaginaries are understood, embodied and reworked from these street-level lives. And, equally important, to critically find ways to unsettle, to call out, and condemn the range of inequalities, terrors, and miseries historically and contemporaneously woven into the soils, political economies, and human and nonhuman beings of Africa and its diasporas thanks to particular configurations of colonial and postcolonial, localized, national and transnational power dynamics and social relationships.

Through their analyses, the contributors to this book in their own way are

---

1. See, for example, his website: http://www.freddytsimba.com/

examining different forms of agency Africans on the continent and in its diasporas deploy against, through, or are even complicit with, the inequalities and injustice pervading our world, as a way to critically reflect on what could or should be. In so doing, their analyses show something new, novel, if not surprising and interesting; expressions associated with the Ga word, *nokoko*, which is the name of the open-access journal in which they were originally published.

*Africa Matters: Cultural politics, political economies, & grammars of protest* brings together insightful articles from the first five issues of *Nokoko*, the journal of the Institute of African Studies at Carleton University in Ottawa, Canada. Since its establishment in 2009, the only stand-alone academic department with a sole focus on African Studies in Canada has helped to galvanize a greater focus on Africa. Refashioning an open-access journal gifted to the new Institute by one of its founding members, Professor Daniel Osabukle, the *Journal of Pan-African Wisdom* then became *Nokoko*, with a renewed commitment to bring a range of views and voices in and on "Africa," some of who are just emerging, all of whose insights are fresh and challenging.

This sampling of articles from *Nokoko* brings together some of the pieces that for the editorial board of the journal are particularly perspicacious in their analysis and resonant in their crafting. Grouping them in this book permits a new dialogue to emerge around the key themes of cultural politics, political economies and grammars of protest. Their intersection here provides a sharp spotlight on some of the seams, knots, and contestations of varied "matters" of import for many Africans in the twenty-first century.

As a verb ("Africa matters to…"), the authors contribute to teasing out the varied ways "Africa" is increasingly important in economies, politics, and daily lives for many outside of the continent of Africa even if, perversely, there is a deeper sense for more and more in different parts of Africa of abjection, of rejection by their governments and corporations and a generalized indifference by those in the Global North and international institutions (Ferguson 2006). As African Studies scholars, if not pan-Africanists, the contributors all are committed to demonstrating why Africa matters in light of the ongoing historicized marginalization of the states, peoples, and sociocultural dynamics from many discussions of so-called global processes and trends: showing, for instance, that not only did much of the wealth that drove the industrial revolution in western Europe come through the exploitative and deadly Atlantic slave trade and the colonial economies in the Americas fuelled by the unfree labour but also the wealth continues to flow out of Africa to Europe, North America, and Asia to the tune of tens of billions of dollars annually through unequal transfer pricing agreements with offshore firms, tax avoidance, and other schemes (Africa Progress Panel 2013). "Africa matters" also in international football and cosmopolitan music and fashion trends, migration patterns and debates, literatures, climate change scenarios and consequences, conservation practices and movements, and securitization infrastructures and panics, among other transnational configurations, apparati and desires enabling new and continued political economies, sociocultural networks, and hegemonies. In other words, we are pointing out that despite apparent indifference and neglect by institutions and opinion leaders that take "the world" as their remit, this continent has been vitally important to a plethora of worldwide processes and imaginaries.

And yet we are adamant that our demonstration of the importance of Africa on a planetary scale does not blind us to the growing economic misery and despair in many parts of Africa. While donor reports declare that the absolute poverty rate in Africa has declined over the last few decades, even these typically sanguine declarations of the importance of the neoliberal policy these organizations promote still show that the number of Africans living in poverty, illiteracy rates remain unchanged and incidences of violence across the continent are on the rise (World Bank 2016). Moreover, even their claims about declining absolute poverty are disputable, in part due to questionable statistical methodologies and analyses deployed to neglect the growing economic inequalities in Africa and beyond (Hickel 2016, 2018). The African Union has created a commendable vision in its Agenda 2063 documents (African Union 2015), but from South Africa to Algeria, Zimbabwe to Eritrea, Lesotho to Nigeria, Burundi to Guinea Bissau, jobs are scarce, government bodies and other institutional nodes of authority are more apt to close down channels of expression and debate, sometimes violently, than enhancing or enabling them and many African populations that are increasingly tapped into social media worlds and connected to family and friends living abroad thanks to the ubiquity of cellphones are feeling left behind.

And it is here in its nounal form ("some African matters include…"), that the chapters in *Africa Matters* trace some of the forms, objects, and lives of differently constituted groups, polities and communities within African and its diasporas. The Africa matters here range from fashion to literature, entrepreneurs to monetary policy, regional administrative bodies to feminist movements, cellphones to cinema, xenophobic violence to political activism. Through incisive analyses of some of these sociocultural lives, objects, ideas and ideals helping to constitute socialities, polities, economies, and imaginaries within and of the continent and its diasporas, the authors of this book provide more enriched understandings of them.

And it is through examining the intersection of these two senses of matters—how explicitly and implicitly "Africa" matters in international, transnational and national domains of policy, activism, and popular culture that in turn help to provide new or different valuations on different matter that become, in part or whole, "African"—that the contributions to this book bring to the foreground. By examining different palimpsests in these intersections—be it the traces of the discursive and nondiscursive that revalue certain ideas, objects, geographies as matters that seem to stand on their own or how different material and nonmaterial items animate the political and intellectual analyses, cultural productions, and economic flows—that these chapters highlight different indexical and iconic moves and socio-political stakes at various scales that are not always apparent.

Let us touch on three such palimpsests one finds threaded through this volume before we briefly examine each chapter.

"African migrants" have screamed across screens, national and subnational legislative houses, and coffeehouses and living rooms throughout Europe and parts of the Middle East, indexing the million asylum seekers entering into these countries since 2010 (also sweeping up the many other Africans who have migrated through other channels, or who are undocumented, or are there on student or work permits, etc.). Both the raced physical corporeality and the idea, if not meme, of "African migrants" have wrought angst, outrage, and suffering and many state and non-state actions ranging from policing, deportations, electioneering, rescuing, xenophobic attacks, protests, and labour practices, especially in states hugging the Mediterranean, from Morocco to Israel, Turkey to Spain (e.g., Flahaux and De Haas 2014, Kalir 2015). It also has led to strenuous efforts by the European Union to enrol northern African governments, including dictatorial regimes, to control and limit the "flows" north of the Mediterranean (Jakob and Schlindwein 2019).

Yet, this intense, disparate and contested focus, particularly since 2015, distracts attention away both from older forms of mobility within and from Africa and a different set of passions, desires, and hostilities. One of the oldest, if not foundational, forms of (forced) mobilities in which a raced sense of Africa was deployed was the Atlantic slave trade, generating a range of changing and different forms of African diasporas in the Americas (and elsewhere) and a range of transnational political economies and cultural forms predicated on particular imaginings of these communities with varying consequences in different parts of Africa (Akyeampong 2000). Such types of cultural politics brims both in W.R. Nadège Compaoré's incisive analysis of the global human hair industry, U.S. cultural industries, and hegemonic visions of black female beauty as well as Suvi Lensu's disquisition on the mediation of the attachments to "Africa" by a small group of diasporic filmmakers.

Another migration route that has grown over the last two decades is between different African cities and regions and cities in China, with a growing number of African individuals and groups heading to China for educational and particularly, economic opportunities (Bodomo 2012) as well as a vast expansion of Chinese governmental, business (including state-owned), and individual visits and migration across the continent (Park 2009). Wendy Thompson Taiwo's photo-essay provides a perspicacious and evocative insight into an element of these human mobility connections.

The mass-mediated version of "African migrants" in Europe also neglects the fact that most African refugees are within other African countries, where they face varying degrees of acceptance or hostilities, particular configurations of state and humanitarian practices from governmental, international, civil society and community bodies, and different sets of grammars of raced, gendered, linguistic and ethnic belonging (Milner 2009, Bakewell and Laundau 2018). For instance, particularly since the political and economic implosions in their country since 2000 (Rutherford 2017), Zimbabweans have become marked as the largest migrant community in South Africa and thus a key representative of "the *makwerekwere*," the Afrophobic term in South Africa to mark African migrants who "don't belong," as Wallace Chuma's sharp analysis makes clear.

The second palimpsest is "African women," one that goes back to at least early European missionary efforts in West Africa, southern Africa and elsewhere with a focus on moulding gender relations and gendered comportment according to their own patriarchal imaginaries (e.g., Comaroff and Comaroff 1991). Along with bilateral and multilateral donor agencies, non-governmental organizations (NGOs)—which in many ways continue the work of missionaries, not only faith-based NGOs but also secular ones (Manji and O'Coill 2002)—have played a crucial role in constituting African women as an object of humanitarian and development concern. At the same time, African ruling political parties and African women's and feminist groups have also galvanized varying legislative, state, and non-state actions directed towards particular socioeconomic, political, and pedagogical projects concerning African women, which can support, contest, or redirect other development initiatives (e.g., Urdang 1989, Nnaemeka 2004). From "FGM" (female genital mutilation) to "economic empowerment," the growth of oppositional feminist African fiction to those challenging the application of Western gender/sexuality classification schemes to precolonial African polities, African women have been iconic figures in many interventions and analyses at multiple and intersecting scales (e.g., Amadiume 1987, Adesanmi 2004, Abusharaf 2007, Tamale 2011). It is also a theme threaded through many of the contributions to this book.

Whereas Compaoré examines the racialized gendering of the transnational human hair industry, Stephanie Urdang reflects on her own feminist awakening as a South African living in the United States in the late 1960s when she learned more about the important African women's anti-apartheid march in Pretoria in 1956. Both Nduka Otiono and Grace Adeniyi-Ogunyankin critically analyse gendered struggles and inequalities in different domains of Nigeria. Otiono draws a vivid portrait of the Nigerian intellectual, activist and leader, Catherine Acholonu, and the gendered struggles she faced in the literary field. In turn, Adeniyi-Ogunyankin insightfully draws on postcolonial and different feminist lenses to show how discourses on culture and religion are deployed to marginalize women in Nigerian politics. Sinmi Akin-Aina also examines women and politics, with a careful analysis of Kenya's oldest and largest women's organization in light of the tensions inherent in African feminisms.

The chapters by Adeniyi-Ogunyankin and Akin-Aina also squarely tease out the overlays of the last palimpsest we will note here: African politics. Politics has become a key index of African matters within and beyond the continent. From corruption to repression, electoral fixing to narrowed classed, ethnic, prebendalist definitions of "publics" that the government serves, "Africa" is often overdetermined by particular connotations of its particular form of necropolitics (Mbembe 2003). Like those by Adeniyi-Ogunyankin and Akin-Aina, several chapters complicate such portrayals. Whereas they examine how "politics" or "feminism" becomes a particular icon that configures uneven and unequal pathways for individual women in specific historical and socio-geographical contexts, other chapters explore both institutionalized political economies and eruptions against such uneven fields of privilege. Jessica Evans smartly examines global political economies, particularly the push for structural adjustment policies by international financial institutions and bilateral donors, that have had ramifications in undermining previous forms of economic livelihoods and leading to a range of transnational pursuits for means of survival in southern Africa and, in response, more stringent border controls against African foreigners in South Africa (also discussed in Chuma's chapter), contrary to the promises of regionalism of the Southern African Development Community. Elizabeth Cobbett also expertly draws on political economy analyses to innovatively show how the South African Reserve Bank uses "monetary stories" as discursive interventions in national political debates as a way to firm up the African National Congress government's neoliberal policy positions. Two other chapters look at creative attempts to provide platforms for those multitudes on the margins of the formal political systems. Wangui Kimari and Jacob Rasmussen carefully examine the possibilities and challenges of a rather ad hoc social movement in Nairobi called The People's Parliament in Nairobi, while one of the key activists in this movement, Gacheke Gachihi, briefly reflects on the promises of Pan-Africanism for new social activists on the continent.

It is here, the to-ing and fro-ing between critical examinations of how "Africa" imbues and energizes particular imaginaries and actions (while marginalizing others) within and beyond continental spaces and simultaneously highlight some particular objects, people, ideas while being tripped up by many other configurations of such material and non-material entities, that the chapters show the doubling of African matters. Although to varying degrees each chapter engages with, if not draws on, issues of cultural politics, political economies and grammars of protest, we are somewhat arbitrarily assigning four chapters to each of these categories as a template of organization for the purposes of this Introduction.

## The matter of cultural politics

All matters of struggle, hegemony, protest, and oppression are infused with cultural terms, symbolic sentiments, and signifying distinctions that help motivate, rationalize, dissemble, and constitute the debates, identifications and socialities on all scales of action: from the murmurings and rumours careening down the proverbial *radio trottoir* to the boardrooms of banks, from state prisons to international development donor workshops (Adesanmi 2011). While all the authors in this book are directly examining and engaging in different forms of cultural politics concerning Africa and its diasporas, the four chapters included under this heading are each explicitly examining and or deploying registers of culture, including some of the aesthetics techniques or discursive genres of persuasion and power.

In her poignant photo essay, "Two Cities: Guangzhou / Lagos," Wendy Thompson Taiwo takes the reader into the lives of Yoruba traders who ply the complicated stream of commerce between Guangzhou, China and Lagos, Nigeria. Drawn into these worlds through reading about a protest by Nigerian traders in Guangzhou over their maltreatment by authorities, Thompson Taiwo examines some of the desires and contestations of the mundane and quotidian in the transnational lives of some of these traders through her words and photos. Making up the largest proportion of the approximately 20,000 Africans living in the coastal Chinese province of Guangzhou in 2009, these Nigerians negotiate a range of boundaries and tensions as they ply their trading endeavours. Reflexively positioning herself—and her camera—in some of the flows of life, Thompson Taiwo vividly captures some of the terms marking the possibilities and borders of business and socialities for these Yoruba men in China and Nigeria.

A very different insight into Nigeria is provided in Nduka Otiono's chapter, "Catherine Acholonu (1951- 2014): The Female Writer as a Goddess," where he offers an elegant unpacking of the gendered struggles of the great Nigerian writer, scholar, and political activist, Catherine Obianuju Olumba-Acholonu. His biographical elucidation of this prominent Nigerian intellectual, writer and public figure not only covers some of her audacious and substantive inquiries into Nigerian history, gender politics, and international politics but also her enchanting mediations on gender, religion and history in her poetry. As insightful as his own analysis is, Otiono's chapter also wonderfully allows the late Nigerian public intellectual herself to note some of the motivations, challenges, and terms of inspiration and opposition that marked her writings and her life in his October 2005 interview with her in Abuja, when she was the Senior Special Adviser on Arts and Culture to President Olusegun Obasanjo.

In "Filming Home, Plurality of Identity, Belonging and Homing in Transnational African Cinema: A Case Study of the Films Restless Wandering, The Place in Between, and That's My Face," Suvi Lensu gives a resonant mediation on the tropes of belonging in a deeply unequal and raced world in three transnational African films. Their filmmakers—Tunisian Nouri Bouzid, African-American Thomas Allen Harris, and French (of Burkinabé heritage), Sarah Bouyain—explore in the films she studies registers and challenges of belonging inside and outside of Africa and along the boundaries of many cultures. This exquisite, theoretically rich, essay speaks to larger issues on digital community formations, an increasingly important medium for generating and informing understandings of continental, raced, gendered and other identifications and affects.

Grace Adeniyi-Ogunyankin's chapter, "'Spare Tires,' 'Second Fiddle,' and 'Prostitutes'?: Interrogating Discourses about Women and Politics in Nigeria," brings the reader back to Nigeria through providing a critical African feminist interrogation of discourses about women and politics in Nigeria. As was clearly on display in the run-up to the February 2019 elections, the grounds of politics in Nigeria, like so many countries in Africa, are treacherous for women candidates. In her incisive analysis, Adeniyi-Ogunyankin lays out the range of barriers against women, as colonial ideologies inflected in postcolonial Nigeria claim culture and religion relegate women to "family matters." Through empirical research in Ibadan, she uncovers some of the key terms marking the moral boundaries deployed to police women's participation in politics.

## The weight of political economies

Political economy analysis in academia is shorthand for a variety of conceptual approaches that examine international and national dimensions of states and markets as key institutional sources of inequalities, hegemonies, and tyrannies. Informed through different configurations of Marxist, feminist, critical race theories, and postcolonialism, those deploying such an analytical approach seek to reveal varied dimensions of economic, political and social power, creating advantages for a few and disadvantages if not misery for many. The four chapters placed under this heading marshal some of these conceptual lenses to examine some of the contours and landscapes of power within and beyond Africa.

In "The South African Reserve Bank and the telling of monetary stories," Elizabeth Cobbett provides a fecund and original analysis of some of the tropes and narratives deployed by the South African Reserve Bank (SARB) to reinforce its (and by extension, the African National Congress government's) neoliberal policies and to undercut criticisms proposed by sympathetic but powerful critics like the main national trade union congress, COSATU (Congress of South African Trade Unions). Situating such monetary storytelling within the political economy of international finance and the particular state formation of post-apartheid South Africa, she illustrates how reserve banks (along with credit rating agencies) have become key arbiters of power in the global governance of finance and some of the discursive techniques and strategies of the SARB to wield this weight on the national scale.

Jessica Evans continues this political economy examination of South Africa with her chapter, "The neoliberal turn in the SADC: Regional integration and disintegration." In it, she shows how the regional development and partnership imaginary of the Southern African Development Community (SADC) when it was created during the transition to post-apartheid South Africa becomes undercut by the pressures for neoliberalism by the global political economy. Anchoring her analysis around the drastic heavy-handed responses of the South African government against the informal cross-border traders of the region who seek to enter it to buy (and occasionally sell) their wares (a growing livelihood in the region thanks to the devastating consequences of neoliberal policies adopted in southern Africa, like elsewhere), Evans spells out the strict border policing as a stark contrast to the open-border promises of the regional body.

Wallace Chuma's sharp chapter, "The Role of Radio and Mobile Phones in Conflict Situations: The Case of the 2008 Zimbabwe Elections and Xenophobic Attacks in Cape Town," also touches on this theme. Yet, his chapter does so through a rich analysis of some of the responses of undocumented Zimbabwean migrants to the most severe outbreak of Afrophobic violence in South Africa in May 2008 as well as some of the strategies by Zimbabweans to cope and reveal the intense political violence in Zimbabwe unleashed by its government and allies after the first round of the presidential elections there in March that year. In particular, he examines how new information communication technologies become deployed by Zimbabwean citizens as well as radio stations in both countries in everyday negotiations of violence, be it coming from state or non-state actors. Drawing on substantial empirical research in Zimbabwe and South Africa, Chuma offers a well-rounded perspective on how new and old media can be deployed in times of conflict.

Through her chapter "Indian Hair, the After-Temple-Life: Class, Gender and Race Representations of the African American Woman in the Human Hair Industry," W. R. Nadège Compaoré traces the political economy of the transnational human hair industry and its part in reinforcing raced and gendered images that play out in diasporic and national circuits. Built around the production of "Virgin Indian Remy hair" in India and its marketing to African

American women in the United States, she establishes the ways in which a gendered construction of blackness is constituted for African Americans and, given the summital position of U.S. cultural industries in Africa, beauty ideals for different black African women in Africa itself, pointing to the inequalities and power dynamics that are part and parcel of intimate bodily aesthetic decisions.

## Grammars of protest

While the chapters found in the previous two headings show Africans on the continent or in the diaspora generating cultural forms for various audiences on the scale of the person or the globe, engaging in debates, carrying out entrepreneurship, performing bureaucratic manoeuvrings, avoiding terror, and the like, the chapters in this final one address specific politic actions. Attending to the specific grammars of protest in particular historical moments shows how different Africans have been generating specific confrontations with power as well as some of the imaginaries driving different commitments to social change. The chapters here attend to weighty matters of organized attempts at social change as well as personal reflections of such change, showing some of the specific grammars of how the personal becomes the political.

The lead-off chapter under this heading beautifully articulates this phrase, "the personal is the political." The renowned South African feminist writer, Stephanie Urdang, critically reflects on her coming-to-awareness in the apartheid state, a reflexivity prompted by her return to her country of birth after fleeing there to the United States (and also conducting research in Mozambique and Guinea Bissau, among elsewhere). In "The Story of Cape Town's Two Marches: Personal Reflections on Going Home," she eloquently inquires into the complicated resonances of "home" (echoing some of the themes in Lensu's chapter) and political struggles for her as well as for so many other South Africans. The semantics of "home" is uneasy for many Africans in the diaspora, even if they do not necessarily recognize themselves as belonging to such a (contested) community, but for Urdang its meanings are laden with struggles for change tied to those multitudes who fought against apartheid South Africa; struggles, she realizes, that continue, albeit in at times different forms, today in the post-apartheid country.

In "Beyond an Epistemology of Bread, Butter, Culture and Power: Mapping the African Feminist Movement," Sinmi Akin-Aina carefully delves into the enduring *Maendeleo Ya Wanawake* (MYW), Kenya's oldest and largest women's organization as a way to assess them as an agent of social change and to critical reflect on wider social movements that could be called feminist. She unpacks the specific cultural logics of advocacy and service of MYW from the colonial period until the twilight of the one party rule in Kenya in the 1990s, showing the tender cross-class (and initially raced) alliances, the necessary but uneasy relationship with the then ruling Kenya African National Union (KANU) party and the tensions with dominant understandings of "feminism" in Kenya that led to what could be called a very feminist organization distancing itself from such a label. This careful analysis of both MYW and "African feminisms" smartly demonstrates the palimpsest through which social actions occur.

Wangui Kimari and Jacob Rasmussen continue the focus on Kenya with their searing chapter, " 'Setting the agenda for our leaders from under a tree': The People's Parliament in Nairobi." Unlike MYW, this is a more rhizomatic initiative, the establishment of *Bunge la Mwananchi*, "people's parliament" in KiSwahili, in a central park where there have been daily gatherings of Kenyans to discuss and debate the matters of the day. Calling itself a "pro-poor social movement," Kimari and Rasmussen carefully examine how it is "political," contesting the spatial and semantic parameters of what generally is constituted as "political" in this East African country. Through a provocative and compelling use of theoretical works and an ethnographic analysis of Bunge la Mwananchi, they show the spatial politics that led to its emergence in the 1990s and innovations of this movement in the 2000s as they trace how it performs a grassroots alternative to political participation.

A short piece by Gacheke Gachihi offers the words and grounded aspirations by one of these activists; words, like Bunge la Mwananchi itself, that invite further reflection and debate. His "Politics Across Boundaries: Pan-Africanism—Seeds for African unity" is a brief reflection on participating in the annual Mwalimu Nyerere intellectual festival in Dar es Salaam, Tanzania, providing one possible call(ing) for a Pan-Africanism that could inform and inspire the myriad of struggles taking place around the continent and among the African diasporas. It is a teasing hint of what could be, of the imaginaries to be reworked through debates and practices of solidarity which Gachihi himself so impressively continues with so many others in Nairobi.

Finally, and sorrowfully, we have had to add an Afterword, a piece that came out in Volume 7, our most recent issue: Blair Rutherford's "Incorporeal words: The tragic passing of Pius Adesanmi." This was initially written a day after the March 10, 2019 passing of the co-author of this Introduction and co-editor of this book, Pius Adesanmi, on the tragic Ethiopian Airlines crash shortly after taking off from Addis Ababa on route to Nairobi. Although it was not published in the first four volumes of *Nokoko*, as Rutherford describes, Adesanmi's passing occurred in the midst of writing this Introduction to this book; a book whose genesis came through his ideas, energy, and efforts. Professor Pius Adesanmi's entire actions as an academic, as a scholarly mentor, as a teacher, and, especially, as a vital public intellectual were geared to show the doubled meanings of Africa matters. In the fibre of his body, if not soul, he demonstrated and performed in his quotidian interactions, his writings, and his public talks, why and how Africa matters. He was an active participant, a creative satirist and social critic, commenting on and working through some of the cultural politics, political economies, and generating new grammars of protest in Nigeria, in Canada, and elsewhere in Africa and its diasporas. He is sorely missed[2] and this book is one of many tributes to him.

*Africa Matters* brings but a sample of *Nokoko* and some of its articles examining "Africa" and its diasporas. Clearly it does not attempt to be a "full" or exhaustive coverage—Nigeria, Kenya, South Africa, Zimbabwe and a few

---

2. See for example, some of the tributes given on Carleton's Institute of African Studies webpage: https://carleton.ca/africanstudies/piusadesanmi-tributes/.

diasporas, are the geographies under investigation here and the actual matters are relatively limited. Yet, the chapters here provide some fresh and novel perspectives on the ways in which Africa matters to transnational, national and local conversations, struggles, and imaginations, even if across a range of inequalities and power imbalances. Many of the contributors are new, some writing these chapters when they were graduate students or in the early stages of their careers and or are activists, the vast majority of whom are from Africa (by birth or descent) and are women. They are excellent exemplars of the mission of *Nokoko* itself as their analyses and debates seek to contribute to varying struggles of creating a world where people are free from all forms of oppression and exploitation, where respect for individuals' varied differences is maintained, and where everyone can realise their full potentials. *Nokoko* aims to be a site for such important conversations related to Africa, the African diaspora, and the continent's relationship with the rest of the world. As a platform for public intellectuals, academics, social movements and organizations that share our vision, this book complements the journal. As we reach our tenth anniversary, we also seek to provide additional ways for enhancing and expanding this conversation, creating, for example, a new open-access podcast series and generating more opportunities for shorter pieces to go alongside our longer, more academic ones. We recognize the depth and diversity of actions that are occurring within and beyond Africa and its diasporas, seeking ways for social justice, and we modestly suggest that *Africa Matters*, like *Nokoko*, contributes to these visceral, artistic and intellectual efforts.

## Bibliography

Abusharaf, Rogaia Mustafa (ed.). 2007. Female Circumcision: Multicultural Perspectives. Philadelphia: University of Pennsylvania Press.
Adesanmi, Pius. 2004. "Of Postcolonial Entanglement and Durée: Reflections on the Francophone African Novel." Comparative Literature 56 (3): 227-242.
Adesanmi, Pius. 2011. You're Not a Country, Africa: A Personal History of the African Present. Johannesburg: Penguin Books.
Africa Progress Panel. 2013. Africa Progress Report 2013. Equity in Extractives: Stewarding Africa's Natural Resources for All. Geneva: Africa Progress Panel.
African Union. 2015. "Key documents of Agenda 2063." African Union Commission, https://au.int/en/documents/20141012/key-documents-agenda2063. Addis Ababa: African Union.
Akyeampong, Emmanuel. 2000. "Africans in the Diaspora: The Diaspora and Africa." African Affairs 99: 183-215.
Amadiume, Ifi. 1987. Male Daughters, Female Husbands Gender and Sex in an African Society. London: Zed Press.
Bakewell, Oliver and Loren Laundau (eds.).2018. Forging African Communities: Mobility, Integration and Belonging. London: Palgrave Macmillan.
Barret, Renaud (director). 2019. Système K. Paris: La Belle Kinoise, Les Films en Vrac.

Bodomo, Adams. 2012. Africans in China: A Sociocultural Study and Its Implications for Africa-China Relations. Amherst, NY: Cambria Press.
Comaroff, Jean and John Comaroff. 1991. Of Revelation and Revolution, Volume 1: Christianity, Colonialism, and Consciousness in South Africa. Chicago: University of Chicago Press.
de Boek, Filip and Marie-Françoise Plissart. 2004. Kinshasa: Tales of the Invisible City. Ghent, Belgium: Ludion.
Ferguson, James. 2006. Global Shadows: Africa in the Neoliberal World Order. Durham, NC: Duke University Press.
Flahaux, Marie-Laurence and Hein De Haas. 2014. African Migration: Trends, Patterns, Drivers. MI Working Paper Series. Oxford, UK: International Migration Institute, University of Oxford.
Hickel, Jason. 2016. "The true extent of global poverty and hunger: Questioning the good news narrative of the Millennium Development Goals." Third World Quarterly 37 (5): 749-767.
Hickel, Jason. 2018. The Divide: Global Inequality from Conquest to Free Markets. New York: W.W. Norton.
Jakob, Christian and Simone Schlindwein. 2019. Dictators as Gatekeepers for Europe: Outsourcing EU border controls to Africa. Montreal: Daraja Press.
Kalir, Barak. 2015. "The Jewish State of Anxiety: Between Moral Obligation and Fearism in the Treatment of African Asylum Seekers in Israel." Journal of Ethnic and Migration Studies 41 (4): 580-598.
Manji, Firoze and Carl O'Coill. 2002. "The missionary position: NGOs and development in Africa." International Affairs 78 (3): 567-584.
Mbembe, Achille. 2003. "Necropolitics." Tr. Libby Meintjes. Public Culture 15 (1): 11-140.
Milner, James. 2009. Refugees, the State and the Politics of Asylum in Africa. London: Palgrave Macmillan.
Nnaemeka, Obioma. 2004. "Nego-Feminism: Theorizing, Practicing, and Pruning Africa's Way." Signs: Journal of Women in Culture and Society 29 (2): 357-385.
Park, Yoon Jung. 2009. "Chinese Migration in Africa." SAIIA Occasional Paper No. 24. Johannesburg: South Africa Institute of International Affairs.
Rutherford, Blair. 2017. Farm Labor Struggles in Zimbabwe: The Ground of Politics. Bloomington, IN: Indiana University Press.
Tamale, Sylvia (ed.). 2008. African Sexualities: A Reader. Cape Town, Dakar, Nairobi and Oxford: Pambazuka/Fahamu Books.
Urdang, Stephanie. 1989. And Still They Dance: Women, War and the Struggle for Change in Mozambique. New York: Monthly Review Press.
World Bank. 2016. Poverty in a Rising Africa. Africa Poverty Report. Washington: World Bank.

# Two cities: Guangzhou / Lagos

Wendy Thompson Taiwo

I was in Nigeria in May, the year I turned twenty-nine. And aside from the few hours of electricity per day, the way most of the food twisted my stomach or burned my tongue, and that the terrible stifling heat made life difficult at times, I was excited to be exactly where I needed to be: Lagos. Once the political center of Nigeria, it is still reigning as the financial and economic capital. And from what I saw, it was a thriving, bustling, chaotic metropolis where swindling police officers, savvy market women, racing okadas, and the occasional goat shared the streets with everyday Lagosians.

Lagos: Women passing along Mile 12 Market in Ketu where one can buy household goods, reusable items, and general foodstuff such as yams, goat, dried fish, pepper, and tomatoes brought in from around the country.

I was pursuing the second leg of a research project devoted to examining everyday lives of Yoruba traders I had met in Guangzhou. In 2009, a series of news reports shifted focus to a sizable West African trading community in southeastern China following a protest by an approximated two hundred African men in front of a police station that drew a crowd and shut down traffic. The protest was in response to earlier events in which an immigration raid staged by Chinese police in a clothing mall frequented primarily by Nigerian traders led to at least two reported injuries, one critical.

*Guangzhou: Chinese soldiers leaving the Guangzhou train station.*

The incidents were examples of the growing tension between Chinese authorities who claimed to be simply doing their job—rounding up and expelling illegals without valid passports or visas—and African traders who felt profiled, discriminated against, and harassed. I went with my camera in hopes of capturing some of these moments but ended up coming away with many more complex images of casual, even friendly interactions. At the very center were the men and women who made the long journey east, following the flow of new money and sellable goods from Lagos to China. And in the end, it only made sense that I continue on with the project in Nigeria where most of the goods ended up.

*Guangzhou: Yoruba trader passing a Chinese man transporting goods on Guangyuanxi Road.*

The camera followed me to Lagos and I made sure to photograph what I saw as Nigerian everyday life. Chasing after a man riding an okada with a goat draped across his lap as an example of efficient livestock transportation and capturing the hand painted images on a wood signboard that advertised the precise cut and appearance of frozen chicken and fish alongside a dignified portrait of the shop's owner. I even managed to photograph personal scenes: a woman brushing her teeth outside of her compound, two boys play fighting with long sticks in a private world of their own.

*Lagos: A Chinese restaurant owner flanked by a Nigerian waiter in a restaurant in Ojota's Chinese Shopping Complex. Inaugurated in 2005 by former first lady, Stella Obasanjo, the complex which resembles a cross between a European fortress and a large Chinese courtyard compound is now a faded pink color with a mix of occupied and empty storefronts.*

I was also schooled in Nigerian Life 101. I watched as black skinned catfish were transformed into a deep red pepper and tomato stew. I curtsied when introduced to a father-in-law, uncles, and aunts. I politely picked up the tab every time a few of us walked down the dirt road to buy something from the provisions seller who kept milk, juice, and beer in a Chinese manufactured freezer powered by a small generator. And I learned to trust Tmony, the trader I had followed from China to Lagos who held a cellular phone steady and illuminated the walls in rooms lightless as the deepest parts of the ocean.

*Guangzhou: A man talks on his cell phone in front of Lotus Market near the Sanyuanli Metro Station. The cell phone, an indispensable tool in China, connects traders with family, potential buyers, sellers, agents, and associates who can quickly send updates about a party or an alert that a police raid is in progress.*

He knew that I had wanted answers and invited me to Nigeria to "see everything"—from his large extended family and childhood home in Ilasamaja to the corruption and lack of jobs that made it nearly impossible to thrive honestly in a country known for fraud.

*Lagos: A man transports a goat by okada*

The latter predicament was what led many Lagosian youth, disillusioned with the long promise of a bright future, to go abroad. Every week it seemed like another one of Tmony's friends, associates, neighbors, or schoolmates had "traveled down." They were in India, China, Malaysia, Egypt, and Dubai armed with student visas, work visas, or tourist visas. Unafraid of the risks and open to the wildest of encounters, these were contemporary explorers riding headfirst into a new global economy.

*Lagos: Customers queue at the bakery counter in Shoprite, an African chain supermarket on Victoria Island.*

At least that's how it felt for many of the men I encountered who had little to no experience in business or travel. When first arriving to China, Tmony had the equivalent of a high school education and had last worked as a machine operator in a Lebanese-owned biscuit factory. He would study briefly in Qinghai before finding his way to Guangzhou after his student visa expired, joining the rest of the undocumented men and women involved in trade.

*Lagos: Schoolchildren passing on a street in Ogba.*

The same year that the protest took place there had been reports that claimed there were approximately 20,000 Africans in China's southern coastal province of Guangdong although many speculated that the total number was actually higher due to the large number of undocumented persons living there (Osnos, 2009). Nigerians made up the largest population of those Africans and comprised an extensive network of buyers, seller, and entrepreneurs. Their constant movement between two cities with the fastest growing economies in Asia and Africa was nothing short of fascinating to me, a recent Ph.D. graduate who had spent six years fixating over historical racial situations in the United States.

*Lagos: Roadside shoe seller. Many sellers in Lagos receive their merchandise directly from Guangzhou. The merchandise is then sold at a higher price with the cost of shipping and taxes factored in.*

Prior to beginning this project, I had done some reading on China's multiple investments in Africa and had even considered claims that China was increasingly engaged in neocolonialism on the continent. However, seeing Africans in China was seeing a different side of the global machine in motion.

*Lagos: A Mobile Policeman (MOPOL) relaxes between two men under the shade of a tree on a busy street.*

I had so many questions and saw this as a once in a lifetime opportunity to sort out some of the anxieties I had about race, borders, and the bodies of my parents—one black and one Chinese. I assumed that many African traders would have had to interpret and negotiate these same themes and embarked on my journey to encounter these new global citizens.

*Guangzhou: Two traders catch a lift on a three-wheeled motorized taxi on Guangyuanxi Road.*

I had arrived during the holiday season and Christmas decorations were everywhere in Guangzhou. Tmony introduced me to small community of Yoruba traders and many were in high spirits despite not being in Lagos to spend time with family and friends. The majority of the men were in their mid-twenties or early thirties.

*Guangzhou: Two Yoruba traders take a night stroll.*

They dressed well in either business casual attire or fashions that looked as if they were lifted from the adverts in a hip hop magazine. If they were married back home, I couldn't tell as most kept an African or local Chinese woman as a girlfriend. And when it came time to asking questions, most answered openly after first greeting me politely.

*Guangzhou: Woman and children passing on Guangyuanxi Road. This is the main thoroughfare where hotels, wholesale markets, barbershops, and export and shipping agents catering to Nigerian clients can be found.*

It actually seemed quite easy to get "linked in" to the trading network in Guangzhou. Not seen were the large debts or underlying stress that the traders carried. From the very beginning, men and women are expected to pay exorbitant fees to agents, employees in the consulate, and informal lenders in Lagos in order to obtain a way into China.

*Guangzhou: A man passes by a police vehicle on Sunday morning. In 2009, it was estimated that twenty thousand Africans were living in Guangzhou; however that number remains unverified since a number of men and women continue to live there off the record—either with expired visas or without passports. Some of the Nigerians without passports had sold theirs to fellow countrymen who wanted to return home.*

Once paid, the person would be given a name, a cell phone number, or a hotel room and address. Upon arrival in Guangzhou, that same person would place a call or take a taxi to the designated contact and the rest would be up to him. Of course, this all came with a price and you could never be sure who was really your friend but most of the traders usually became seasoned after their first few months or the second time being ripped off, whichever came first. Several times Tmony had merchandise destroyed or stolen by customs officials, shipyard workers, or middle men who promised to personally deliver the goods to Lagos. But it was all still worth it.

*Lagos: Men rest along the road at Mile 12 Market.*

Tmony and most other traders each turned enough profit to continuously order shipments of goods to be sent to Nigeria while some had even gone on to start their own business working as barbers, restaurateurs, shipping agents, wholesalers, and consultants. A small number of women supplemented their income by braiding hair, selling food, and providing sexual services. And children, while few and far between, occasionally assisted their parents on shopping trips and provided the everyday joy. But there was a dark side to life as a trader.

*Guangzhou: Men inside of a Yoruba owned barber shop in the Tong Tong Hotel. The hotel's staff would occasionally notify Nigerian patrons ahead of time if the police showed up looking for illegals. The men—both Igbos and Yorubas—come to the shop regularly, not only for a touch up but to socialize and hear about the latest news.*

For the undocumented living in Guangzhou, the added burden of having to conceal one's status in order to prevent harassment, arrest, or jail time forced many men and women to operate within the peripheries. Tmony was one of those people. He explained that while he often relied on other traders to give the "all clear" via calls made to his cell phone, he usually avoided certain areas and ventured out only when it seemed safest. This meant we had to watch where we went and that it was up to me to book both our transportation arrangements and hotel rooms using my American passport as identification for the both of us.

*Guangzhou: Chinese staff inside Bestway African Restaurant where an Igbo cook prepares such staples as pepper soup, egusi soup, and semo for a predominately Nigerian clientele.*

In spite of this, Tmony remained eager to answer my questions and show me the everyday grind of traders living and working in Guangzhou. He introduced me to his personal shipping agent and barber. He maneuvered me past countless stalls in wholesale malls that sold everything from infrared goggles to sequined halter tops.

*Yoruba man walks along side a Chinese woman in Ojota's Chinese Shopping Complex. In addition to restaurants and small shops selling clothing, textiles, shoes, and accessories imported from China, there are residential apartments in the complex with most of the tenants hailing from Mainland China.*

He directed taxi cab drivers in pidginized Chinese phrases that I hadn't heard since girlhood. And we shared a meal of egusi soup and semo with another trader which was a change from the cheap meals they frequently had at McDonalds, KFC, or any of the myriad of cafeteria style fast food Chinese restaurants in Guangzhou.

*Guangzhou: A Yoruba female trader carrying a home theater system in Dashatou. Accessible by bus, Dashatou is home to a large electronics bazaar where traders buy laptops, cell phones, and other electronic devices in bulk.*

It seemed oddly fitting that I was in China eating Nigerian food in the company of Yorubas who had picked up basic Chinese. Yet, I would see a similar kind of hybridity in the experiences of Chinese and Lebanese men and women in Lagos that following spring. For them, learning pidgin or any of the five hundred plus languages spoken in Nigeria as well as creating relationships with local people and adopting particular customs and social norms were essential to a smooth survival. Like the traders in Guangzhou, Chinese and Lebanese small business owners, contractors, and their spouses and children were grappling at the edges of a new cultural world where life was complex and required certain adaptations.

*Guangzhou: Trader pricing shoes in Canaan Market. Canaan Market is the main wholesale market catering to Nigerian traders, known for selling garments, shoes, and accessories. However, some Chinese sellers have begun selling products targeting to African buyers: hair extensions and wigs and Chinese produced imitation wax and lace fabric.*

One of those adaptations was being prepared for the possibility of change. For Tmony, this meant staying afloat amidst the daily cycle of births and deaths in Lagos after permanently returning there a month after we last saw each other in China. He had found a way to raise the money needed to pay off fines associated with his overstay and had bought a one-way plane ticket home. Since then, he had been selling what few goods his older brother in Sichuan Province could ship down. But with business being slow, he often found himself idle and thinking about traveling abroad again.

*Guangzhou: Laborers take a break to eat lunch by the side of the road in Tienhe.*

If anything, Tmony's experience reveals not only how fast money passes through the hand but how hungry Nigerian young people are for a taste of their own destiny; hungry enough to risk safety, leave the familiar, and live suspended between two cities, continents apart. I had gone to Guangzhou to see how capitalism was motivating ordinary African men and women to change the direction of their futures and left Lagos having witnessed the other side of the trade.

*Lagos: Mile 12 Market.*

It was, in fact, nothing short of inspiring: young people finding creative ways to become powerful, exercising their economic freedom beyond their wildest imaginations, and running ever so fiercely after the edge of their own dreams.

*Guangzhou: Goods packed and ready to be shipped to Lagos.*

## References

Branigan, Tania. (July 16, 2009) "Africans Protest in China After Nigerian Dies in Immigration Raid." *The Guardian*.
Osnos, Evan. (February 9, 2009) "The Promised Land: Guangzhou's Canaan Market and the Rise of an African Merchant Class." *The New Yorker*, 85(1), p. 50-55.
Quanlin, Qui. (July 16, 2009). "Africans Protest in Guangzhou After Passport Checks." *China Daily*.
(July 15, 2009).
"Africans Surround China Police Station to Protest Alleged Death." *Xinhua*.

# Catherine Acholonu (1951- 2014): The female writer as a goddess

Nduka Otiono

> *The goddess that is everywhere*
> *streams into my veins*
> *that I may live*
> *that you may drink*
> *I am the goddess*
> *Of the market square.*
>
> —Catherine Acholonu, "The Market Goddess" (*The Spring's Last Drop*)

By the time she died on March 18, 2014 at the age of 62, Nigerian writer, scholar, and political activist, Catherine Obianuju Olumba-Acholonu had established a reputation as a goddess of the intellectual market square. She achieved this reputation through her enigmatic persona and interest in esoteric ideas, as well as through her provocative and eclectic publications.[1] Catherine Acholonu first caused a stir in the Nigerian literary firmament when, in the mid 1980s, she launched eight books at the same time. It was a Nigerian publishing record that only Ken Saro Wiwa, the writer and environmental rights activist who was hung in 1995 by the dictator General Sani Abacha, surpassed. Within the same decade, Acholonu sparked another literary squall when she queried some winning entries for the literary prizes of the Association of Nigerian Authors (ANA), especially one awarded to another female writer. But it was in the political terrain, where she doggedly earned considerable recognition in a field dominated by male gladiators and chauvinists, that she proved her mettle as a fearless fighter and promoted her irrepressible spirit of a goddess. People still tell stories of her controversial bids for Presidential and Gubernatorial tickets in the past, and on one occasion squaring off with her then husband who had been the Deputy Governor of Imo State. Her activism fetched her appointment as Senior Special Adviser on Arts and Culture to President Olusegun Obasanjo. Not surprisingly, she resigned the position at a critical stage to contest the senatorial election against one of Nigeria's dreaded politicians, Senator Arthur Nzeribe. Feeling short-changed when she didn't get the ticket, she resigned her membership of the ruling Peoples' Democratic Party (PDP) and joined the Na-

---

1. It should be noted that in one of the earliest critical engagements with Acholonu's work, Obi Maduakor (1989) compares the poet to a "priestess" and a "diviner" (p. 78). For a more detailed list of her intellectual achievements see the Igbo Hall of Fame web site: http://igbohalloffame.org/people/details.php?id=17&name=Prof.-(Mrs)-Catherine-Obianuju-Acholonu&cat=Education,-Research-and-Literature Accessed January 13, 2015.

tional Democratic Party (NDP) to challenge the dominant politician. She lost the election and later told journalists that her rival had sent her death threats via her ageing mother. Afterwards, Acholonu was appointed Nigeria's Cultural Ambassador to the United Nations.

Between her audacious political activism, perhaps the best known example of a Nigerian female intellectual who has dared to wade into Nigeria's male-dominated treacherous political waters,[2] Acholonu sustained her passion for scholarship, and remained prolific throughout her productive life. This is understandable for a writer whom The Guardian of June 14, 1985, awkwardly described as "The most notable woman poet among the new additions to Nigerian poetry…, a very gifted… poet". At the 2002 International Convention of the Association of Nigerian Authors (ANA) in Asaba, her academic background served her well. Her Keynote Address, published as a monograph, was an impressive intellectual output on the theme Literature and National Development. She earned a standing ovation for her presentation entitled *Africa, the New Frontier: A truly Global Literary Theory for the 21st Century.*

Born in Orlu, Imo State, as the first of four children, Catherine Acholonu obtained her Doctorate degree in English and African Literatures from the University of Dusseldorf, Germany. She is the "author of over 16 books, many of which are used in secondary schools and universities in Nigeria, and in African Studies Departments in USA and Europe."[3] Her first monograph was a seminal study, *The Igbo Roots of Olaudah Equiano* (1989), which investigated the origins of the great slave autobiographer Olaudah Equiano (Gustavus Vassa). Although University of Benin Professor of English, Steve Ogude, has challenged her thesis, the study served notice about Acholonu's radical intellectual ambitions, and opened fresh insights into our understanding of the narrative on slavery.[4] She soon followed with her most influential work in Women Studies, *Motherism: The Afrocentric Alternative to Feminism* (1995), rightly described as "Africa's alternative to Western feminism" (Nayer 2008:135). The book originated as her Fulbright Scholar project, and an early

---

2. Although some gains have been made with regard to women representation in Nigerian politics, Udodinma Okoronkwo-Chukwu offers more revealing critical insight into the situation. See "Female Representation In Nigeria: The Case Of The 2011 General Elections And The Fallacy Of 35% Affirmative Action" published in Research on Humanities and Social Sciences, Vol. 3, No.2, 2013, 39-46, is very revealing. See http://www.iiste.org/Journals/index.php/RHSS/article/viewFile/4407/4475 Accessed Jan 15, 2015.
3. See catherineacholonu.wordpress.com/about.
4. The book sparked debates on the roots of Equiano, with Vincent Caretta (1999, 2003, 2005) and Steve Ogude (1989) being some of the most strident critics, and Paul E. Lovejoy (2007) supporting Acholonu. Acholonu evidently took the challenge seriously that in an email to me on February 5, 2008, she revisited the controversy: "You might wish to check the Internet for ongoing controversy on Equiano. I made a response in a public lecture delivered last year at the Community College of Southern Nevada and at our Equiano Conference in IMSU [Imo State University] also last year. It's all on the Net. Ogude has retracted his position on an Edoborn Equiano and now favours an Igbo origin, which nullifies him as a voice to be reckoned with in that discourse. I attach a copy of the paper." The lengthy paper entitled "Caretta-Gate and Igbophobia: The Facts, the Fallacies and the Grand Conspiracy to Deface Olaudah Equiano" is published in Acholonu's blog:
http://catherineacholonu.blogspot.ca/2007/09/caretta-gate-and-igbophobia-facts.html

draft was delivered as a Hitachi Public Lecture at Manhattanville College, New York on April 23, 1991.

With a remarkable appetite for intellectual storms, Acholonu earned a special commendation letter from U.S. President Bill Clinton not long after she interrogated former Vice President Al Gore's views on the search for alternative options for development. Restating her position in an interview with me, Acholonu said that Al Gore was not courageous enough to identify the Third World as the missing link in the world's search for solutions to further development. Hence, she undertook a holistic research to rediscover Africa's "lost knowledge" in her book, *The Earth Unchained, a Quantum Leap in Consciousness: A Reply to Al Gore* (1995). This perhaps accounts for her intellectual interest in the provenance and significance of the South-Eastern Nigeria stone monoliths at Ikom.[5] The research provided a more spiritual framework for her thesis in the book *The Earth Unchained*. At the ANA-Enugu conference and first Eastern Nigeria Book Fair in 2003, during which she was presented with an award for outstanding contributions to humanity, Acholonu gave a two-hour presentation on the Ikom monoliths, and afterwards conducted collaborative projects with the Institute of African Studies, University of Nigeria, Nsukka.[6]

Acholonu's intellectual interest in the Ikom stone monoliths evokes the mystical overtones of *The Spring's Last Drops*, her poetry collection which I shall closely examine here. Her other creative works include *Nigeria in the Year 1999* (poems); *Abu Umu Praimari and Children's verses*, and the plays: *Trial of the Beautiful Ones, The Deal, Into the Heart of Biafara* and *Who is the Head of State?* Her poems are included in the Heinemann Book of African Female Writers. The volume also features her as a short story writer with her often anthologized story with the arresting title, "Mother was a Great Man." Acholonu's provocative, non-fictional works include the oft-cited radical feminist study, *Motherism: the Afrocentric Alternative to Feminism*, and *The Earth Unchained*, which argues that positive thinking can unchain the earth.

Acholonu's creative works evince her versatility and restless spirit as she boldly explores her themes and engages in stylistic experimentation. The *Spring's Last Drop* has been rightly introduced as "a collection of poems that glow from the depths of the soul. The theme of cultural awareness is spiced with mystical profundity and social criticism".[7] Indeed, the epigraph to this article excerpted from one of my favorite poems of hers, "The Market Goddess," immerses us at once into the world of the writer. The metaphor of the goddess, served up early in the collection, conjoins with the two opening poems, "life's head" and "the way" to read like an Introit. The metaphor reminds one of

---

5. For a brief expose on the monoliths see Apollos Ibeabuchi Oziogu's easily accessible article, "The Mystery Called Ikom Monoliths..." Vanguard Online, on March 08, 2012. http://www.vanguardngr.com/2012/03/the-mystery-calledikom-monoliths/. Also see Keith Ray's "The Ikom Monoliths." In Andrew M. Reid, and Paul J. Lane, Eds. African Historical Archaeologies. New York: Kluwer Academics/Plenum Publishers, 2004. 192-194.

6. Acholonu's work with the University culminated in the Catherine Acholonu International Conference, November 17th—19th, 2012, hosted by the University of Nigeria Institute for Africa Studies, Nsukka, Nigeria.

7. From the book's blurb.

the opening lines of Christopher Okigbo's collection of poems, *Labyrinths* (1998), with its tribute to the goddess, Mother Idoto. But here, Acholonu's ritualistic evocation is not purely spiritual or votive, but also both "womanist" and sociological. Interestingly, in the preceding poem, she prepares the reader for this domestication of the spiritual: After introducing the reader to "The way/ that is the tree" from which the poetpersona can climb and pluck cotton seeds, she notes: "these beads of coral/drag me down/take off this regalia/ these ivory anklets/ cripple me with weight" (p.12). In the final, stanza she laments that she be set free "to paddle/my astral canoe". Evident at the outset, therefore, is the tension between the astral (spiritual) and the physical planes. Hence, "the market goddess" reigns over a recognizable place, a most 'common' place which in stereotypical and traditional perspectives are seen as the domain of the African woman, and which is a source of survival for humanity. For what is life without the marketplace!

Significantly, Acholonu humanizes the market goddess in a manner that some devotees may consider sacrilegious or profane:

*Listen to the stirring*
*Of her limbs*
*Listen to the heaving*
*Of her chest*
*Eke the market goddess*
*Squats at the village square*
*Breast resplendent with milk...*

Beyond the enchanting lyricism which overlaces Acholonu's poetry, the poet here sows the seeds of her theory of "Motherism" which celebrates matriarchal powers:

*Market deity squats in readiness*
*Immense thighs thrown*
*Wide apart*
*Come my children*
*Come to the one*
*That brings life*
*Food*
*Your daily needs...* (p.14)

Apparently, cultured irreverence is permissible in Acholonu's poetry. The image of thighs thrown apart with its amorous connotation is transformed into an enduring metaphor "that brings life/food/daily needs." In another poem from her book *Nigeria in The year 1999*, she speaks of forms of slaughter occurring during the Biafran War "when rods of aggression / rip through sealed valves/ of flutes of reed (p.32). This image has become somewhat a recurring trope in our literature. Those familiar with the performance of the polemical poet, Odia Ofemum, would better appreciate the point being made here by recalling his refrain in the memorable poem *"Thighs fall apart, the General (dis)appears"*. In the same vein, the popular columnist and publisher of *Classique* magazine in Nigeria, MEE Mofe Damijo of blessed memory, had written a searing satire on men under the title "Thighs Fall Apart", deliberately parodying Chinua Achebe's celebrate novel, *Things Fall Apart.*

For Acholonu, naming the private aspects of her femininity is a celebration of the distinct features of womanhood. In "lost virtue", she speaks of painting the "breasts/with red camwood", polishing the "ivory fingernails" and "ebony face/which soon shall be corroded/by modern cosmetics". Then, a poem that seems to delight in the physical appearance and beautifying routines of women, is finally translated into a neo-negritude intervention: "you may be happy/ with a colour/neither white nor black" (p.21).

Throughout the three sections of *The Spring's Last Drop* (1985), the poet establishes her familiarity with African and Western civilizations. Perhaps the poem that best exemplifies this is "the dying godhead" (pp 44-47). One could hear a skilled "speaking voice" rich in traditional resources and Western allusions to food and drinks. Like a priestess, the voice is oracular: "he who eats without defecating/gets the belly swelling" (p.11). There are also strong evocations of the African intermingling of the living and the dead: "The souls of the dead/dwelt on my branches/ at nights" (p.52).

Although no pantheon of gods as one may find in the works of other African writers such as Okigbo and Soyinka is identifiable in this collection of poems, the collection ripples with ritual elements, and is occasionally processional in rendition. In the long poem *"the message"*, Acholonu writes:

> *You have completed*
> *My midday offering*
> *Freeing me from the gods of air*
> *Now the gods of light*
> *Receive my offering....* (p.57)

There is a muted obsession with the gods in this collection. Far from the seeming Christian influence identifiable with a monotheist belief, the poet-persona proves to be at home with Africa's many gods. This is in tandem with the poet's philosophical musings in some of her non-fictional works. Nevertheless, the use of local expressions for words with easy English translation is sometimes distracting. In spite of the use of italics and footnotes, one comes away with the impression that the poet was a victim of the anxiety of early modern African writers to localize their works through such vernacular referencing. Fortunately, this is not the case with her other collection of poems, *Nigeria in the Year 1999*. A searing, poetic exploration of the ravages of war, the urgency of the theme of conflict doesn't seem to offer the poet the space for such indulgence.[8]

Taken together, Acholonu's poetry, accentuated by her gifts as a fine artist and the cover illustrator of the collections, draws attention to her artistic

---

8. Ogaga Okuyade offers a more detailed contextual analysis of the poem in his essay, "The Re-Articulation of Hope from Grief: Nigerian Civil War Poetry as Ledger, published in Novitas-ROYAL (Research on Youth and Language), 2010, 4 (2), 201-215. See especially pages 211=212. Remarkably, Okuyade evokes another useful study, Funso Aiyejinâs "Recent Nigerian Poetry in English: An Alternative Tradition". In Perspectives on Nigerian Literature, Ed. Yemi Ogunbiyi. Vol. I, Lagos: Guardian Books Ltd., 1988. 112-128.

temperament. Her drawing on the cover of *The Spring* (1985) suggests an influence of the Igbo Uli art form. At the time of her death, Acholonu was the founder and Director of the Catherine Acholonu Research Center, Abuja (CARC). The Centre focused on "research into Africa's prehistory, stone inscriptions, cave art, and linguistic analyses of ancient symbols and communication mediums from the continent."[9] The Centre published most of her later works between 2005 and the time of her death. The significant titles included: *The Gram Code of African Adam, Stone Books and Cave Libraries, Reconstructing 450,000 Years of Africa's Lost Civilizations* (2005); *They Lived Before Adam: Pre-historic Origins of the Igbo, The Never Been Ruled* (2009) which won the International Book Awards, USA, and two Harlem Book Fair Awards); and *The Lost Testament of the Ancestors of Adam* (2010). Thus, the recipient of numerous awards and honours, including the Africa Renaissance Ambassador by the Pan African arm of African Union, gravitated more from her creative writing stream to largely esoteric scholarship in History, Archeology, Cultural Anthropology, Sociology, and Geophysics. This much is evident in the following interview which she granted me in October 2005 while she was the Senior Special Adviser on Arts and Culture to President Olusegun Obasanjo (1999-2002). The interview took place in her office in Abuja, Nigeria.

## The Interview

**OTIONO: What, really, is the driving force behind your intellectual project in African Studies?**

**ACHOLONU**: I'm into Fundamental Studies. There is a new discipline that is called Fundamental Studies and this is an area where you think deeply about the origin of things. You don't deal with effects; you deal with causes. I am a humanist, and as a humanist, anything concerning the human condition, the progress of man, civilisation, the human thinking, knowledge especially, are some of the things that I take very personally.

**OTIONO: What are the circumstances surrounding the letter President Bill Clinton of the US, sent you?**

**ACHOLONU**: It was sent in by the American Embassy. Actually, I wasn't in town then. I was on leave and when I came back, saw the letter. When I read it, I was very, very pleased and I was wondering how his Presidency had gotten to know me. But then, I remembered that my works have been in circulation, especially after my book, *The Igbo Roots of Olaudah Equiano* was published in 1989; it was distributed to libraries in the U.S., including the Library of Congress. After the publication of the book, I was sponsored to visit the U.S. as part of the international visitors program. The USIS (United States Information Service) in Nigeria organised for me to travel to several U.S. universities to give lectures and do readings from my work.

---

9. See https://catherineacholonu.wordpress.com/about/

**OTIONO: Your works demonstrate considerable commitment to thinking about humanity and the environment...**

ACHOLONU: Yes of course. But mine is an environmental philosophy. And my suggestion is that we should have a holistic approach, that all sectors should come together and work together for the progress of humanity. And I am essentially a thinker. I think all the time. I'm always trying to work out solutions to problems. Once I see a problem I don't leave it there. No matter what aspect of life, I analyse it. Even if it's in science, religion, philosophy, theology, the arts, culture, you name it. Whether it touches youths, children, parenting, education, any problem I see goes home with me and I don't rest until I find a solution to that problem, including political issues. I take them home with me and I keep thinking, brain-storming with myself, working it out: thinking, dwelling on it. So these things have a way of getting right into my soul and I continue to seek for answers and I'm always researching. I was doing my doctorate degree and the topic was the clash of culture/civilization in African Literature. I took the Igbo example. I studied in Germany. It was when I came back to Nigeria and I decided to go into African studies that I stumbled upon Equiano, and the moment I read about him and the materials he gave and the story he wrote, I started having a suspicion of you know... I thought that with the instances of culture and language he gave, it shouldn't be difficult to trace him. So I said I was going to do something about it. I finished my doctorate and then attended a conference, the Ibadan conference on Pan Africanism. It was the first conference I had ever attended in my life. I presented four papers! [Laughs] I was hungry to learn and to get knowledge. One of the papers was tracing the pioneer of Igbo literature. The Equiano thing, I can't remember. So I gave some instances and added my own voice to the debate. I knew there was a debate. Then I sent the paper to the *Journal of Commonwealth Literature* in London. They read it and said I should go and do more research on that because I was suggesting that archaeologist should to do it. They said, no, no, you go and do it... [*Laughs*]. So I now decided to go further. That was how I got into this [the Equaino book]. Then, the *Motherism* work was... you know... I'm not a feminist, I'm a humanist. Being in Women Studies and being in African Studies and being a woman, you often find this discussion coming to you.

**OTIONO: Looking back several years after, and in relation to the way Gender Studies have evolved, how do you feel about your central thesis in your often cited book, *Motherism*?**

ACHOLONU: The thing I always do in any field I go into—any topic I pick—I give it my all. I never give halfheartedly and I find that when I say it, people don't fully appreciate it when I say it. Years after, I always have a way of saying things long before time. Because thinkers are those people who are able to pierce into the future and catch glimpses of light and bring it down. Many people do not often see what you are seeing until years and years later. Every year it opens, some aspects opens from year to year, decade to decade, until it fully blossoms. But the joy in it is that you challenge people to think, open up to see, and it's a gradual process. The thing is that any work of art that has something in it will always challenge people: Some, in one respect; the others, in another respect. But you will find out that people keep on going back to that work because there is always something challenging in it. That's the thing with Christopher Okigbo's work. It is a bud, you go in there to take any part you think you can digest, you go with it. But the real thing is still unopened. The poetry of Okigbo is yet unopened and that poetry is a process of initiation which the poet went through himself and until you go through what initiation that he went through and hit what he hit, you can't open it all.

**OTIONO: Okay, in proposing the idea of "Motherism," was there an immediate dominant idea or scholar —say Alice Walker or Elaine Sholwalter— that you thought you had to challenge while promoting your own African perspective of feminism?**

ACHOLONU: Well, you see, I went through the different perspectives [on Feminism] we had at that time. The person who appealed to me more among black women feminist would be Philomena Steady. I don't think she has a book but I know I read her essay; I appreciated her work, her perspective, I thought she was objective enough but Alice Walker…

**OTIONO: What about Chikwenye Okonjo-Ogunyemi?**

ACHOLONU: She hadn't written her book then. But we had Alice Walker, we had Ama Ata Aidoo. Those were the people making a lot of waves at that time. Ama Ata Aidoo was okay but she was too extreme.

**OTIONO: And Buchi Emecheta…**

ACHOLONU: [Laughs]…. And Flora Nwapa… .She was really very bitter, but we can't train our daughters hating men. We just can't do it. Give them the opportunity to love, let them have their own experience. Don't tell them men are distasteful or evil; don't do that. I can't do that to my children. I want my children to know that the world is full of love, even if there is lots of hate around. The light is there and invariably, the light will overcome darkness. And if you arm your children with love, love conquers evil all the time. If you arm them with hate, you've already defeated them—you destroy them.

**OTIONO: In other words, through *Motherism* you are operating both as a scholar and as a mother?**

ACHOLONU: Oh yes, oh yes, I'm a mother to the core. If you see my children, you will know I'm a mother to the core. I give my all to child upbringing. I give every minute of my life because I don't have a social life. All I have is a family life and a working life. I don't have time for social life because if I should have time for social life, I won't have time for my children. I work a lot, I write a lot, I think a lot. The remaining part of the time I sit with my children: we chat, talk, laugh, I lie on their bed. If they have questions, they ask me. I give them my time and it's not wasted, because when they grow up anybody seeing them will know you planted a seed in them. More so because you know they won't have you all the time. You have to plant all the seed, give them all the knowledge you have, and all the love you can give; make sure that they know love from you so that they can extend it to others in their life.

**OTIONO: Now, how correct would it be to describe you as a restless scholar because you are always moving on to new areas? Apart from being engaged with Fundamental Studies, I am thinking about your current research into the Cross River State stone carvings, and so on.**

ACHOLONU: Yes, I'm very restless [*Laughs*] because I move from field to field. The reason being that I know there is a lot of work to be done in African Studies. There are so many untouched areas. And one thing that makes me unhappy: African scholars don't research these untapped areas especially in the arts. There are very few people doing deep research. When our people get a professorship, they relax. How many of our professors are working? They are all gone to gone rest, once they get Professorship, they now go to rest. I don't feel that, that is right. Years ago I said it when I was still in the university. I was saying we have a lot of need for new materials. Nobody is giving it to us because our professors are no longer working. They will go and rest. But fortunately we still have scholars like Ernest Emenyonu. But you won't hear [Romanus] Egudu, I don't know where he is now, and a number of them. It's really worrisome because I know they have a lot to offer, and I feel that they should still come out there and start working, give us what they have so that our children can grow with it.

**OTIONO: Couldn't it also be attributed to the parlous state of the country and the deterioration in the Ivory Tower?**

ACHOLONU: Many of them live outside the country as I'm talking to you. I experienced this during my two to three years lecturing in the university. I started publishing a journal, using my paltry pay as Lecturer 1 to finance the journal.

**OTIONO: What was the name of the journal?**

ACHOLONU: *Afa: Journal of Creative Writing.* I started it so that my colleagues could publish. I have that knack to find solution to problems. I'm restless with academics. Now you find me in History, Environmental Studies this moment, the next moment you find me in Women Studies, Language Studies—I am a linguist also—you find me in Education. We have just brought out a book on "Youths and Non Violence in Nigeria" towards a culture of non violence for youths.

**OTIONO: How did you get into this new direction with regard to the stone monoliths you're now researching?**

ACHOLONU: I went to Lagos for one program and I used that opportunity to visit our installations at our Ministry's parastatal in Lagos. I was at the museum. I had been seeing the monoliths in pictures for years but I always said to myself, there is something there. I felt this whenever I looked at the monoliths, it blows my mind. I would ask myself how did these things come here? What are these things? So when I saw them face-to-face, I was like trapped. I touched them for the first time. I looked, and went from one to the other, looking at the symbols. I took some pictures. I went home and couldn't get them out of my mind. I would go to bed dreaming of them. It was like an obsession. I kept asking myself what are they? When it kept worrying me, I called the museum and told them to send more pictures. They did. I looked at the photographs and saw some things which began to give me some messages. I saw a symbol like a multi-cross. What is the multi-cross doing on the monolith? If by archaeological results/explanations we are told that the monoliths go back at least to 1200 BC, can you tell me what the multi-cross was doing on the monoliths. Christ was not born yet. You see, you have million-dollar questions on these monoliths. I went into deep meditation and then I began to see the light, it started opening for me and I began to study it. It was as if old women who were no longer bearing children or seeing me would go along with a virgin, they would go and take their different colors of chalk and trace those symbols on the monoliths. They are dressing them for the new yam festival. And on the D-day, they will bring food and feed them and pray for progress and protection. I kept asking, they told me "Madam, since the history of Ejagham, no foreigner has ever dressed the monoliths." I was the first foreigner to dress the monoliths.

Also, they said nobody ever dressed the monoliths on any day other than the 14th of September; it's never done. So as they said so I was tracing the monoliths by myself and taking the pictures. There was one they called the Wisdom Stone. They all have names, e.g. Queen Stone, King Stone, etc. with various significance. As I was tracing the Wisdom stone they told me I was imbibing wisdom. The monolith gives people wisdom. People come from far and wide to touch the Wisdom stone to obtain wisdom. They told me a story of a British commissioner who had gone to Ikom. He was leaving Nigeria and he wanted to visit Ikom before leaving. He went with a former British army colonel. They said when the colonel saw the Wisdom Stone, he said this is Israel in Africa. He went and embraced it three times, saying, I have obtained wisdom before people know the meaning of this thing and the whole world will be coming here. That was what they told me the British Colonel said. I said to the monoliths: "Give me wisdom…" [Laughs] But I understood better the significance before then because I already connected with the monoliths even before visiting there.

**OTIONO: Having established these foundational ideas, how long would it take you to complete the research?**

**ACHOLONU**: I started about four months ago. I finished before presenting it at that event. I went to Ikom after seeing the monoliths in the museum in Lagos. I decided to go deeper. Initially I wanted to do the interpretations only. But after visiting Ikom, I thought of going deeper. I started looking for similarities between those symbols and others in other parts of the world. And nobody had ever studied the monoliths in detail. Artists mention them but nobody had ever gone into it. When I found out this was the place of origin, I said I have to go deeper to find out what more we could know about the stones and the people. I already suspected that the Olmec (of Mexico) were from there. I asked them [the Olmec] to give me some of their words. And I was seeing this stool, it kept on coming and that is one truth that you find in almost 90% of the words, among the Olmec, it surpassed Mayan language. All their names ended with TL. I see a connection because the TL I encountered in South [Central] America and here, I see a connection. The man was surprised that I knew so much about it. There are things they know and don't tell people. I lectured him about the monoliths, who made the monoliths, when they were made, what they stand for and so on and so forth.

**OTIONO: Are you concluding the research now?**

**ACHOLONU**: I'm about to. But when I came back from my trip to lkom, I went into meditation again, I had questions. I said, God, open it for me, because I'm very religious.

**OTIONO: How religious—orthodox or African?**

**ACHOLONU**: I told God. So I was led... I gave a friend my book *The Earth Unchained* to read. After reading the book, he brought another book and said, Madam have you read this book, it was the Hebrew Kabala. He said, Madam have you read this book, I said no. He said, it looks like you are breaking into some fundamental secrets of life. I said to him, the book *The Earth Unchained* came to me in a dream and I wrote it in two weeks. And it was at a time when I was going through excruciating difficulties in my life. I couldn't even have done anything but the book kept pouring and would not be stopped. I had to give two weeks of my life: It was pouring and pouring. I wrote it in a stretch, no correction, no revision. I sent it raw to the publisher. I have my publishing company, if I have to subject what I have to institutional publishers, politics would come in, and anybody who does not want Africa to make progress, will not publish me. So I publish myself. I don't subject my creativity to any politics, definitely not international politics of knowledge production. The book was a revelation from God. So the man went home—and brought me a book titled "Kabala". I was afraid to open it but I kept it. One day when I was meditating on this, I was led to go and bring that book. I opened it, and behold, I could see how the monoliths jammed with some elements of the Kabala. After I saw more, when King Solomon came and he prayed to God to give him wisdom. These were in the monoliths, and also in the Kabala. I saw the Kabala signs in that place. You can now see that these things go further than we think.

**OTIONO: How much longer would we have to wait to see this book in print?**

**ACHOLONU**: The second part will be on the Ejagham people [of northern Cross River region], the place of origin of the monoliths and Nsibidi symbols... Maybe by December [2001], the first book will be out. The second one will come out around February [2002].

**OTIONO: There is a connection here between the work you are doing as a scholar and your present public appointment. In what official ways have you been able to use your position as a Senior Special Adviser to the President to advance arts and culture in Nigeria?**

ACHOLONU: I do design projects for different ministries and for the parastatals. I give them ideas. I don't want to talk about my advice to the president.

**OTIONO: What has been your essential vision?**

ACHOLONU: The new thing I want to add to knowledge is: I want to connect culture and education, science and technology. I have seen the link between culture and science, culture and education, culture and technology, and that's what I think I can establish.

**OTIONO: Could you please open up more on your research findings?**

ACHOLONU: My research goes in two parts. The first part of it was that after seeing the monoliths, I said I'm going to zero in on them based on what I see. I do Fundamental research all the time wherever I find literature that can help me. Fundamental Studies take me to the root of things; to the origin. But I've been seeking for answers to Blackness, to Africa: Who we are? There was once I was in the U.S., I think it was in Boston. It was at an exhibition of African masks but it was done by an American, raffia and all that. All the masks were black. It was a masquerade, whole masquerade regalia. About four or six people, all of them were Black. The whole raffia was black, but there was no human being inside, they position it as if someone was inside. I looked at these things; I saw some of our works there. Those things like Ikenga, like the ones they get from the shrine. I saw those things in the museum. And when I looked at them, each of them commanded presence as if they would take you back in time if you could let yourself go, you would see them in their original setting with the whole village surrounding them, playing music. There was such presence, such silence you would cut with a knife; such presence, such power in each of those things especially the Egungun [masquerade] man. That thing kept haunting me. I said these things are not just pieces of wood. There and then, it dawned on me that these people were just taking away our soul. These are things that were taken away from here; they took everything. These were all we had. This was us. Our ancestors had put in so much energy into these symbols. They had put in so much collective energy into it and somebody came and took it away and we are left with nothing. No wonder our people are wandering. So when I saw those masks, I had this feeling. At that moment I said there is… in blackness. Blackness goes beyond light. Blackness was before light. I felt that it was too deep, it's indescribable. There was such awesome power, I could feel, even in the silence, it was too much. It went beyond time and light. You could feel the statement: In the beginning, there was Blackness, Blacknesss belonged to time before the beginning…So these things make you want to know who you are, want to know what is the meaning of Blackness, why we are dark and who we are, why we are talented. And I know also that the intelligence we have that is in-built is beyond the knowledge that you see being valued about right now. Our knowledge is beyond the technology that we study. It is higher than that. If we were to expose what is in us, there would be no comparison between this science and that science. The science that we embody, we carry it, you see it on the dresses we wear, the way we move, the way we speak, the way we dance, smile, everything we do! If you take a Kente or an Adire cloth, or whichever, you will appreciate it.

**OTIONO: You are beginning to sound like a neo-Negritudist...**

**ACHOLONU**: When you look at all those things, you will know there is something overwhelmingly powerful than anything we can imagine. And if could translate what we have into portable technology what we are seeing here would be nothing.

**OTIONO: So by the time you see all these monoliths, you'll establish a reconnection.**

**ACHOLONU**: I could see that the monoliths go beyond our time. They don't belong to our time. There is nothing anywhere that has the appearance of the monoliths. If you look all over Africa, all African art, people will always make cubic kind of structures, if you see the statues our ancestors made, you will see a human kind of figure. The anthropomorphic head, neck, etc, even if they look geometric... With the monoliths, you have the eyes, the mouth, you see something that looks like a hand, but none of them has a leg.

**OTIONO: Have you been able to establish any connection with either the Adinkra or the Nsibidi symbols?**

**ACHOLONU**: Yes, I have now found out that the Nsibidi symbols originated from the monoliths. Many of the Nsibidi symbols are on the monoliths but many are not on the monoliths. But one could see the Nsibidi connection with the monoliths that they originated from the same source. Whoever carried the monoliths gave the Nsibidi signs. And also, I found out that the community, the clan, the tribe where we have—geographically—where we find these is the Ejagham clan, and it is the original home of Bantu language. Many words in Ejagham language have this tone. You don't find it anywhere else.

**OTIONO: What is the phonetic symbol?**

**ACHOLONU**: It is TL. It sounds like "eti". Nobody else speaks like that in Africa: That you have two consonants and no vowel in-between. Even the Bantu have lost that, but we still find it in South [Central] America...

**OTIONO: What does it mean?**

**ACHOLONU**: It is in my notebook. So I found this similarity and also find the connection to "red Indians" [indigenous peoples in the Americas].[10] The major thing you find in their attire is the feather. That's almost the first and last thing. It's unique to them. It is also the same with the Ejagham people. If you make one achievement, you wear one; if you make two, you wear two.

**OTIONO: The Igbo have that also?**

ACHOLONU: If you kill 10 people in battle, you wear ten feathers. If you are portraying leadership, you wear a different kind of feather, e.g. eagle feather to prove leadership in battle or that you are a business magnate. They clothe themselves with feather. Also in South America.

**OTIONO: How has this fashion diffused over time?**

ACHOLONU: Originally, the Ejagham people were well travelled, to Guinea, Angola, etc. There is some place where you have very strong ocean currents, that easily lifts a boat and throw it within a matter of days into South America. It has been reported a number of times by geographers and oceanographers. When you read these things you find out how people migrate. Christopher Columbus was travelling to India and landed in America, before he was diverted somehow. It was Ejagham people that populated South America. They brought civilisation there. Olmec were the first, and it has been proved by writers and scholars that the Olmec were West Africans from the Delta part of Nigeria... Language is a weapon for connecting culture and people. How did scholars know that the Bantu language is spoken all over Western to Southern Africa? South Africa, Zimbabwe, Ethiopia, Kenya Congo, Angola, Sudan, name it, they speak Bantu. It was the Ejagham people that populated the whole place. They made the other tribe become small. They rendered them redundant. These people have always been migrating from time to time because the place is small and does not contain them, and they are very enterprising people. They introduced agriculture to different parts of Africa today. The iron culture came from Ejagham. If you go there today, you will still find pieces of iron or metal that shows that there must have been a prehistoric melting and mining centre there.

**OTIONO: How much of archeological work have been done that you've been able to utilize?**

ACHOLONU: Some have been done. I know that Ekpo Eyo have done some, but not much have been done. I knew that there was iron there before I went there, and I could tell.

**OTIONO: How?**

ACHOLONU: By looking at the monoliths, I knew it was not done by human hands. There was some sort of technology that was able to melt the rock like volcanoes do and remould it or use a tool to bore through the rock. A tool that

---

10. Many Africans in former British and French colonies continue to use this term innocently, without awareness of the derogatory connotations that have inspired opposition to the term in North America.

melts the rock as it is moving and gives specific symbols that are very sharp, and the circles are perfect. No human hand created by God can ever make a perfect circle.

**OTIONO: How have you been able to establish that they are perfect circles?**

ACHOLONU: Oh you can see it. You find concentric circles that are perfect. I use my compass and math set to measure it. I approach it from a very scientific point of view: equilateral triangles, squares are perfect. What human hand makes that, especially for a rock that is very demanding? Only a sophisticated tool and mind can make that. And I find that sophisticated tool among the Olmec.

You could see some image holding something that looks like equipment and you would see fire coming out of it. At the Olmec week in South America in 3000BC they made perfect heads, giant heads. I also found that in the olden days they had dens, so everything is….in place.

**OTIONO: Would you consider these preliminary findings or do you have enough authority based on your research to say that these findings can be put up to any kind of test?**

Like I said, I had finished writing my book before I went there for the first time. I wrote based on what I saw at the museum. And I presented it at the UNESCO (Badagry) meeting. After that I went Ikom. But it was like I just went there to prove myself right. I was telling the curator that my thesis is that they were made with some sort of sophisticated technology. He told me that they had iron which he showed me. He told me that it has been there scattered all over the place and nobody knows. And also, the very notion that there was no connection between the people who made the monoliths and the present people living there and their ancestors speak volumes. If ancestors hand down tech from age to age, then it means that there was a major interruption. No, break in transmission. That interruption can only happen with a major event like the "deluge" which destroyed history and mankind started afresh. These are things I'm trying to trace. I go as far as I can and leave it for others to continue from where I stopped. I don't make sweeping statements unless I have to.

**OTIONO: What is the next level for your research in this area?**

ACHOLONU: I finished the first phase of my book and went to Ikom and found more things. Something interesting happened; I prayed for sunshine when I was going because it was in the rainy season and I know that it rains a lot there. When we got there, just as we were approaching Ikom we had sunshine and we were there for four hours. At the first location, cameras could not snap the images very well so I requested for native chalk so that I can trace the line. They seem not to understand what I asked them. They said nobody does it. It's a taboo, only our people do it and only on the 14th of September before the New Yam festival.

**OTIONO: How has it been like, advising the President on Arts and Culture?**

ACHOLONU: Not easy, because the President [Olusegun Obasanjo] is a person with very strong ideas… [Laughs] But he has respect for good ideas. And he will respect you if you know what you are talking about, and you have to convince him. He is a good listener. I've been able to get quite a number of ideas across to him. The priority is trying to organise the national cultural program. If you operate everything in an adhoc manner you achieve nothing, waste time, opportunities, etc. You must have a long-term programme. We want to set up a national cultural programme on a 4-5 year plan in Culture. It will involve every aspect of culture. I have this program on the table and UNESCO is cooperating with us.

**OTIONO: Being an artist and a scholar, haven't there been times when you've been embarrassed by some of the President's acts, for example the sale of a national artifact which was reported by *TELL* magazine?**

ACHOLONU: That is where some of the frustrations come in, some of the things that can't change immediately. You need time. All African countries have been robbed. As an adviser, I can only advise. And the museum, the National Commission for Museums and Monuments has also been working. They've travelled all over the world trying to identify those Nigerian artifacts that were stolen. They brought some back. And are still working to get more…Recently, *Time* magazine published a report on that. The problem we have here is that our people are not aware of the significance of culture. That's why people like me are here. It's a slow process but we'll get there.

*The Ikom stone monolith. Daniel Williams Cobhams, DW Photography, Calabar, Nigeria.*

## Acknowledgements

This article originated from two separate pieces originally published in *The Post Express Literary Supplement* (October 28, 2001) by The Post Publishing Company, Lagos Nigeria and edited by me, and in *The Sun Literary Series—Women Writers*, (December 1, 2004), edited by Olu Obafemi, and published by The Sun Publishing Ltd. I am grateful to Ikechi Uko, publisher of *African Travel Quarterly* (ATQ) for the illustrative photographs taken as part of his Seven Wonders of Nigeria project.

## References

### Creative Writing

Acholonu, Catherine. Abu Umu Praimari: A Collections of Poems for Junior Primary in Igbo, University Publishers Ltd., 1985.
———. Nigeria in the Year 1999, (poems), Totan Publishers, 1985.
———. Into the Heart of Biafra, (war poems), Totan, 1985.
———. Trial of the Beautiful Ones, (a play), Totan 1985.
———. The Spring's Last Drop, (poems), Totan, 1985.
———. The Deal & Who is the Head of State? (plays), Totan, 1985.

### Research Publications:

Acholonu, Catherine. *Motherism: the Afrocentric Alternative to Feminism*, Afa Publications, Owerri, 1995.
———. The Earth Unchained: A Quantum Leap in Consciousnes; a Reply to Al Gore, Afa Publications, 1995.
———. Afa Journal of Creative Writing, Vol. 1, No. 1 (Founding Editor)
———. The Igbo Roots of Olaudah Equiano, (a Linguistic and Anthropological Research), Afa Publications, 1989, Revised Edition, 2007
———. The Gram Code of African Adam, Stone Books and Cave Libraries, Reconstructing 450,000 Years of Africa's Lost Civilizations, CARC Publications, Abuja, 2005.
———. They Lived Before Adam: Pre-historic Origins of the Igbo, The Never Been Ruled (CARC Publication, Abuja, 2009.
———. The Lost Testament of the Ancestors of Adam, CARC Publication, Abuja, 2010
Acholonu, Catherine, and Naja Levoe and Sidney Davis. *Eden in Sumer on the Niger: Origin of Aryans of Eri-Land, Hebrews, Moors and Vedic Indians*, LAP Lambert Academic Publishers, Germany, 2013/2014.

Web sites

Catherin Acholonu's blog: *https://catherineacholonu.wordpress.com/*
Igbo Hall of Fame, *http://igbohalloffame.org/people/details.php?id=17 &name=Prof.-(Mrs)-Catherine-Obianuju-Acholonu&cat=Education,-Research-and-Literature*

Others

Achebe, Chinua, *Things Fall Apart*. Knopf Doubleday Publishing Group, 1994 (1958)
Aiyejina, Funso. "Recent Nigerian Poetry in English: An Alternative Tradition". In Perspectives on Nigerian Literature, Ed. Yemi Ogunbiyi. Vol. I, Lagos: Guardian Books Ltd., 1988. 112 – 128.
Carretta, Vincent. *Equiano, the African: Biography of a Self Made Man* (University of Georgia Press, 2005).
———. "Introduction" in *The Interesting Narrative and Other Writings*, edited with an introduction and notes by Vincent Carretta (London and New York: Penguin, 2003), pp. x-xi.
———. "Olaudah Equiano or Gustavus Vassa? New Light on an Eighteenth-century Question of Identity", *Slavery and Abolition*, 20, 3 (December 1999), 96-105.
Lovejoy, Paul E. "Issues of Motivation—Vassa/Equiano and Carretta's Critique of the Evidence." *Slavery and Abolition*, Vol. 28, No. 1, April 2007, pp. 1–5.
Maduakor, Obi. "Female Voices in Poetry: Catherine Acholonu and Omolara Ogundipe-Leslie as Poets." In *Nigerian Female Writers: A Critical Perspective*, Eds. Henrietta Otokunefor and Obiagel Nwodo, Lagos: Malthouse Press Ltd, 1989. 75-91.
Nayer, Pramod K. *Postcolonial Literature: An Introduction*. India: Dorling Kindersley Pvt Ltd., 2008.
Ogude, Steve E. "No Roots Here: On the Igbo Roots of Olaudah Equiano." *Review of English and Literary Studies*. Ibadan: Bookman Educational and Communications Services, 1989.
Okigbo, Christopher, *Labyrinths and Path of Thunder*. Trenton, NJ: Africa World Press, Inc., 1998.
Okoronkwo-Chukwu, Udodinma. "Female Representation In Nigeria: The Case Of The 2011 General Elections And The Fallacy Of 35% Affirmative Action," *Research on Humanities and Social Sciences*, Vol. 3, No.2, 2013, 39-46. http://www.iiste.org/Journals/index.php/ RHSS/article/viewFile/4407/ 4475 Accessed Jan 15, 2015.
Okuyade, Ogaga. "The Re-Articulation of Hope from Grief: Nigerian Civil War Poetry as Ledger, published in *Novitas-ROYAL (Research on Youth and Language)*, 2010, 4 (2), 201-215.
Oziogu, Apollos Ibeabuchi. The Mystery Called Ikom Monoliths..., *Vanguard Online*, on March 08, 2012. http://www.vanguardngr.com/ 2012/03/the-mystery-calledikom-monoliths/
Ray, Keith, "The Ikom Monoliths." In Andrew M. Reid, and Paul J. Lane, Eds.

*African Historical Archaeologies*. New York: Kluwer Academics/Plenum Publishers, 2004. 192-194.

# Filming home, plurality of identity, belonging and homing in transnational African cinema

Suvi Lensu

## A Case Study of the Films *Restless Wandering*, *The Place in Between*, and *That's My Face*

> *Are you lost?*
> *Me, lost? I never get lost. When you don't remember where you're going, remember where you come from. And you will never get lost.*
>
> A griot in Restless Wandering

## Introduction

To feel at *home*, to feel one *belongs*, is essential for identity construction. For long the prevailing premise has been that because people develop emotional ties to a place and to community, nomadic life-style engenders a sense of homelessness (Cuba and Hummon 1993: 547-8). Although the first claim is unquestionably true, the latter belief is being challenged by our ever more transnational and multicultural world, where the concepts of home and belonging are going through significant transformations. For many, 'home' has lost its meaning as being something rooted in one particular place or community. As people are increasingly more mobile and de-territorialised, home becomes imagined and invented through diasporas, and their memories, and through new, digital forms of community. The subfield of intercultural cinema in particular has tackled the issue of belonging in transnational space. It has explored questions such as what does it mean to have a plural meaning for home, and for belonging that can move in-between various cultures and borders? Consequently, intercultural filmmakers have discovered new affective methods and techniques to depict the quest for identities and homes. The objective of this article is to study these discoveries by analyzing three African transnational films *Restless Wandering* (2009), *The Place in Between* (2010), and *That's My Face* (2001).

*Courtesy of Digital Diaspora Family Reunion, LLC. Photo by Mary Kirstin for Chimpanzee Productions, Inc.*

Central to my analysis is what it means to be at home. As stated above, home and identity are closely linked concepts. They form and shape one another. Just as our identities go through transformations in different stages of life, our identities can also be reconstructed and recreated during the course of migration and moving. Stuart Hall usefully defines identity as a "production, which is never complete [and] always in process" (1996: 210). Hall's description allows us to see identity as something ever fluid and dynamic. Due to its adaptable and plural characteristics it can be attached to multiple places and layers at the same time. This article translates Hall's notion of identity-as-process to the idea of home, discussing home as a production in a process. In this article home is understood as an abstract concept, a feeling of belonging to a place or places. Home can be imagined and/or it can be a psychological state of mind. When referring to a place or a territory where a person has created a deep attachment, I use the word *homeland*. Naturally, these concepts can overlap and are sometimes inseparable.

Throughout my research I found the quest for finding home particularly significant for filmmakers from the African diaspora. They have increasingly explored what Africa has meant to those outside the continent and how to return to Africa metaphorically (Hall 1996: 218). For many, pan-Africanism has been an important facet to be included in their work. To define the ideology and the movement of pan-Africanism, I borrow the definition by Lemmelle and Kelley (1994: 4) who discuss pan-Africanism as the contact between Africa and its diaspora. The running theme in pan-Africanism has been the historical links between countries resisting slavery, colonialism and imperialism (Ibid). Similarly, the contact between the continent and the diaspora has been one of the central themes in African transnational cinema. In this paper no boundary is created between continent-based African filmmakers over African diaspora filmmakers. I see all three filmmakers reviving memories and heritage of African cultures that invoke a feeling of home and a sense of belonging. The films call attention to the process of how to recreate African and/or diaspora identities and belonging in transnational space.

Although Africa is the connecting theme between the three works discussed here, these films not only discuss home inside and outside of Africa but also one's place in between many cultures. Without focusing on specific ethnicities, African nationalities or diasporas, the aim is to study the filming of home in African 'intercultural cinema,' which is defined by Laura Marks as a form of moving picture art representing experiences of living between two or more cultures or living as a minority. Because intercultural cinema cannot be confined to a single culture, and it moves between and within cultures, it is a valuable genre in the exploration of the concept of home in an increasingly transnational world (Marks 2000: 1, 6). As Hamid Naficy accurately observes, transnational filmmakers create "sites for intertextual, cross-cultural, and transnational struggles over meanings and identities" (Naficy quoted in Marks 2000: 7). Both Naficy's and Marks' theories help us to analyze transnational cinema and its representations of home.

I start the article by mapping out the literature on transnationalism and identity construction, and intercultural cinema. The literature selected specifically discusses belonging and feeling at home. In particular, I draw on the works of Liisa Malkki, Gaim Kibreab, Avtar Brah, Laura Marks and Hamid Naficy. This discussion will be followed by a close analysis of how the three case study films 'film home.' Finally, before the conclusion, the section 'Home as a Journey' will explore some of the joint findings of the films.

The first film analyzed is a short film titled *Restless Wandering* (2009) by Tunisian filmmaker Nouri Bouzid. It explores issues of modernity, nation-statehood, and border control in contemporary African societies. Further, the film explores how sedentarist metaphysics is a challenge for some people with more traditional notions of belonging and feeling at home in Africa. In this film, the confrontation between tradition and modernity is represented through two characters: a West African griot and a Tunisian security officer. The second film analyzed is *That's My Face* (2001) by African-American filmmaker Thomas Allen Harris. In this biographical documentary Harris goes for a one man's journey to discover his African spirituality in Brazil. The final film analyzed is *The Place in Between* (2010) by a French director of Burkinabé heritage, Sarah Bouyain. *The Place in Between* is a fictional film, though it also has some autobiographical features, portraying a young woman's return to Burkina Faso from France in search of her biological mother.

All three films can be considered to belong to the genre of intercultural cinema and therefore they share a common foundation from which we can explore the concept of home. However, the differences in their styles and narration are also very useful to draw comparisons. In relation to Bouzid's and Bouyain's work the cinematic style in Harris' documentary is much more alternative and experimental. Additionally, since there are fewer female than male filmmakers working today (in Africa and the West), Bouyain's *The Place in Between* is a useful example to account for the female perspective, which in diaspora cinema has often been marginalized (Foster 1997:1). Finally, it is important to note that the conceptual approach of each artist is distinct. Whereas Bouzid's griot longs for continental Pan-African reconstruction, Sarah Bouyain's film studies postcolonial exile identity. Harris, on the other hand, is in search of African diasporic belonging. Indeed, the artists are situated in different historical, geographical and conceptual positions, yet their quest for what is home is a consequence of globalization. Instead of focusing on each of their conceptual positioning as such, my aim is to understand how home in African transnational cinema can be perceived and explored in various ways.

## Literature review: Identity and home in transnational space

Increased global cultural interaction has brought people closer and made them more aware of each other than ever before; the increasing movement of people has become a defining character of global politics, economics, and culture. The world is more condensed due to the accelerated movement of information and capital. While different populations are more interlinked, they have also become increasingly deattached from their countries origin and their original homes (Malkki 1992: 25). De-territorialization, a weakening of ties between culture and place, has been described as the central force of the modern world (Appadurai 1990: 11). Edward Said (1979: 18) also describes this period of globalization as the "generalized condition of homelessness." Further, Daniel Warner characterizes the contemporary world as being a place where "we are all refugees" or "tourists" (Warner quoted in Kibreab 1999: 385).

Although exile and territorial displacement are not new or exclusively postmodern phenomena, they have more analytical visibility today due to a higher degree of research on the topic (Malkki 1992: 24). In her research, anthropologist Liisa Malkki suggests that people's deep attachment to a place is significant in identity construction. However, drawing from nomadic metaphysics, one's territory does not necessarily define identity itself. Malkki further observes that in this time of 'generalized condition of homelessness,' it is more visible than ever before how identities are more fluid rather than fixed. During the process of de-territorialization, identities continue to be reconstructed and recreated throughout a person's life-time. Consistent with Hall's notion of identity discussed above, Malkki sees identity as "always mobile and processual, partly self-construction, partly categorization by others, partly a condition, a status, a label, a weapon, a shield, [and] a fund of memories" (Malkki 1992: 37). The emphasis in her work is on plurality of identity, which may be attached to multiple places while living in them, remembering and imagining them.

While Malkki has emphasized the de-territorialization that is seen to be underway in the global world, Gaim Kibreab (1999) has argued that the era of globalization has in fact reinforced re-territorialization of identity, home and homeland. Accordingly, Kibreab believes that, increasingly, people are leaning towards their own cultural, racial, historical and spatial belonging (Kibreab1999: 385). He draws from sedentarist metaphysics, which conceives that one's culture and identity derive from a specific place and from a sense of belonging to somewhere. Moreover, sedentarists believe that territory provides the basis of morality. Sedentarist thinking has led to a belief that people who are uprooted from their own culture and sense of belonging can suffer from immorality and a lack of identity (Malkki 1992: 31-2). Therefore, the exclusion and alienation of 'the other'[1] is greater than ever. As the displaced 'others' can be received with hostility, the desire to return to one's 'natural place', or physical home, has become increasingly important (Kibreab 1999: 408).

Acknowledging Kibreab's notion of the desire to return home, especially in circumstances when one has been violently de-territorialised, it is also important to outline that desire is not always material, but rather imagined. Avtar Brah (1996: 181) argues that in an era which is so strongly defined and driven by the movements of people, the "'[diaspora space]' is 'inhabited' not only by those who have migrated and their descendants, but equally by those who are constructed and represented as indigenous." By indigenous Brah means those who do not live in exile or posses a multicultural background. Yet they are deeply affected by transnationalism through multicultural people close to them and through the blending of various cultures. In her discourse about belonging Brah takes into account a 'homing' desire but distinguishes it from the desire to return to a homeland, which may not be as compelling, as we all already live in a diaspora space. Home can simultaneously be a mythical place of desires and imagination while also being the lived experience of locality (Brah 1996:192). Thus, "[t]he *concept* of diaspora places the discourse of 'home' and 'dispersion' in creative tension, *inscribing a homing desire while simultaneously critiquing the discourses of fixed origins*" (Brah 1996:193; italics in original). Brah believes that because of diaspora and the diasporic space in which we live, the concept of home can be perceived in new and more creative ways. Understanding that every human has a strong desire to belong and to feel at home, this feeling does not need to derive from a person's natural place or place of origin. This 'homing' desire (rather than the desire to return to a homeland) is central to transnationalism and multiculturalism and to the films discussed here.

Since the beginning of the 1990s academia has seen a growing interest in the issues of identity and transnationalism. This research has increasingly focused on subfields of post-colonialism, multiculturalism and diaspora studies. Similarly, mainstream-media has also given an increasingly larger space for narratives of transnationalism (Shohat and Stam 2003:1). The engagement of the media with transnational identities can be very prominent in the process of fulfilling the homing desire. For people who live outside of their homelands, who belong to more than one culture, or who may be disconnected from their families, imagination begins to play a vital role in social life.

Arjun Appadurai (1990) has suggested that the image, the imagined and the imaginary are the components for the new global order. For people living geographically distanced from the places and people they feel attachment to, the imagination has become a new social practice. Media creates imagined lives for those living outside of their physical homelands. Moreover, subjects

---

1. 'The other' can be seen as someone who differs from the majority population, for example on the basis of ethnicity, religion or nationality. For a more detailed discussion see Julia Kristeva's Powers of Horror (Kristeva & Roudiez, 1982) and Edward Said's Orientalism (1988).

of home, homelessness, identity formation and transnationalism have become ever more popular in artistic expressions. As Appadurai (1990: 11) writes: "[D]eterritorialization creates new markets for film companies, art impresarios and travel agencies who thrive on the need of a de-territorialized population for contact with its homeland." Media engages people, places and imagined communities with distant places significantly impacting on national and transnational identity and communal belonging (Shohat and Stam 2003:1-2). In other words, the media has become a catalyzer for multicultural affiliations and transnational identifications, and a significant way of accessing 'home'.

## Cinema as a catalyzer for transnationalism

In intercultural and transnational cinema, filmmakers draw from various cultures, memories and attachments. For transnational filmmakers questions of home, identity, nation and belonging are often central to their work (Naficy 2001: 6-9). The importance of their work lies in the way they challenge cultural separateness. Since their films are multicultural and hybrid, giving voice to multicultural scenes and settings, they can move between the dominant cultural relations and make racist and colonial settings visible (Marks 2000: xii). Hamid Naficy (2001) has further emphasized that films made by filmmakers with multicultural backgrounds often share similarities in the cinematic style and narratives. If we simply categorize transnational films under, for example, genres of national[2], Third Cinema[3], ethnic cinema[4] or identity cinema,[5] we misread films that reflect transnationalism and multiculturalism (Naficy 2001: 19). As a result, Naficy proposes a more appropriate term, 'accented cinema.' However, it is important to keep in mind that these filmmakers do not only work on the borders, but also "inhabit the interstitial spaces of not only the host society but also the main film industry" (Naficy, 1999: 133).

Naficy discusses three overlapping types of films which all have characteristics of what he calls accented cinema: exilic, diasporic and ethnic films. John Durham Peters (1999: 18-20) distinguishes the differences between the categories. To Peters, exile is a painful banishment from home and is often experienced in solitariness rather than in community. Exile invokes home and homeland via longing and fantasizing. Diaspora is often a collective experience

---

2. National cinema can mean a government funded film-industry or a cinema specifically concentrated on representing a country or a nation. It often concentrates on informing the viewer much about the nation, people, and national issues occurring. The term "national cinema" is a subject of debate in the field of film studies, disagreements deriving from questions such as how to define "a nation". Some of the famous examples of national cinema are Russian and Iranian cinemas. For further interest see Vitali and Willemen (2006).
3. Third Cinema started in Latin America in the late 1960s as a political cinematic movement strongly resisting colonialism and neocolonialism, and artistically challenging hegemonic Hollywood cinematic style and its representation. See Solanans and Getino (1969).
4. Ethnic cinema emerges from the conflict between descent relations, emphasising the bloodline and ethnicity of the filmmaker. See Naficy (2001: 15).
5. Identity cinema often focuses in the country in which the filmmaker resides, and in that context discusses spilt identities or minority identities within majority identifications. See (Naficy 2001: 15-16).

in which people are tied via a network to their compatriots. Home is more comfortably imagined and return is not seen as necessary or even desired. Whereas, ethnic films are most concerned with a specific group and they are associated with identity cinema. As Naficy (2001:15) explains:

> [E]xilic cinema is dominated by its focus on there and then in the homeland, diasporic cinema by its vertical relationship to the homeland and by its lateral relationship to the diaspora communities and experiences, and postcolonial ethnic and identity cinema by its exigencies of life here and now in the country in which the filmmaker resides.

Thus, diasporic cinema becomes the crossing point in the filmmaking of these three different types. The emphasis of accented films is on their heterogeneity. They can overlap with each other and establish different relationship to places. Some highlight their relation to their host while others to their home country.

Despite the different approaches Naficy argues there is a frequent theme in accented films, which is a return narrative. The filmmakers are often situated at borders. These can be physical or metaphorical marked by, for instance, race, class, gender, or membership or a citizenship (Naficy 2001:31). They articulate the place in between which the transnational filmmakers occupy. Naficy (2001:33) highlights that the return, crossing the border or seeking or escaping home can be as much psychological and metaphorical as physical. Further, the films tend to have an autobiographical signature, where the filmmakers draw deeply from their own memories and experiences. As in Third Cinema, the films are often politically engaged. But unlike Third Cinema, they do not focus so much on national allegories, but reveal the racist, colonial and hegemonic power relations between cultures through more personal and private storytelling (Ibid).

Although Laura Marks does not clearly categorize intercultural films as a genre, as Naficy does with 'accented cinema', they both attempt to theorize how the imagination is a key component used in intercultural cinema. The imagination discussed here is constructed by memories and experiences. Because we feel, remember and sense most strongly with our bodies, the conclusion of both authors is that imagination in film is sensed strongest via cinematic elements and narratives, which excite an embodied experience in the viewer. The human body is experienced externally through mediums such as mirrors, photography, films and the gaze of others, and internally by our own vision and proprioception (Naficy 2001:28). Considering the body itself as a home, "it provides our original and initial opening upon the access to the world" (Sobchack 1999: 47). In exilic experiences the body can be traumatized by, for instance, the hostility and racism of the new living environment, or it can be alienated because of a deviant dress, style or skin color (Naficy 2001:28). Moreover, the exile can become a "somatic experience, in which the subject's own body, or image, is appropriated by an external agency" (Wagstaff and Everett quoted in Dovey 2009b: 60). Therefore, Naficy proposes that through bodily experiences memories and associations of home can be evoked. They can be sensed by a touch, a smell or perhaps a mother tongue heard spoken in a street. Accented filmmakers tend to use tactile optics which evoke senses such as touch and smell and other sense memories, thereby memorializing and "recollecting the images, sounds, smells, people, places, and times they left behind" (Naficy 2001:29).

Instead of talking about 'tactile optics' like Naficy, Marks proposes that many intercultural films are 'visually haptic'. Her argument is that filmmakers, when positioned in between cultures, tend to look for new methods of visual expression. Whereas Western art has prioritized the sense of sight to express knowledge and experience, intercultural filmmakers in search or longing for home and memories draw on and evoke 'embodied' experiences in their film. Marks describes this as follows:

> Haptic visuality is distinguished from optical visuality, which sees things from enough distance to perceive them as distinctive forms in deep space: in other words, how we usually conceive a vision. [...] Haptic looking tends to move over the surface of its object rather than plunge into illusionistic depth, not to distinguish form so much as to discern texture. It is more inclined to move than to focus, more inclined to graze than to gaze. (Marks 2000: 162)

In other words, she argues that senses such as touch and smell are primary senses. Through touching, for instance, the whole body engages with the sensation. This is because a touch is experienced on the surface of the body; the sense is inseparable from us. On the other hand, sight or sound can be distanced from the viewer or listener. In films where haptic visuality is present, we are more engaged with the picture, which can evoke more intense feelings and memories. Marks (2000:163) continues:

> [H]aptic perception privileges the material presence of the image. ...[I]mages that are so 'thin' and unclichéd that the viewer must bring his or her resources of memory and imagination to complete them. The haptic image forces the viewer to contemplate the image itself instead of being pulled into the narrative.

Marks offers several examples of techniques which can provoke haptic visuality in relation to a film, such as: close-to-the-body camera positions, characters in actions of smelling, touching, or tasting, changes in focus and under- and overexposed film. These observations by Marks and Nacify's, together with Brah's notion of 'homing desires', will be utilized when analyzing the films *Restless Wandering*, *That's My Face* and *The Place in Between*.

## Representation of Africa and exilic people

It is important to briefly state why the films discussed here have been selected. While both Africans and exilic peoples (immigrants, refugees, diasporic peoples), as subjects, have often been marginalized and victimized, the films here are narratives where the protagonists and filmmakers are locating their own destiny and place.

In his essay "How to Write about Africa", Kenyan-born Binyavanga Wainana (2005) writes about how *Africa* (as though it were *a country*) has been represented in media and literature only as a continent suffering from endless wars, illnesses and disasters. Africans are victimized and alienated in the eyes of the reader. They are voiceless and homogeneous people without an active role in their own destiny. In his article Wainana (2006) satirically comments how Africans have been stereotyped:

> [The typical] African characters may include naked warriors [and a] loyal servant, [who] always behaves like a seven-year-old and needs a firm hand... [and the characters should] always include *The* Starving African, who wanders the refugee camp nearly naked, and waits for the benevolence of the West.

In the early days of motion pictures, Africa was not only homogenized and victimized, but its cinematic representation was also racist. For filmmakers in the early 20th century, Africa offered a new, exotic and bizarre setting for films. As Peter Davis (1996:3) writes: "[T]he pictures of the native people [were] scarcely distinguishable from those of the animal trophies. Africa was a hunting-ground for the white man and when Hollywood seized on Africa, this was the Africa it offered." Over a century later, Hollywood still stamps stereotypes of Africans (Davis 1996: 4). By looking at most of the blockbuster films made in or about Africa such as *Hotel Rwanda* (2004), *Lord of Wars* (2005), *The Last King of Scotland* (2006), or *Machine Gun Preacher* (2011) the observations by Wainana about stereotypical Africa remain true. Africa is a war-torn place, and Africans themselves appear to be helpless victims. The continent is still a white man's playground, where 'he' can make a change in the lives of Africans.

But it is not only the Africans who have been marginalized. Amongst the other colonized populations and nations, diasporas and exilic people have also often been represented as victims and 'the Other'. In the second half of the 20th century, an enormous number of people and nations have been displaced due to a failure of socialism, communism, nationalism, religious and ethnic wars, and the fragmentation of nation-states (Naficy 2001: 10). These peoples are the products of postcolonial displacement and postmodern scattering. Simultaneously, in the process of globalization, many have moved voluntarily. Without making a distinction between voluntarily and involuntarily deterritorialised peoples and people coming from multicultural backgrounds, these groups are represented in cinema in new ways. Instead of seeing the displaced peoples as mere victims and marginalized groups, they are increasingly represented as active agents connecting links between the borders of nations (Ibid).

Through the agency of exilic people, we can explore ideas of home in a very intimate way, through individuals who live in between places and cultures, who journey inside themselves, to discover where they belong. It is important to note that all the filmmakers and the protagonists in the films have a choice. Being in exile or being alienated is not necessarily due to a hostile environment. Malian-Mauritanian filmmaker Abderrahmane Sissako, who has lived most of his life abroad, says:

> I'm not a whole entity as such. I'm a multiple. And this multiplicity is fragility. This fragility becomes nearly a lightness. So I surf over things, perhaps with more ease.

By that I mean that I'm not someone who is saddened by exile. I'm not a victim. It's a choice. (Sissako in Whitfiel 2002)

As Lindiwe Dovey (2009 b: 56) discusses in her article 'Subjects of exile: Alienation in Francophone West African cinema', exile is not always painful and negative, but rather it can be reinvented as a positive and strengthening experience. Julia Kristeva (quoted in Dovey, 2009b: 56) also writes that "Being alienated from myself, as painful as that may be, provides me with that exquisite distance within which perverse pleasure begins, as well as the possibility of my imagining and thinking, the impetus of my culture." The protagonists in the films discussed here are not victims of alienation or represented as 'the other'. They are active pursuers in the search for home and belonging.

## Homing in transnational African films

### Restless Wandering in L'Afrique Vue Par, 2009

Nouri Bouzid's *L'Afrique Vue Par*[6] is a collection of ten short films by some of the most prominent African filmmakers such as Flora Gomes, Gaston Kaboré, Mama Keïta and Abderrahmane Sissako. The films portray contemporary Africa in different parts of the continent and diaspora. The short film *Restless Wandering*, by the famous Tunisian filmmaker Nouri Bouzid,[7] is a story set in the old ruins in Tunisia. An encounter between a West African griot[8] and a group of Tunisian children is interrupted when a Tunisian security official suspects the man of having illegally immigrated to the country and drives him away.

The film is a remarkable representation of pan-Africanism. It is an encounter, and a meeting point of the north and the south. In the center of the discussion is what separates North Africa from Sub-Saharan Africa. The film articulates how Africans have been, and still are, affected by rules and ideologies introduced and imposed by colonialism. To highlight the changes occurring in African societies, Bouzid portrays the dichotomy of old and new; inclusion and exclusion is represented through the two characters—the griot and the security official. The griot character symbolizes African traditions and customs and the continent's rich cultural heritage. His role is played by the famous Sotigui Kouyaté[9]; a real Malian-Burkinabé griot, who during his life was hailed as one of the

---

6. Translation: 'Africa seen by'
7. Nouri Bouzid is arguably one of the most renowned filmmakers in Maghrebian cinema. Born in 1945 in Tunisia and trained in Belgium, Bouzid then returned to his home country and worked for several film productions. He was later imprisoned for five years for radical left wing activism (Armes 2006: 91).
8. Griot is a French word for a prestigious keeper of oral cultural traditions and heritage in West Africa, specifically referring to Mande culture (Panzacchi, 1994, Belcher, 1999).
9. Sotigui Kouyaté (1936-2010) was an internationally acclaimed actor and a founder of a theater company in Burkina Faso. The Kouyaté family is part of prestigious clans of griots. Also Sotigui's son Dani Kouyaté is a griot and an important filmmaker (Guttman 2001). His film Keïta! l'Héritage du griot, is a fundamental work in African cinema, in which Sotigui plays the key character, Jeliba, the griot (Armes 2006: 168).

most significant contributors to West African cultural heritage (Guttman, 2001). Although griots belong to a particular West African cultural tradition, the griot's ethnic and regional background is never highlighted in the film. In the cast he is referred to as *L'Africain*. Thus, I read him to represent the rich African cultural heritage in general as well as the unity of Africa.

First, the spectator sees the griot silently resting in the ruins, representing what could be interpreted as sleeping, forgotten traditions. The children play near him and as soon as they spot him they wake the griot up. This suggests that it is the curiosity of the children and the new generations that could revive the ancient traditions back to life. When the griot teaches proverbs to the children, he describes Africa as a big tree. The many branches of the tree symbolize all the countries in Africa. Applying the metaphor of a tree into sedentarist metaphysics, a tree has represented fixed roots and belonging, particularly in Western history (Malkki 1992:28). However, here the roots are a symbol of a mutual substrate. The roots provide the history and foundation of Africa, but from that point all the countries and nations grow in different directions. The symbolism here can be linked to the ideology of pan-Africanism, which draws the historical links between African countries and the diaspora, thus uniting Africa (Lemmelle and Kelley 1994).

The location of the film is particularly important. The story is set in Tunisia, which is not only the country of origin of the filmmaker, but it is also an important transit point for illegal immigration from Africa to Europe. In consequence, Tunisia has in past years passed more restrictive laws to limit such traffic. It has pursued a bilateral agreement with Italy to send illegal immigrants arriving in Italy back to Tunisia, positioning immigrants in very vulnerable situations (Baldwin-Edwards 2006:12-3). Through the character of the government official, the film critiques these laws and agreements.

The ruins represent Africa as a place. The ancient walls and buildings have been destroyed by colonialism. It seems everyone has forgotten the place except the griot. In the turning point of the film, a car drives into the ruins. The vehicle is a symbol of modern and materialistic values, which intrude into the space. An aggressive security official steps outside of the car, frightening the children away. The security official's only interest in the griot is whether he has legally immigrated to Tunisia, has valid identification, possesses money or is a terrorist. For him, these factors define one's purpose, identity and belonging. But the griot does not need official papers to define his identity. Being a griot is a continuation of ancient traditions. His profession and identity are defined through his belonging to the community and its acceptance and appreciation to Africa at large. A griot enjoys a unique position where he is enabled and expected to speak up and critique society, and therefore partaking in its development (Smith 2010: 28-9).

The clash of pan-Africanism and nation-statehood becomes highlighted when the griot states: "I'm not an illegal immigrant. I'm at home here […] A griot feels home everywhere he goes." The security official is resentful of the griot's idea of them being brothers and belonging to the same living space. The official is a product and a guardian of nationalism, border control and modernity, whereas the griot knows no borders in Africa. What is implied clearly is that the concepts of nation-statehood and nationalism imported from the West to

Africa divided the united struggle against colonialism and neo-colonialism. Cultures are being disturbed when imposing homogeneous national identities (Sethi 2011:46). The borders, nationalism and increased control of citizens are a threat for the unity and the traditional African lifestyle that the griot represents. The film suggests that the artificial exclusion and a weakening of old customs in modern society are slowly alienating Africans in their own continent.

There are no alternative experimentations in the cinematic style in the film. However, Bouzid utilizes some filming techniques to empower the narration. When the griot steps outside of the cave the camera creates distance by zooming out. The griot walks at a slow pace in the front of the screen and the children are unfocused and blurred in the background. The diegetic sounds constantly grow. We hear the walking stick hitting the soil and the rocks. Simultaneously as the sound of the wind grows, the movement of it becomes more vivid on the screen. This kind of footage creates a feeling of a revival of ancient Africa.

Throughout the film the narrative construction is simple and rather slow paced. However, despite the slowness, and simplistic structure much is said and implied in the film. Moreover, these features highlight the meaningful content and message of the film. Oliver Barlet explains that the slowness of the footage in African cinema is typical, as it allows the spectator to engage with the film. Senegalese director Ababacar Samb Makharam once said that in oral story-telling the slowness of narration is crucial. Because the oral tradition is so deeply rooted in African cultures throughout the continent many African filmmakers have aspired to sustain the tradition in new digital forms of narrations (Barlet &Turner 1996: 171, 191).

Drawing from the oral tradition, proverbs play a significant role in the film. The griot explains to the children "We have one mouth and two ears, haven't we? It means that we have to speak once and listen twice." It can be interpreted that we, as spectators, also need to listen twice. The usage of sounds supports the proverb. Every scratch of the sand on the ground and the sound of the soft wind are clear. Outside the cave, the picture is almost silent, therefore all the sounds created by movements of the people and movements in nature catch our attention. As Barlet points out: "African cinema tells us, then, that we gain not only from looking at Africa, but also from listening to it" (Ibid: 192). This is the message of Bouzid as well, conveyed through the narrative, *mise-en-scène*, and slow shots and finally the soundtrack: we should listen to Africa.

The film ends with a scene where the griot is taken away by the security official. He leaves with him voluntarily but seems to realize the official's dubious motives. The camera zooms out high above the ruins. The children return to the middle of them and a close-up-shot shows one of the girl's faces. She and the viewer are left with confusion. How will the future generations preserve the memories of their African heritage?

*Restless Wandering* is not only an encounter between the griot, the children and the Tunisian security officer. It is also an encounter of Africans who are across borders, which are still, to this day, strikingly controlled by outsiders. It is an encounter of modernity and historical cultural heritage, and finally, it is an encounter of pan-Africanism and the artificial division of people. The griot feels at home everywhere. That is the essential content of the film. His identity constitutes from the past as much as it does from the present time. His belonging and right for being in a place is defined by the people, and not by immigration laws. Therefore, the film proposes an important question: does the obsession of sedentarist metaphysics of inclusion, exclusion and control over people's memberships alienate those with more nomadic or plural identity and belonging?

## That's my face / É a Minha Gara, 2001, by Thomas Allen Harris

Thomas Allen Harris is an African-American filmmaker, raised in both the Bronx of New York and Dar es Salaam in Tanzania. In his career, Harris has filmed subjects of identity, sexuality and race. Although Harris's work can be considered as American rather than African, in his film *That's My Face* Harris creates a bridge between the two cinemas. *That's my Face* is an experimental documentary about race, but in relation to his earlier films, it is much more personal, autobiographical and explicitly discusses identity construction in relation to Africa. The film is shot following three different generations, from the 1960s to the early 2000s, with all footage being silent (Harris added voice-over narration in the editing stage). The film explores African spirituality and identity, first discussing what it was like for Harris to grow up in New York in a black community and later on in Tanzania. Harris expresses that he felt equally at home in both places. However, he could never identify himself with Christianity and was entreated—or 'haunted', as he puts it—by African spirits. The documentary thus follows his journey to Brazil where Orishas, Yoruba gods, are worshipped and where the Yoruba religion is merged within Catholic traditions.

The opening shot of the film shows people in the streets in Brazil. In a voice-over, Harris explains how he has had a double vision ever since he was a child. His left eye sees everything normally, but the right eye is incapable of focusing, as if it only sees the essence and the aura of the object. This duality becomes the theme of the film: his growing up in two different countries; his feeling both American and African; his trying to follow his grandmother's teachings of Christianity but having dreams about the African spirits. Therefore, he finds the Orishas in Brazil consoling. Their duality, which evolves from two religions, is an aspect that Harris identifies with strongly.

The film is executed in a way that leaves space for other interpretations, since, as Harris states "[it is made to have] enough holes in the narrative that you could add your own narrative to it" ("That's my face: An interview with Thomas Allen Harris," n.d.). 'Leaving holes' can be interpreted via what Marks calls haptic visuality. Harris uses a lot of his own family home-video material and photographs. This footage is very grainy, and the camera is rarely still and focused. The footage from Brazil is shot with Super 8 film, which Harris believes brings nostalgia into pictures (ibid). Moreover, the film is almost always either over- or under-exposed with light. The framing of people's faces brings them very close to the screen and they hardly ever stay still: they dance, move and often stare straight at the viewer. Sometimes pictures are superimposed, creating duality and blurring views. The techniques which Harris uses can, as Marks has noted in her study of the techniques of intercultural filmmakers, "discourage the viewer from distinguishing objects and encourage a relationship to the screen as a whole" (Marks 2000:172). This is because the images prevent an easy connection to the narrative and therefore, the viewer is forced to complete the images, filling them with his or her own memories (Marks 2000: 163, 177).

In a process of completing the images the imagination becomes essential. Appadurai (1990) has expressed how the image, the imagined, and imaginary are central components in connecting people in contemporary world. They interlink the moving groups such as diasporas and the people who cannot afford to move, but who can move through the imagination created by the media. In *That's My Face*, it is not only the blurred, unfocused footage that creates the space for the viewer's imagination, but also the mismatching of the picture and sound. In addition to the visual, the soundtrack of the documentary highlights and encourages imagining. Harris' own voice is very mystical and soft. Sometimes there are several voices on top of one another. Sometimes Portuguese is mixed with English; sometimes it is translated into English, with the spectator still hearing the original Portuguese voice. The filmmaker explains that he wanted to create a 'dreamscape' ("That's my face: An interview with Thomas Allen Harris," n.d.). This is for the viewer to complete the picture with their imagination and to create their own dreamscape.

The reflections on plurality in the identities of the Orishas become essential for Harris's sense of belonging. Orishas in Yoruba religion are deities, which play the role as intermediaries between the gods and men. During the cross-Atlantic slave trade the religion merged with Catholicism. The Orishas and the saints in Catholic religion were seen to reflect each other and both deities occupied same roles as spiritual intermediaries between god and men. Further, the whole religion of Yoruba is stated to have developed into a transnational and pan-ethnic religion (Cohen 2002:17). The double roles and crossover of cultures and traditions are identifiable for Harris. His aim is to find his spiritual home. Although his journey is physical, finding it requires inherent imagining. He goes to Brazil and participates in religious festivals and celebrations to become closer to the Orishas. However, in the end, finding his spiritual home is more a psychological state of mind that he effectively creates through the film. *That's My Face* (in Portuguese *É a Minha Gara*) is explained as 'my thing'. It can be anything that one feels he or she can identify with, something, which represents him or her. Many characters in the film are in search of their *É a Minha Gara*. One says she came to Brazil from the United States to feel how it is like to be part of the majority. She wanted to feel home, not physically, but rather spiritually. In the black community in New York, where Harris grew up some people chose to ignore their African cultural heritage. For Harris this was not appealing. He states it was like putting up a mask. In Brazil the history of Africa is constantly present and celebrated. Harris' homing desire may not be completed but he finds the idea of a plural identity soothing; there he finds a space to belong.

## The place in between/ Notre étrangère, 2010, by Sarah Bouyain

*The Place in Between* is the first feature film by the French-Burkinabe filmmaker Sarah Bouyain. The story is set in both Paris and in a second largest city of Burkina Faso, Bobo-Dioulasso. Amy, the protagonist in the film, is a mixed-race young woman; her mother is Burkinabé and her father, who has passed away, is French. Since Amy was eight years old, she has been living in France with her father and his new wife. In her early days of adulthood, Amy wants to reconnect with her biological mother and therefore travels to Burkina Faso in search of her. To her disappointment, her mother Mariam has left the village a long time ago and Amy stays with her aunt Acita and her maid Kadiatou trying to learn about her past. What the viewer knows, but Amy does not, is that Mariam has migrated to Paris, where she works as a cleaner and teaches Dioula language to a French woman, Esther, who works in the building where Mariam cleans. Esther is about to adopt a child from Burkina, but only reveals this to Mariam in at the end of the film.

Through foregrounding the encounters of the five women, Bouyain highlights the kind of transnational space, which Brah (1996:181) calls a *diaspora space*, in which we all live. According to Brah and Bouyain, it is not only people with a multicultural background[10], but rather everyone who is affected by intercultural relations, differences and their challenges. In the film, only Amy's character belongs to two cultures. Yet the sense of a search for belonging and feeling at home is not a feeling reserved only for her. Both Mariam and Amy feel lost between the two countries and do not know where they belong. Esther, Kadiatou and Acita, although more grounded, are affected deeply by the uprooting of people like Amy and Mariam who they are close to.

For all the characters in the film, language plays an essential role; it both separates and unites the women. Acita and Amy have no mutual language to communicate with each other, but the young maid is able to translate their conversations. Mariam lives an isolated exile life in France, and refuses to establish connections with the African diaspora community. However, the language lessons she gives in her mother tongue to Esther provide glimpses of happy moments in her life. During the lessons, she feels useful.

As Naficy (2001: 28) points out, the mother tongue in a strange environment can evoke strong feelings and memories of home. These moments are a way for Mariam to feel at home. Esther learns a foreign language to prepare a foundation for her family relationship. Thus, language is a tool to connect and disconnect. In the Burkina Faso scenes, the viewer (if not a Dioula speaker) is always positioned within Amy's perspective. For her, conversations with her aunt are never subtitled. When the two argue, their feelings can be sensed and Amy's words understood, but only Dioula speakers would know how Acita responds. In this scene the viewer is forced to complete the image and understanding through reading Acita's expressions and listening closely to her voice. Here Bouyain utilizes the technique which Naficy call tactile optics. Thus, the viewer interprets the feelings of characters with a deeper engagement and is not distanced from the conversation through subtitles. However, the

---

10. Multicultural as a person who comes from more than one country and/ or cultural background.

scenes of Mariam teaching Dioula to Esther, and the dialogues between Acita and the locals of Bobo are translated. The conscious choice of the filmmaker to exclude the viewer with Amy is to emphasize how hard it can be to communicate (Amarger, 2010).

Language is one of the key components of our identity. Without Amy being able to communicate with her aunt she is forced to face her alienation from her family and culture and find alternative means of communication, which she does by employing universally recognized indications of different emotions. In order for Amy to express herself she uses physical contact, without the use of verbal formulation. In a scene where Amy and Acita converse in their own languages, they express themselves through smiling, laughing and touching each other. But it is not only language that makes Amy and Mariam feel estranged from Burkina Faso and France respectively.

The separation of the mother and the daughter creates estrangement. Whereas Amy tries to find her mother but fails, Mariam isolates herself, perhaps punishing herself, perhaps blaming herself for the separation they both experience. Also, a distant culture and non-integration are central to the women's feeling of homelessness. Mariam's roommate, for example, has made an effort to integrate into French society. She has made friends, decorated her room, and enjoys her life in Paris. Mariam has made a choice to stay detached from her surroundings. We see her wandering the streets in the suburbs on her own, and when a priest from the community church approaches her she retreats more into herself. Mariam's exile portrays the loneliness that is experienced as not due to a hostile environment but because she determinedly positions herself in a no man's land. Her experience is complementary to that of John Durham Peters, who sees exile as a painful banishment (see chapter *Cinema as a Catalyzer for Transnationalism*).

When Amy returns to Burkina, she is not prepared to feel disconnected. After the first disappointments she complains about everything from flies and hot weather to miscommunication with her aunt over the phone to her brother in France. She has an African dress tailored but is not comfortable wearing it. Her blunt, white hotel room in Bobo becomes her place of escape. When she is discontent with her aunt, she returns to the hotel. After Amy's African dress falls off her in public because she does not know how to tie it properly, she returns to the room, and aggressively throws the dress away. She is considered a European tourist. The locals call her white, the taxi-driver charges her extra and her aunt decorates a room for Amy to feel at home. Acita says: "White people always hang things on their walls." As Bouyain notes, this is a legacy of colonialism: "[Amy's] family history could just as well have been lived by a French family living in France" (Bouyain quoted in Amarger 2010).

Amy's feeling of homelessness in Burkina Faso is further emphasized in the shot of her feet. Naficy remarks that close-up footage of a body is often a way to show alienation in accented films. Further, Dovey (2009 b: 61) discusses how there have been "a surprising number of close-up shots of feet in francophone West-African film".[11] According to Said, exiles are often thought to be cut off

---

11. In her article (Subjects of exile: Alienation in Francophone African cinema) Dovey discusses closely the images of feet in films by Ousamane Sembene (La Noire de..., 1966; Niaye ,1964; Xala, 1974), Samb

from their roots, their land and their past (Dovey 2009b: 60). Feet are the part of the body, which connects a person to the ground. Therefore, symbolically one is uprooted from her or his feet. In *The Place in Between*, only Amy's feet are shot closely. After she goes to see her aunt for the first time she returns to the hotel. After her showering, the camera focuses on her wet toes, restlessly rubbing against the floor. In another scene in Acita's house, Amy stands in the terrace looking at the rain. Again, the camera shoots her feet closely, while she plays with the water with her feet. To connect with her past, she needs to attach her bare feet to the soil, and ground herself again to Burkina Faso.

According to Naficy (2001: 289) the visual style used in intercultural cinema is often incomplete and rough, as can be seen as the defining characteristic in *That's My Face*. However, in *The Place in Between* the camera is very still as it follows Amy and her journey. The still, sometimes completely stagnant camera is frequently used in the works of West African filmmakers such as Abderrahmane Sissako, Ousmane Sembene and Mahamat Saleh Haroun. Bouyain explains the fixity of the frame is to highlight Amy's anxiety and movement, her search for home (Amarger 2010). The everyday life in Bobo is calm and relaxed. Therefore, the anxious behavior of Amy, her nervousness and uncomfortable state of being, are emphasized. Further, the extra-diegetic signature music of the film gives a further sense of Amy's anxiety, following the events fom Paris to Bobo and the other way around. Even though the locations are distant and different they are connected, not only through the soundtrack and anxiety of the characters but also through the style of editing. After the footage of Acita and Kadiatou washing clothes and pouring water the camera follows Esther pouring water for Mariam. When Amy and Acita are shot sleeping, the music and camera moves to film Amy's French mother lying down on her couch, focused on a picture of Amy as a child. Later in the film Esther receives a mango fruit as a gift from Mariam. Soon Amy is picking fruits from a tree in Bobo and leaves one beside her resting aunt. This parallel editing style reaffirms the intense dialogue between the women as well as showing the character's loneliness and lack of belonging in different parts of the world.

## Home as a journey

*Restless Wandering*, *That's My Face* and *The Place in Between* all share a common feature of highlighting the issue of return and reconnection to home and the homeland. In the first film, modern enforcement of nation-state boundaries alienates the griot, representing the traditions of Africa, from his homeland and livelihood. The latter two films discuss the issue of what it means to belong to different cultures and the complexity of reconnecting to one's origins in these cases. Naficy writes how the trope of the journey is a dominant element in accented cinema. The journeys of de-territorialization and re-territorialization take different forms but just as importantly, they are not only

---

Makharam (Et La Neige N'Etait Plus,1965), Djibril Diop Mambety (Hyenas, 1992) and by Abderrahmane Sissako (Waiting for Happiness, 2002).

physical and geographical but also cultural, metaphorical and psychological (Naficy 2001: 222).

In *That's My Face*, Harris detaches himself from his physical home even before beginning his journey to Brazil. The first half of the film is a preparation for his journey. As Sissako (quoted in Armes 2006:198) says: "We make true exile within ourselves even before we depart. It's a sort of interior exile." This interior exile translates into a 'no man's land.' One does not belong to the place of departure, nor to the destination. Similarly, Mariam in *The Place in Between* resents herself into interior exile. Amy feels internally alienated as well, as she finds it hard to re-connect to her past, whereas for the griot in Bouzid's film, the alienation is forced through an outsider. Naficy (2001: 6) writes that:

> Journeys are not just physical and territorial but also deeply psychological. Among the most important are journeys of identity, in the course of which old identities are sometimes shed and new ones refashioned. In the best of the accented films, identity is not a fixed essence but a process of becoming, even a performance of identity.

Throughout the three films there is a binding theme, that identity and belonging, the sense of being at home, is a psychological state of mind. The homing desire is in one's imagination. Although, the protagonists are actively seeking their place in between cultures, they have no need to fix their feet on one specific place. Instead, they re-construct and reattach to multiple places and identities. The films effectively perform identity and belonging as a process. This conception of home and belonging being fluid and plural is essential for those who have lived through experience of exile.

## Conclusion

Since the end of the twentieth century there has been a profound shift in the understanding of spaces of cultures. The conventional premise has been that people and cultures are rooted in their natural places and territories and therefore, sense of belonging and feeling at home are inseparable elements from peoples' homelands. However, the process of globalization has accelerated the flows of capital, transport and people. Thus the world and people have become more inter-linked than ever before. Territorialized spaces and borders are constantly compromised and challenged by de-territorialised people, as they occupy multiple places and inter-link them to one another, creating ambiguous borders. As a consequence, the concept of home has gone through a transformation, from being something rooted and fixed to fluid and 'processual.' As people are scattered from their homelands, communities or are chronically mobile, the images and imagination are essential part of social process, reconnecting the people and places. As the images and media create connectedness amongst the displaced and transnational people and places, the homing desire translates into an imaginative connectedness.

Transnationalism has not only triggered debates about belonging, nation and home in academia, but has also become more visible in media. The voices of transnational artists have been increasingly influential, especially in cinema. In an era where people are more nomadic than ever before, the diaspora space is inhabited by not only those who belong to several cultures, but also by everyone who is affected by globalization. Therefore, a work that articulates the basic human need and desire of homing and belonging is more valuable than ever before. By understanding home and belonging as only a physical attachment to a place, we dismiss the lived experiences and memories of those with multiple attachments. It is then the plural, nomadic and transnational views, which provide us with fresh perspectives on the concepts of home and belonging. As Deleuze and Guattari state:

> History is always written from a sedentary point of view and in the name of a unitary State apparatus, at least a possible one, even when the topic is nomads. What is lacking is a Nomadology, the opposite of a history (Deleuze and Guattari quoted in Malkki 1992:31).

I see intercultural cinema as a prominent medium to represent 'Nomadology': the missing side of the history written from the point of view of those who have often been marginalized and yet have contributed to and significantly shaped the contemporary world. In this article I have analyzed three films: *Restless Wondering* by Nouri Bouzid, *That's My Face* by Thomas Allen Harris and *The Place in Between* by Sarah Bouyain, and demonstrated their success to portray home as a journey, a fluid and plural concept which can be re-invented and re-constructed in the process of de-territorialization. The artificial division of people is not only controlled by the physical borders, but also by the legacy of colonialism and sedentarist metaphysics. The characters in the films are in search of plural, more nomadic identities, through which they can establish attachments to multiple places, especially to Africa. Therefore, the films call attention to what the griot in Bouzids's Restless Wandering describes as the African tree. Africa and the African diaspora share mutual substrate, from where they grow in different directions. The imagination becomes a profound element to reinforce these connections and keep alive the memories of African heritage.

# References

Print

Amarger, M. (2010, October). *Film Africa 2011 Press Pack*
Appadurai, A. (1990). Disjuncture and Difference in the Global Cultural Economy. *Public Culture, 2*(2), 1-24. doi:10.1215/08992363-2-2-1
Armes, R. (2006). *African filmmaking: North and south of the Sahara*. Edinburgh: Edinburgh University Press.
Baldwin-Edwards, M. (2006). "Between a rock & a hard place": North Africa as a region of emigration, immigration & transit migration. *Review of African Political Economy, 33*(108), 311–324. doi:10.1080/03056240600843089

Barlet, O. & Turner, C. (2000). *African cinemas: Decolonizing the gaze*. London: Zed Books.
Bouzid, N., & el Ezabi, S. (1995). New realism in Arab cinema: The defeat-conscious cinema/ الواقعية الجديدة في السينما العربية: سينما الوعي بالهزيمة. *Alif: Journal of Comparative Poetics*, 242-250. doi:10.2307/521690
Bordwell, D., Thompson, K., & Bordwell, P. D. (2004). *Film art: An introduction*. New York: McGraw Hill.
Brah, A. (1996). Cartographies of Diaspora: Contesting identities. New York: Taylor & Francis.
Cham, M. B., & Bakari, I. I. (Eds.). (1996). *African experiences of cinema*. London: BFI Publishing. In-line Citation: (Cham & Bakari, 1996)
Cohen, P. (2002), Orisha Journeys: The Role of Travel in the Birth of Yorùbá-Atlantic Religions, Archives de sciences sociales des religions , 47e Année, No. 117, Les Religions Afro-Américaines: Genèse et Développement dans la modernité (Jan. – Mar., 2002), 17-36.
Cuba, L., & Hummon, D. M. (1993). Constructing a sense of home: Place affiliation and migration across the life cycle. *Sociological Forum, 8*(4), 547–572. doi:10.1007/bf01115211
Davis, P. (1996). In darkest Hollywood: Exploring the jungles of cinemâs South Africa. United States: Ohio University Press.
Dovey, L. (2009a). African film and literature: Adapting violence to the screen. New York: Columbia University Press.
Dovey, L. (2009b). Subjects of exile: Alienation in Francophone west African cinema. *International Journal of Francophone Studies, 12*(1), 55–75. doi:10.1386/ijfs.12.1.55_1
Foster, G. A. (1997). Women filmmakers of the African and Asian Diaspora: Decolonizing the gaze, locating subjectivity. United States: Southern Illinois University Press.
Guillen, P. L. (2002). *The changing face of home: The transnational lives of the Second generation*. United States: Russell Sage Foundation Publications.
Guttman, S. (2001, October). Talking to Sotigui Kouyaté: The Vice Man of the Stage. *Unesco Courier*. Retrieved from http://unesdoc.unesco.org/images/0012/001237/123798e.pdf
Hall, S. (1996). Cultural Identity and Cinematic Representation: In H.A. Baker (Ed. alt.), *Black British Cultural Studies: a reader*. (pp. 36-58). Chicago: University of Chicago Press.
Kibreab, G. (1999). Revisiting the debate on people, place, identity and displacement. *Journal of Refugee Studies, 12*(4), 384–410. doi:10.1093/jrs/12.4.384
Kristeva, J., & Roudiez, L. S. (1982). *Powers of horror: An essay on abjection* (19th ed.). New York: Columbia University Press.
Lemelle, S., & Kelley, R. (Eds.). (1994). *Imagining home: Class, culture and nationalism in the African Diaspora*. United Kingdom: Verso Books.
Marks, L. U. (2000). The skin of the film: Intercultural cinema, embodiment, and the senses. Durham, NC: Duke University Press Books.
Malkki, L. (1992). National geographic: The rooting of peoples and the Territorialization of national identity among scholars and refugees. *Cultural*

*Anthropology, 7*(1), 24–44. doi:10.1525/can.1992.7.1.02a00030

Naficy, H. (Ed.). (1999). Home, exile, homeland: Film, media and the politics of place. London: Routledge.

Naficy, H. (2001). *An accented cinema: Exilic and diasporic filmmaking*. United States: Princeton University Press

Panzacchi, C. (1994). The livelihoods of traditional griots in modern Senegal. *Africa, 64*(02), 190–210. doi:10.2307/1160979

Peters, J. D. (1999). Nomadism, Diaspora, Exile: The Stakes of Mobility within the Western Canon: In H. Nacify (Ed.), *Home, Exile, Homeland: Film, Media, and the Politics of the Place* (pp. 17–41). New York: Routledge.

Said, E. W. (1979). Zionism from the standpoint of its victims. *Social Text*7. doi:10.2307/466405

Said, E. W. (1988). *Orientalism* (25th ed.). New York: Knopf Doubleday Publishing Group.

Sethi, R. (2011). The politics of Postcolonialism: Empire, nation and resistance. London: Pluto Press.

Smith, K. B. (2010). Questions of source in African cinema: The heritage of the griot in Dani Kouyat's films. *Journal of African Media Studies, 2*(1), 25–38. doi:10.1386/jams.2.1.25/1

Shohat, E., & Stam, R. (Eds.). (2003). *Multiculturalism, Postcoloniality and transnational media*. United States: Rutgers University Press.

Sobchack, V. (1999). Is Anybody Home? : Embodied imagination and visible evictions. In H. Nacify (Ed.), *Home, Exile, Homeland: Film, Media, and the Politics of the Place* (pp. 45–62). New York: Routlege.

Solanans, F. and Getino, O. (1969). Towards a Third Cinema. Rpt. In Bill Nichols, ed., Movies and Methods: *An Anthology Vol. 1* (1976), Berkley/ London: U of California, 44-64.

That's my face: An interview with thomas allen harris. Retrieved July 6, 2015, from http://blackfilm.com/20030523/features/thomasallenharris.shtml

Vitali, V., & Willemen, P. (Eds.). (2006). *Theorising national cinema; Ed. By Valentina Vitali*. London: British Film Institute.

Wainana, B. (2006, January 19). *How to write about Africa*. Retrieved July 5, 2016, from Essays & Memoir, http://granta.com/how-to-write-about-africa/

Filmography

Bouzid, N. (Director). (2009). *Restless wondering: L'Afrique Vue Par* [DVD]. Algeria: Laith Media.

Bouyain, S. (Director). (2010). *The Place in Between /Notre étrangère* [DVD]. France, Athénaïse, Abissia Productions, Centre National de la Cinématographie (CNC).

Harris, T. A. (Director). (2001). *That's My Face/É a Minha Gara* [DVD]. USA: Chimpansee Productions.

Harris, T. A. (Director). (n.d.). *Twelve Disciples of Nelson Mandela* [Video file]. USA/ South Africa, Chimpansee Productions.

Whitfiel G. (Director). (2002). Interview with Abderrahmane Sissako: special features in Waiting for Happiness, [DVD] Artificial Eye.

# 'Spare Tires', 'Second Fiddle' and 'Prostitutes'? Interrogating discourses about women and politics in Nigeria

Grace Adeniyi-Ogunyankin

One theme that emerged from my PhD fieldwork research on gender and the urban political economy during the 2011 elections in Ibadan, south western Nigeria, is the marginalization of women in politics.[1] So dominant was the theme that in a conversation with a male colleague he declared that he would not vote for me if I contested as a politician because I was a woman and politics was not meant for women. I thought he was joking, but as our conversation progressed, I realized he was adamant. This paper is inspired by that encounter, and the need to explore in some detail women's marginalization in colonial and postcolonial Nigerian politics.

This paper examines discourses on women and politics in Nigeria[2] and analyzes why the political is gendered in ways that leave women out. Drawing largely on in-depth interviews carried out with local women in Ibadan, Nigeria, I argue that women are aware of, and critical about, the gendered nature of politics in Nigeria as a key factor operating against the participation of women in formal politics. They openly speak out against culture and patriarchy but are cautious to criticize their religious affiliations[3] even when they recognize the role religious discourses play in their exclusion. Moreover, though women disagree with hegemonic patriarchal cultural discourses that propagate women's

1. In Nigeria's Fourth Republic (1999 to the present), men overwhelmingly dominate politics. No woman has ever been elected president or governor of any of Nigeria's thirty-six states. There have been a few deputy governors, the highest being six in 2007. In the lower house of the Nigeria's national assembly, called the House of Representatives, the highest number of elected women occurred in 2007 when, of 360 representatives, 25 (7.5%) were women. In the upper house of Nigeria's national assembly, called the Senate, the situation of women's representation is no different. In 2007, out of 109 the highest number of women senators also occurred in 2007 where nine (8.3%) out of 109 senators were women.(see Agbalajobi, 2010; European Union Election Observation Mission to Nigeria, 2011; Federal Ministry of Women Affairs, 2004; Irabor, n.d.; International Federation for Human Rights, 2008).
2. Nigeria is a very populous country with various ethnic and cultural groups. This paper, while using Nigeria has an umbrella word, focuses on South West Nigeria. It is probable that there are inter and intra regional differences not captured in this paper.
3. The women I interviewed were Muslims and Christians. The Christians were Anglican, Catholic and from charismatic African initiated churches. Note that when the Christian women stated their religion, they would most often state their denomination as well. Or they would mention their church/denomination in passing during the interview. The Muslim women would just state that they were Muslim. Note that most Muslims in Nigeria are Sunni. The most prominent sects are Ahmadiyya, Sanusiyya and Quadriyya.

political exclusions, they hesitate to challenge the status quo because of their desire to be perceived as respectable women.

I begin the paper by discussing the influence of Victorian ideologies of gender in the gendered formation of the Nigerian state and the consequent impact upon women's exclusion from formal politics. I argue that these gender ideologies have played a key role in shaping discourses that construct women as "spare tires," "second fiddle" and "prostitutes." I next show that culture, religion, and violence through political godfatherism play a central role in constructing women as outside of the political landscape and women political participants as deviants. I also highlight that when women do partake in the political sphere, it is often in gendered ways that do not challenge hegemonic patriarchal structures. I posit however that allowing women to participate in politics in a manner that values their gendered knowledge, perspectives and experiences is a key step towards gender equality. I conclude by examining women's proposal for transformative change in gender relations in Ibadan.

In this paper, the reference to women as "spare tires" in politics is when rare exceptions are made to justify women's entry into politics based on essentialised notions about women as non-violent, moral, and caring mothers. "Second fiddle" refers to the popular belief that women are supposed to play a subordinate role to male in politics. My use of "prostitutes" in this paper reflects the commonly held assumption that a woman's primary role is to be a "good" wife and mother who values domesticity. Thus, a woman who participates in politics is oftentimes viewed from a moral perspective as a "bad" woman who transgresses her assigned gender role because she is outside the home, where she does not belong, mingling with men in the political arena.

This paper draws on data from the semi-structured interviews I conducted with forty-eight women, ages eighteen to eighty-three, in two local government areas of metropolitan Ibadan, Oyo state. Within each local government area, I chose twenty-four women through purposive sampling. The major variables of concern for the study were income-level and age. I use data from ten key informant interviews with local government workers in the departments of Community Development and Town Planning and the Oyo State Ministry of Women Affairs, two local politicians, as well as discourse analysis of Nigerian newspaper articles (print and web), spanning three decades, on women and politics to support the arguments advanced in this paper.

## Culture and the rendering of women as "Spare Tires," "Second Fiddle" and "Prostitutes"

> The woman is the helper. By virtue of that, they are to play an assisting role [...] it's like a spare tire so when the real tire is defective, I mean burst or has a problem, then you can pick the other one and put it there (E. Awoniyi, personal communication, July 10, 2011).[4]

---

4. This comment was made by one of my male colleagues at the University of Ibadan during our discussion on women and politics in Nigeria.

During my interviews with women in Ibadan, the most cited reasons (across class, age and educational levels) for the marginalization of women in politics were cultural and religious. All the women interviewed clearly asserted that politics has been created as a man's world and women's right to participate on an equal footing is suppressed. The interviews highlight C. Otutubikey Izugbara's (2004) argument that "Men and women enter national [imaginaries] differently" (p. 25). In this imaginary, in Nigeria, men are viewed to be natural leaders. As expressed by one participant:

> It seems […] men […] choose to be in the positions. The women, perhaps they look at them and say, what can these people do? What can women do? [They think] that wherever men are, women should not be there to occupy those positions, and that if they get there they won't even know how to do it at all. They come to these conclusions without ever giving women a chance (Ayobami,[5] interview by author, Ibadan, Nigeria, 02 Aug. 2011).

Men's 'presumed' natural right as leaders is predicated on the notion that they have authority and power over women. Many participants highlighted that this apparent inherent political right of men cheats women by presuming that the political is the domain of men.

Women, however, enter the national imaginary as biological and social reproducers who are supposed to stay out of public affairs, or only enter as supporters of men. One participant clearly illustrates this point through her argument that, "They don't like to hear women's voices in public. Only men want to be the ones who will be talking [and] who will become a big person. The thing that [a] woman [is] for is that, she cooks the food, takes care of the children, that she also eats and takes care of her husband" (Mojisola, interview by author, July 15, 2011). Participants posited that women are often unwanted political participants and they see them as being incapable of making sound decisions or that it is culturally unbecoming for women to expose themselves in public for political activities outside of domestic and supportive roles. They consider women who overstep this boundary to be 'culturally deviant.'

The reason why the Nigerian political imagination excludes women as political subjects, and views them mainly as mothers, wives and reproducers of culture, is partly located in the gendered formation of the Nigerian state. An understanding of the history of gender politics in Nigeria enables an analysis of the construct of women as outside of politics. As Mire (2001) argues, "African social and political thought cannot be understood in abstraction from the history of colonial encounter between European colonial conquest and African society" (p. 4). Contemporary narratives about politics—who belongs and who should participate—cannot be divorced from British Victorian ideologies of gender.

In Nigeria, British colonial administrators implemented indirect rule as a tool of governance. The British believed that leaving local community affairs in the hands of local chiefs and rulers was a means of keeping Nigerian culture intact (Kirk-Greene, 1965, p. 246). The appointed chiefs and rulers were usually male and this system of indirect rule disregarded the fact that female leadership was part of culture in many Nigerian societies.

---

5. Real names have been altered to help protect research participants.

The British also superimposed the Victorian ideologies of gender on many societies/communities in Nigeria. It was inconceivable to the British that Nigerian women could be chosen as indirect rulers because in Britain, the public duty of women was an extension of private role and as Mba (1982) asserts, the "British administrators worked for a government in which there were no women at any level" (p. 39). Helen Callaway (1987) also notes that the colonizers "assumed African women generally to be in a dependent and subordinate position to men even in areas where women were noted for their independent trading activities and their political power" (p. 51). Thus, colonial administration was based on the ideology that women should occupy the domestic sphere and men the public sphere. This rendered Nigerian women invisible in the governing of British Nigeria. It made the exercise of control they had over their own affairs in precolonial Nigeria irrelevant. Colonial rule subdued the representation and voice they had in decision-making (Mba, p. 38; Petsalis, 1990, p. 197; Okoh, 2003, p. 22). Under indirect rule, the British administrators and the 'native' administrators of indirect rule, "rarely consulted women on matters that affected them" (Johnson-Odim & Mba, 1997, p. 11). Colonial rule relegated women solely to the status of child bearers and housekeepers.

Victorian ideologies of gender and domesticity were not only used as a frame of reference by the British for administration in Nigeria, but also instilled through the colonized education of boys and girls. The 1909 Code of Education was gendered (Okonkwo & Ezeh, 2008) because it emphasized training males to become professionals while females were trained to become good wives and mothers (Denzer, 1992). By the early mid-twentieth century, girls' education had reformed slightly. Girls were allowed to pursue education that would allow them to contribute to the colonial economy. Nevertheless, their education continued to stress the importance of devotion to home and family regardless of economic status or education (Denzer, p. 122).

On the eve of Nigeria's independence of October 1, 1960 there were more women, albeit few by comparison to the total population of women in Nigeria, who possessed tertiary education and professional training. However, the gendered education system contributed to the "preponderance of the male population in the new emerging social elite, which provided the political leadership of the nationalism of the [mid] twentieth century" (Okonkwo & Ezeh, p. 189).

Women and men collaborated in Nigeria's struggle for independence from British rule. However, not many women were involved in the nationalist movements and when women were involved it was class based (Pereira, 2000). Postcolonial Nigeria was built on a "male privileging colonial ideology" that quickly forgot women's contribution to nationalism (Nzegwu, 2001, p. 6). In line with Yuval-Davis' (1997) and McClintock's (1995) approach, gender is crucial to understanding Nigeria as a nation. Nigeria was directly gendered through the feminization of Nigeria as a domestication project and through the imported ideologies of gender that shaped colonial society. In the post-independence era, Nigeria became further gendered by the continual exclusion of women from the public sphere and the reinvention of tradition.

In addition, women's role as gatekeepers of customs and culture shapes

Nigeria as a gendered nation. As Yuval-Davis (1997) notes, women's role as custodian of culture and custom is pertinent in reproducing the nation. This has been exemplified in Nigeria in the post-independence era by the National Council of Women's Society (NCWS). Elite Nigerian women formed the NCWS in 1959 as a non-partisan and non-political organization (Mba, 1989, p. 71). The NCWS's aims were to "promote the welfare and progress of women, especially in education and to ensure that women [were] given every opportunity to play an important part in social and community affairs" (Pereira 2000, p. 118). The NCWS was recognized as the only organization representing women's interest. However, NCWS has mainly served the interests of a sub-group of women. At the organization's prime, it assured the federal government that it did not desire political power because women had not forgotten their traditional roles as mothers and wives. The NCWS, as Pereira argues, "employed the discourse of motherhood, and the concomitant responsibility for family affairs and child rearing as the ultimate destiny of all women" (p. 123). Thus, for women, their involvement in national affairs in the public realm is limited to the extension of their domestic role (p. 124). This discourse resonated with Victorian ideology. As such, the NCWS did not make inroads in serving or capturing Nigerian women's interests, needs, and priorities, nor were women included in decision-making processes. Notably, based on Nigeria's precolonial history, these women did not uphold the 'traditional' roles of women in Nigeria given that women historically were involved in making decisions.

In light of the preceding discussion, women are expected to honour their duties as mothers and spouses first and foremost. As such, political engagement was assumed to distract women from successfully performing these roles. Even when women are politicians, the validity of their leadership depends on proving that they are "good and responsible housewives and mothers" (Ibrahim, 2004, para. 42). A male politician I interviewed clearly demonstrates this point:

> If you say you have a meeting by 6 in the morning and your children will go to school, you have to care for your children and your husband. This will portray you better and show you're a good woman and you can be a good leader. But if your home is not tidied up, you cannot come outside and say you want to be a leader. You have to show them a good example (Mayowa, interview by author, March 16, 2011).

The expectation is that women should be doting mothers and dutiful wives which, according to this discourse, entails being at home. During the interviews, most women said political participation requires attending evening meetings. Fadeke noted that there is gender imbalance in political representation at the local level because "responsible women" rarely partake in politics:

> [...] women are not participating in politics like men because of the odd
> time they meet. You know they always meet at night. It is not easy for a *responsible woman to leave her home for a meeting at night. Our religious and cultural aspects [do not] even give the women enough opportunity to participate in politics* (interview by author, March 16, 2011; emphasis added).

These late-night political meetings contravene the cultural and religious expectation that a woman will be at home in the evening, and not "gallivant about." Because of these expectations, it is then assumed in popular discourse that women who dabble in politics are prostitutes. Seun mentioned that, "a lot of people have erroneous ideas about women participating in politics. A lot of people are biased; they think if you go into politics you become a prostitute" (interview by author, March 23, 2011). Jade, also remarked, "but you know any woman that wants to get there… it's a problem we have in Africa I mean Nigeria. Any woman in top office must be a flirt.[6] They believe that" (interview by author, August 22, 2011). Tobi, further explicated the prostitution narrative below:

> **Tobi**: …if any woman joins politics they'll be like, *"ah she must have been sleeping with men. How can a woman be having meetings in the night?"…*
>
> **Grace**: Do all political meetings take place at night or is it just a rumour?
>
> **Tobi**: It's not a rumour because they think that's the only time they can [meet]. I don't know why. But they do it in the night. Okay maybe they allow themselves to go and do their business during the day then they now come and I don't know why, and they feel a woman should not be there in the night.
>
> **Grace**: That she should be at home?
>
> **Tobi**: Yes
> (interview by author, July 18, 2011; emphasis added).

Since the political meetings take place at night, there is an assumption in popular discourse that a woman surrounded by several men would be sleeping with them. In addition, given that the political sphere is dominated by men, it is believed that for a woman to make it in politics, she must be using her 'bottom power' to rise.

Although women aspirants are not prostitutes, the moral narrative is nevertheless leveraged against them. Many Nigerian women aspirants are subjected "to smear campaigns [centering] on their alleged loose moral standing, [while] some are insulted directly" (IDEA 2006, p. 10). This is problematic because male privilege and double standards obscure the applicability of the same line of questioning to males. As Ibrahim (2004) asserts,

> It is well known…that many male politicians go on the campaign trail with girlfriends and/or sex workers. Male supporters see such behaviour as a normal sign of the virility of their leaders. Women candidates, however, even if they are not sexually promiscuous, indeed, even if they are saints, are expected to shoulder the burden of proof to show that they are morally upright. This suggests that the moral standards set for women politicians are higher than those for male politicians (para. 42).

---

6. The way Jade talked about being a flirt during the interview included engagement in sexual intercourse.

Moreover, husbands are sometimes ridiculed for not having control of their politically-oriented wives. The derision leverages the discourse that only "loose" women go into politics. As such, ridicule or the fear of ridicule makes it more difficult for women to obtain their husbands' support. A husband's support, beyond the need for adequate finances, is considered a paramount prerequisite for political participation. Even if a woman has a supportive spouse, it is possible the support may be only transient. As one interviewee explained,

> [The husband] will just wake up and tell you he's no more interested or maybe he starts sleeping outside with another woman too and then when you now accost him, 'Why are you doing this?' He will say, 'Hey you don't have time for me again, it is this your career political thing you have pursued.' That's it (Titilayo, interview by author, March 8, 2011).

There also seems to be a palpable fear that if women were to become dominant in the political sphere, gender relations would be ruined. This poses a threat to national stability—as the discourse that males are head and therefore *de facto* leaders—will no longer be tenable. This narrative was common in the newspapers I read and was also proffered, during interviews, as an explanation for why men are so resistant to women participating in politics. Concerns centered on the fragility of men's natural dominance and the decline of women's role in reproducing proper morals and culture. There is an underlying fear that women will no longer be under men's authority. As one interviewee pointed out, "It may not all go well with a man. You understand? And no man wants to play the *second fiddle*" (Ayo, interview by author, August 23, 2011; emphasis added). Other women during interviews noted that some men have a complex and cannot handle competition from women, and that they view themselves as superior to women. For them, it does not make sense that they would fall under a woman's leadership. In this way, women's leadership is often viewed by men as going against the natural order.

Religious cultural discourses play a central role in propagating patriarchal gender norms because "the belief that God destined men to be in charge and women to be governed by men is evident in many passages of the Islamic and Christian Holy Books" (Izugbara, 2004, p. 13). In this vein, religion is "used as an instrument in defense of patriarchy. Christian and Islamic law gives central place to paternalistic interpretation to women's appropriate roles and socio-political arrangements of the society" (Ndubuisi 2006, p. 2). During my interviews, people often explained leadership as something that is considered by society as inherently male because males have been ordained as head by God. Atinuke and Zahra for example highlighted the blurring of the Yoruba culture and Christianity/Islam in constructing women's political role as unnatural:

> **Atinuke**: Yoruba people they want women to respect men in the house even in the society. Maybe that's the major reason why they don't give women opportunity. They believe men have the power to be ruling because from the Bible woman was created from man (Interview with author, June 30, 2011).
>
> **Zahra**: I think in a situation you know God has made men to be our head so if we

look to that as per our culture if we believe in our culture men must always be the leader.

**Grace**: And do you agree with this view?

**Zahra**: I quite agree. Biblically, Islamically if you look

**Grace**: But you yourself do you agree? Let's say for now you have all the qualifications to become President, but somebody now says no you cannot become president because you are a woman like do you agree with it?

**Zahra**: Um, Islamically? Due to my religion?

**Grace**: Hmm. But, lets say religion. Now I know religion is very important so lets say religion put aside. What about your own personal feelings? Like I know that's what it says in the Qur'an and in the Bible

**Zahra**: I know if women if we were given chance. I think we will still be able to perform better than the men [...]
(Interview by author, June 30, 2011).

Many women I interviewed think that the ordaining of male as head and female as submissive is unfair because of the male tendency to exploit this designation. The women participants consequently called for increased participation of women in decision-making and governance. However, they did not want to challenge the dominant patriarchal cultural and religious discourse. Inasmuch as women acknowledged the egotistical[7] behaviour of men and a male fear of losing control over women if women were to enter politics, they did not critique the Bible or the Qur'an. Although women understood the position of their religious texts on gender relations, some women did not wholly believe that politics is not a place for women. They used religious teachings to highlight that women should not be excluded:[8]

**Ebun**: [...] Women don't have high positions [because the men think] women will be the one making rules for them [especially] when the bible says women do not have custom to make rules [...] That's what they are quoting. But, the world is more modern than that now. God left [the] command for everybody to love each other. (Interview by author, July 7, 2011).

**Nike**: Why should I be in the kitchen? I can be in the kitchen to take care of my family. That is what God sent us to this world to come and do. But it's not the only thing. You see when I traveled to Jerusalem [...] the guards that were taking us to the places where we were supposed to go and visit, when we were in the bus we were discussing the bible and discussing [that] women are next to God. In that sense, God has made women. We are mothers. We are the ones taking care of these children that he has sent to this world. Not men. How many men can put diapers on

---

7. By this, I mean some males' inflated idea of their own importance and selfish reluctance to include women in the political sphere.
8. By 'love', Ebun means that focusing on loving each other would reduce the propensity to promote women's exclusion.

their children? How many men can take his child and feed the child like a mother? So we are next to God. And they misuse it. Our men. That is the reason why God is taking it away from them.
(Interview by author, July 12, 2011).

As illustrated by Nike's comment, sometimes even when women's place in the political sphere is justified, the interviewees ensured that they did not stray far from cultural and religious notions of women's role. They seemed to do this because they want to be, and also desire to be perceived as, a good woman, wife, and mother, who is respectful to her husband and cherishes her matrimonial home.

## Violence, "thuggery" and intimidation: The masculinization of Nigerian politics

The most cited reason that my interviewees provided for their non-participation in politics or lack of interest in political participation was the issue of violence that pervades Nigerian politics.[9] Many research participants, like Damilola, highlighted the "do-or-die"[10] nature of Nigerian politics:

> **Damilola**: I see politics in Nigeria like do or die.
>
> **Grace**: What if it wasn't do or die? Do you want to become president?
>
> **Damilola**: If there was no do or die .
>
> **Grace**: So you are interested?
>
> **Damilola**: Ah, ah! I like it.
> (interview by author, August 30, 2011).

In another context the following exchange occurred:

> **Vivian**: [...] There was a woman sometimes ago that they killed, the politicians want[ed] people to vote for them [...] We can't have women there. The men won't accept it.
>
> **Grace**: Why?
>
> **Mary**: They will kill her (interview by author, July 13, 2011).

Godfathers, political gatekeepers, in Nigeria dominate politics and dictate who participates in politics. They are also responsible for most pre- and post-election

---

9. Note that violence was the most popular reason cited by women during the interviews, other cited reasons, which are beyond the purview of this paper, include low-levels of education and high cost of elections.
10. A popular phrase used to describe politics in Nigeria.

violence. Politically motivated violence is synonymous with politics in Nigeria. This violence affects women as well. Nigerian women electoral candidates have been "kidnapped, beaten up, sexually assaulted, and shot at in order to deter them from participating in elections" (Denny, 2011, para. 6). United Nations Women (UNWomen), in collaboration with a coalition of Nigerian civil society organizations and activists, spearheaded a pilot study in response to the issue of electoral violence against women. The study tracked incidents of violence against women aspirants in real-time during the 2011 elections (UNWomen 2011, para. 3). Preliminary findings reveal

> 75% of the field monitors report[ed] an incident or incidents of violence that were targeted specifically at women. The largest number of these incidents reportedly took place during political campaigns or rallies, while others occurred at political party events. The perpetrators were identified as primarily party supporters and agents (Coalition of civil society Nigeria/UNWomen/UNDP, 2011, p. 1).

As such, women do not like the insecurity of politics (Akindele et al, 2011, p. 192). Women would rather avoid politics altogether than face the violence. Since politics is "do-or die", it becomes gendered male through the discourse that "those who possess the wherewithal take politics by force when force is required" (Agbalajobi, 2010, p. 78). Women are excluded because they often opt out of exercising force. The pervasiveness of violence thus gives more credibility to the discourse that the political is a male prerogative and domain. Solape pointed out that women are unable to contend with the violent nature of politics:

> There are too many risks involved in Nigerian politics that I have to admit when it comes to physical strength, women are not as strong as men definitely [...] and that's one admission I'm not ashamed to make. We're not built that way (interview by author, July 26, 2011).

Moreover, there is a fear to speak out against the government because they believe that the godfather's foot soldiers are always "around the corner", ready to harm critics:

> The person who talks and says this [and] that concerning politics—they quote them and kill them—that's why nobody wants to talk. Try to understand. And I want you to really understand. Ah ah! If we both do it, it will be good. Do you understand me? If we both do it, it's for it to be good. But when they are killing people—who wants to die? Why don't you just wait until it's your time to die? Focus on your work... That's why I don't see some women who will [contest]. As for me, they can never call me to contest. I don't want trouble (Sike, interview by author, July 16, 2011).

Politics is gendered via violence because violence is associated with masculinity. Violence is not considered a deviation but an accepted part of masculinity and there is a growing connection in society between being a man and being violent (Jhally et al., 1999). The danger in accepting violence as a masculine norm is that in Nigeria, the validation of violence also allows politics to continue to be gendered and normalized as masculine. Accordingly, because violence is gendered masculine, and politics in Nigeria have become synonymous with violence, it is easy to say women do not belong. In this vein, since violence is gendered masculine, it is normal when men engage in politics and by this logic, when women participate in politics, it is considered abnormal. Thus, there has been a normalization of political violence in Nigeria. Terms such as 'tough', and 'strong' are used to describe 'real' men while the antithesis is often ascribed to womanhood. Using this reasoning, since political power in Nigeria is often attained through violent struggle, 'real' men then belong in politics, and 'real' women do not. This explanation normalizes and masculinizes violence and praises women for staying true to their nature by fearing violence and not participating in politics. The women who transgress risk having their womanhood called into question and are often labeled negatively.

In sum, not dismantling the notion of violence as natural and politics as masculine, and restricting women and men to a particular gendered script does not change anything; it only continues to situate women as outsiders and foreigners to the political terrain. Rather than problematize violence and condemn it as unnecessary, it condones it. Masculinity and femininity needs to be recognized as performances learned via socialization in order to disrupt the notion that politics is the purview of men.

## Does more women in politics equal meaningful change for women?

So far I have tried to demonstrate the marginalization of women in Nigerian politics. Now, a pertinent question needs to be asked: Does having more women in politics mean that things will get better for women? Not necessarily. Women politicians do not necessary support women's rights. For example, Nigerian Senator Eme Ufot Ekaette, a high profile woman politician, proposed an indecent dressing bill in 2008. The rationale for the bill was that a dress code is a solution to rape and sexual violence against women. However, the bill's proposed discourse blamed the victim, rather than recognize the existence of gender inequalities that promote a culture of violence against women.

The existence of a *femocracy* in Nigeria serves as a potential impediment to gender equality. Amina Mama (1997) defines *femocracy* as " an anti-democratic female power structure, which claims to exist for the advancement of ordinary women, but is unable to do so because it is dominated by a small clique of women whose authority derives from their being married to powerful men" (p. 81). In a similar vein, Jibrin Ibrahim (2004) posits that the:

> First Lady phenomenon has opened doors for women that had previously been closed. At the same time, it has created a dynamic in which political space has been appropriated and used by the wives and friends of men in power for purposes of personal aggrandisement, rather than for furthering the interests of women (para. 1).

The primacy of wives of men in leadership also means issues concerning Nigerian women are often not part of formalized decision-making, and are instead placed under the purview of the wives. This is a gendered and classed process. It is "gendered" because it makes it seem like women's issues are not significant enough for formalized decision-making and politics. It is "classed" because it limits who participates in contributing to what is considered and/or what is done about women's issues.

During my interviews with staff in the Women Affairs Division of the Department of Community Development and a senior official with the State Ministry of Women Affairs and Community Development, it was mentioned that there are frequent liaisons between the governor's wife and the wives of Ibadan local chairmen. For example, on issues pertaining to women at the local level, the Women Affairs branch of the Local Government Community Development Department hold meetings with the governor's wife. When the Local Government Women Affairs staff meets with the State Ministry of Women Affairs and Community Development or the Commissioner, the wife of the Chairman is usually present. Whenever there are top-down initiatives that the State Ministry of Women Affairs and Community Development want to pursue, the State Ministry discusses strategies with wives of the chairman. Moreover, the State Ministry of Women Affairs and Community Development uses the wives of the chairmen to hold local governments accountable to women with regards to programming and initiatives. This genders politics through not accounting for how women's issues might be taken up if woman assumed leadership roles. It assumes that leadership is male, and that women will always be by the leader's (their husband's) side.

Despite the foregoing negative analysis, there have been cases in which First Ladies have been instrumental in advocating for women's increased involvement in politics. An example is Patience Jonathan, the former First Lady of Nigeria, who worked to increase the number of women in decision-making her project during and after the 2011 election campaigns. Rumours suggest she pushed her husband to choose a 'large' number of women as cabinet ministers. Should politics be played out via influence, especially bedroom influence? Though gains are made for women, bedroom politics of this kind does not begin to address the root causes of women's marginalization from politics.

Women's success in politics is often questioned in popular discourse, and some people have noted that iconic female politicians gained their posts via patronage. Reuben Abati (2011), writing in the Nigerian *Guardian* newspaper, notes, "many of the women in politics are in public positions not because they merit them, but because they have been put there by their husbands, parents, or Godfathers. In that wise, they are agents of male domination, and not flag bearers of women empowerment" (para. 13). A few interviewees, especially professional middle class women, shared this opinion with regard to political appointments. The following expresses this sentiment:[11],

> I have seen a few women like this Okonjo Iweala who has been brought back a few times and other women who are doing well. But, unfortunately again, apart from this Dora Akunyili, who was [in charge of] NAFDAC you find that those ones who are now ministers, I'm sorry to say so, many of them are political appointees more on connections than on their own ability (Solape, interview by author, July 26, 2011).

---

11. NAFDAC is the National Agency for Food and Drug Administration and Control (NAFDAC)

Even when women are in the political sphere, it is possible that they may not serve the best interests of women. They may make anti-democratic decisions and they may be accused of using godfathers to get ahead. This does not mean that all women in the political sphere are tainted in this way. It also does not mean that it is hopeless to agitate for increased participation by women. Rather, it means being more critical of narratives that assume complacency when a token woman is represented. We need to ensure women in leadership roles do not move us in a backward direction, but a step towards promoting gender equality.

## A woman's touch?: The case for women's political participation

Despite the negative and dominant narratives on women politicians, there are some discourses that promote the participation of women in politics. Some of the newspapers[12] when they had positive things to say about women, were usually within a particular discourse about women that continues to gender politics. This discourse posits that women will bring sanity and decorum into politics and therefore they should participate. Their participation is based on the possibilities of what women will do to reduce the pervasive violence and corruption rather than on the fact that they should be given the equal opportunity to participate regardless of what they will do or not do for the political landscape.

Some of the women I interviewed strongly believed that because women are wives and mothers and conversant with domesticity as well as compassionate, caring and more moral than men, they will perform better in politics than males. Below are three examples from the interviews that illustrate the foregoing narrative:

> We women are not so stubborn or hard-hearted as men [...] [We] will do it well because people use to say you women are our mothers [...] though we haven't seen any woman who has been maybe head of state or head of anything, [...] I know that if women come to power they will do well (Toni, interview by author, August 23, 2011).

> Let the women try even this Presidency [or] governor[ship] let us see what we have [...] [Women] have the fear of God in them more than the men [...] and I pray that one day we [will] get there in Jesus' name (Fadeke, interview by author, March 16, 2011).

> You know women. Women are different from men. We are more kind, right? We

---

12. Women in Government (Sunday Tribune, March 31, 1991); Who shall go for us? (July 16, 1992); Are you ready for a female leader? (Sunday Times, July 27, 1992); Women to the rescue (Guardian, July 7, 1994); and That Iyabo's Interview, Nigerian women and 2007 Nigerian elections (Nigeria World, July 15, 2006).

are close to our children so we will do better than men (Sade, interview by author, August 23, 2011).

However, the women's narratives do not redress the current patriarchal discourses surrounding women and politics in Nigeria. Rather, the narratives proffered by my interviewees fit neatly into the patriarchal discourse on women and continues to gender politics as masculine as it remains exclusionary and expects that women can only be painted in the political landscape in particular ways. The male-female binary is retained and only serves to further reinforce patriarchy and gender roles. The narrative also privileges specific forms of femininity as well as obscures the fact that it sets particular barometer for evaluating women politicians. Moreover, if this narrative is prevalent, when a woman deviates from these expectations, she may not be seen as the exception but rather a wake-up call to re-evaluate whether women should continue to participate in politics. For example, there is a prevailing narrative that women are more moral, and therefore less corrupt. Since Nigerian politics is known for its high level of corruption, some people have called for women to take on their "spare tire" role to reduce corruption. However, when the first female speaker of the House of Representatives, Patricia Etteh was impeached in 2007 on allegations of corruption, the usefulness of women in politics became questionable in popular discourse. For example, in an article on the news website *Nigeriaworld* Bayo Omolola (2007) wrote,

> The heart-disturbing news about the involvement of such a highly placed female politician reduces the hope that the masses have for a better country that women are expected to build when they have the chance to be at the helm of affairs. The news also signals that women can be as guilty as men in doing damages to the nation (para. 7).

Nigeria is infamously known for its corruption, yet Patricia Etteh's level of corruption is situated within a gendered discourse while countless corrupt men have not been judged in a similar manner that discriminates against the male gender. A perfect example would be the former speaker of the House of Representatives, Dimeji Bankole, who was accused of corruption towards the end of his term. The judgments levied against him were on an individual basis, not on his gender. As such, it is important that women are not included in politics on the basis of gendered notions. Otherwise, they will never be valued as 'true politicians but rather viewed as foreigners with special entry visas to the political landscape.

However, arguing that women should play a significant role in decision-making and governance on the basis that they have different experiences and perspectives, alongside the democratic argument, is more relevant (de la Rey, 2005; Kamau, 2010; Kethusegile-Juru, 2003). Some of the women I interviewed also engaged with this discourse when I asked them if Ibadan would be different if more women occupied decision-making and political positions. Some reasons proffered for why women would be better were that they have better knowledge about the city, food security issues, and water and sanitation issues. Therefore, their inclusion in decision-making processes would entail investment in infrastructure and a reduction in the 'reproduction tax'[13] on women (Chant, 2007, p. 52). Here is a sample of my exchange with one of the women:

> **Adeola**: If a woman is councillor or governor [...] She may look at all the things that—like right now you know for us to fetch water and throw out the garbage that is women's work, not men's. [...] So a woman may think, people are suffering from things like this. Like the water, I said we don't have right now, she could find a neighbourhood and provide water for them. She may look at things and say, "ah, the women they don't have where they will be throwing trash." She'd provide a vehicle that will be throwing the waste away for them (interview by author, August 1, 2011).

Such reasoning was more common among low-income class women because most of these issues are connected to the socio-spatial inequalities present in the city and their social-reproductive work, which have little resonance for middle-class women. For example, the major challenge Bukky, a middle class woman, identified in her life is:

> **Bukky**: You know the challenges I face now as a housewife really have to do with staff. You know as I said, I'm out of the house all day. I can wake up in the morning and the housekeeper may not turn up. [...] Now I have a running battle with my gardeners. I have two of them. I've not seen them and my flowers are due for trimming. So you know you don't have people who can do it. The quality of services that you get now is very bad (interview by author, August 26, 2011)

In contrast, Tayo, describes her challenge as: "We don't have a toilet here, we also don't have water here. We have to go to Oke Ado to get water" (interview by author, July 20, 2011). Thus, the low-income women argued that because of their experience, they would have more insight on how to formulate, plan, and implement policies and programs to address these issues. This is clearly a more productive narrative because it places more value on women's experience and also provides a stronger argument for the inclusion of women.

## Conclusion: The road towards social transformation

> We need one another [...] we need to complement one another we must both be there we must both develop the nation, it must not be a one sided issue and I believe if we have that in mind we will be able to go far [...] (Funmi, interview by author, July 14, 2011).

> You know they are just starting. And one day they will get there. At least we now have women commissioners, women ministers, women senators, women honourables women as deputy governors [...] (Ayo, interview by author, August 23, 2011).

Although, my interviewees were not impressed by the ways women are

---

13. This refers to the social reproductive work women engage in such as the collection of water, house work, cooking and unpaid care work in addition to their income generating activities.

excluded from politics, they were still optimistic that things would improve. Some praised the Jonathan administration for its progressiveness in selecting the greatest number of women cabinet ministers (13) that Nigeria has seen to date. However, while an unprecedented inroad has been made with regard to the appointment of women to key posts, we must not celebrate too soon. As Lisa Denney (2011) has argued, "It is doubtful whether the top-down changes that President Goodluck Jonathan has made through political appointments of women will transform the role of women in politics without similar results achieved from the bottom-up" (para. 10). Thus, it remains pertinent to continue to challenge the discourses and factors deterring women.

Fortunately, many gender activists and organizations have been, and remain, active in challenging the marginalization of women in politics and advocating for change in Nigeria. Groups such as Women Rights Advancement and Protection Alternative (WRAPA), Gender and Development Action (GADA), and Forum of Nigerian Women in Politics (FONWIP) have done a lot to raise more awareness among society and government. Their current priorities are for the government to follow through on the National Gender Policy's aim to advance 35% affirmative action for women in all governance processes as well as the domestication of the Convention on the Elimination of All Forms of Discrimination Against Women (CEDAW).

However, in the push to reduce the marginalization of women, there is a disproportionate focus on sensitizing, educating and empowering women. For example, the Oyo State Ministry of Women Affairs and Community Development as well as the Women Affairs branch of the Department of Community Development usually target women for their sensitization programs. But is it possible for transformation to occur if only half of the population is being sensitized? There is a need for "a political environment that empowers women and simultaneously sensitizes men and transforms masculinist structures and processes on the importance and strategic relevance of increasing the role of women in national and sub-regional political decision-making processes for the advancement of democracy" (Mensah-Kutin, 2010, p. 30). Tola, suggested that men can become more sensitized once they actually hear what women have to say and recognize that women have contributions to make:

> **Tola**: You know that men act and behave in a way that asserts that they are the head of everything, so they use that to cheat women. Men would think that they are the ones who can plan and make everything work so that's the reason that I would give for why it is usually males who do it.
>
> **Grace**: What do you think we can do about it?
>
> **Tola**: *As women, we are the ones who know how things work in the city. We are the ones who know what's going on in the city very well.* If they leave some room for women to occupy some positions, that would be good.
>
> **Grace**: What are the steps that you think we can take to get there?
>
> **Tola**: ... so let's say they do a meeting they say that those women who have the

opportunity or the time, they should please come o. ... And [when] they allow women to talk or be part of the meeting, you know from there they would observe the intelligence of the woman that if she's in office, she will also succeed and do good things for the city ... (Personal communication, August 2, 2011; emphasis added).

The women I interviewed noted that the way forward, with regards to transformative change, starts at a young age:

We should correct it from the home front.... they should let the boy-child and the girl-child perform the same role so that there won't be discrimination in the workplace about the position to be occupied by a female or a male (Seun, interview by author, March 23, 2011).

We should not discourage our female children. You know these things started from when we were young, if the men are talking, a woman should shut up—even if they are talking nonsense. Anytime we have the opportunity to contribute to pour our mind ...we should not allow inferiority complex to pull us down. If we continue like this...hmmm...I am afraid. But we should start it from our home. We should encourage our female children to be even [participating in] school politics (Fadeke, interview by author, March 16, 2011)

My interviewees also emphasized that in addition to teaching their daughters to be confident and telling them that they should not play the "second fiddle", they will also socialize their sons in a way that deviates from prevailing gender stereotyping and norms. Hopefully, this type of socialization will pave the way for gender equality in the political arena. As one interviewee cogently remarked, "Things like that should change. They should be saying it in stories that 'once upon a time o, men were the only ones who were doing politics. But now, women are also doing it'" (Tola, interview by author, August 2, 2011). Clearly, women envision equal access to Nigeria's political landscape where they would no longer be considered "spare tires," "second fiddle" and "prostitutes."

## References

Ajayi, Y. & Ogbu, A. (2011). President Jonathan's 13 women: Can they deliver? THISDAY LIVE. Retrieved from http://www.thisdaylive.com/articles/president-jonathan-s-13-women-can-they-deliver-/95176/.

Ajayi-Soyinka, O. (2005). Who is afraid of agency?: Theorizing African women out of the victim syndrome. In J.R. Chepyator-Thomson(Ed), *African women and globalization: Dawn of the 21st century* (pp. 67-94). Trenton, NJ: Africa World Press.

Akindele, S. T., Adeyemi, O. O. & Aluko, K. (2011). The myth and reality of women in politics: A discourse of the core issues. *African Journal of Political Science and International Relations* 5 (4): 190–207.

Anderson, B. (1983). Imagined communities : Reflections on the origin and spread of nationalism. London: Verso.

Bolaji, K. (2008). Towards greater participation of Nigerian women in democratic governance and development: Challenges and prospects. *Gender and Behaviour* 5 (2): 1406–1420.

Center for Asia Pacific Women in Politics. (2012). Women heads of state. Retrieved from http://www.capwip. org/participation/womenheadofstate.html

Coalition of civil society Nigeria/UNWomen/UNDP. (2011). Statement on violence against women in politics in Nigeria. Iknowpolitics. Retrieved from http://www.iknowpolitics.org/node/41654.

Davin, A. (1997). Imperialism and motherhood. In F. Cooper and A. L. Stoler (Eds.), *Tensions of empire: Colonial cultures in a bourgeois world* (pp. 87-151). Berkeley, Calif.: University of California Press.

de la Rey, C. (2005). Gender, women and leadership. Agenda 19 (65): 4–11.

Denney, L. (2011). Nigeria: Women on the outskirts of politics. openDemocracy. Retrieved from http://www.opendemocracy.net/5050/lisa-denney/nigeria-women-on-outskirts-of-politics.

Denzer, L. (1992). Domestic science training in colonial Yoruba land. In K. Tranberg Hansen (Ed), *African encounters with domesticity* (pp. 116-142). New Brunswick: Rutgers University Press.

European Union Election Observation Mission to Nigeria. (2011). Final report on the 2011 general elections. European Union Election Observation Mission. Retrieved from http://www.eueom.eu/nigeria2011/reports

Guzmán, V. (2004). Democratic governance and gender: Possible linkages. Vol. 48. United Nations.

Ibrahim, J. (2004). The first lady syndrome and the marginalisation of women from power: Opportunities or compromises for gender equality? *Feminist Africa*, 3. Retrieved from: http://agi.ac.za/sites/agi.ac.za/files/fa_3_feature_article_3.pdf

International Federation for Human Rights. (2008). The Nigeria NGO coalition shadow report to the CEDAW committee. Retrieved from: http://www.unhcr.org/refworld/docid/48a0007a2.html.

International Institute for Democracy and Electoral Assistance. (2006). *Nigeria: Country report based on research and dialogue with political parties.* Stockholm: International IDEA.

Inter-Parliamentary Union. (2011). Women in national parliaments. Retrieved from http://www.ipu.org/wmne/classif.htm

Irabor, F. (2011). Review of women's participation and performance at the 2011 General Elections in Nigeria. Baobab Women. Retrieved from www.baobabwomen.org

Izugbara, C. O. (2004). Patriarchal ideology and discourses of sexuality in Nigeria." In *Understanding Human Sexuality Seminar Series*, 2:1–34.

Jhally, S, Ericsson, S, Talreja, S., Katz, J., Earp, L. & Media Education Foundation. (1999). Tough guise: Violence, media, and the crisis in masculinity. Northampton, MA: Media Education Foundation.

Johnson-Odim, C. & Mba, N. (1997). *For women and the nation: Funmilayo Ransome-Kuti of Nigeria*. University of Illinois Press.

Kamau, N. (2010). *Women and political leadership in Kenya*. Retrieved from http://www.hbfha.com/downloads/Women_in_Leadership_Study.pdf.

Kandawasvika-Nhundu, R. (2010). International women's day 2010.

International IDEA. Retrieved from http://www.idea.int/gender/womens_day_2010.cfm.

Kethusegile-Juru, B. M. (2003). Intra-Party democracy and the inclusion of women. *Journal of African Elections* 2(1): 49-62.

Kirk-Greene, A.H.M. (1965). The principles of native administration in Nigeria; selected documents, 1900-1947. London: Oxford University Press.

Mama, A. (1998). Khaki in the family: Gender discourses and militarism in Nigeria. *African Studies Review*: 1–17.

Mba, N.E. (1982). Nigerian women mobilize: Women's political activity in southern Nigeria, 1900-1965. Berkeley: Institute of International Studies, University of California, Berkeley.

McClintock, A. (1995).Imperial leather: Race, gender, and sexuality in the colonial conquest. New York: Routledge.

Mire, A. (1998). In/through the bodies of women: Rethinking gender in African politics. *Polis* 6 (2): 1-19.

Mutame, G. (2004). Women break into African politics. *Africa Recovery* 18 (1): 4

Nzegwu, N. (2001). Gender equality in a dual-sex system: The case of Onitsha. *Jenda: A Journal of Culture and African Women Studies* 1(1):1-32.

Okoh, J. (2003). Feminism: An African perspective. In N. C. Ejituwu & A.O.I. Gabriel (Eds.), *Women in Nigerian history : The Rivers and Bayelsa states experience*. Port Harcourt, Nigeria: Onyoma Research Publications.

Okonkwo, U & Ezeh, M. (2008). Implications of missionary education for women in Nigeria: A historical analysis. *Journal of International Women's Studies* 10(2) : 186-197

Pereira, C. (2000). National council of women's societies and the state, 1985-1993: The use of discourses of womanhood by the NCWS. In A. Jega (Ed.), *Identity Transformation and Identity Politics under Structural Adjustment in Nigeria (109-133)*. Uppsala : Nordiska Afrikainstitutet in collaboration with the Centre for Research and Documentation, Kano.

_____. (2002). Understanding women's experiences of citizenship in Nigeria: From advocacy to research. In CODESRIA/Arab Research Centre Symposium on "African Gender Research in the New Millennium: Perspectives, Directions and Challenges", Cairo, Egypt, 7–10.

Petsalis, S. F. (1990). *The silent power: A portrait of Nigerian women*. Montreal: Meridian Press.

UNWomen. (2011). Nigeria: Tracing electoral violence against women in real-time. UN Women. Retrieved from http://www.unwomen.org/2011/04/nigeria-tracing-electoral-violence-against-women-in-real-time/.

Yuval-Davis, N. (1997). *Gender and nation*. London: Sage Publications.

# The South African Reserve Bank and the telling of monetary stories

Elizabeth Cobbett

Stories about the new South Africa—its miraculous and peaceful transition to democracy, its macroeconomic stability, and its strong regional and continental diplomatic role—abound and serve to reinforce a master narrative of a transformed country rising from a violent past and now heading in the right direction. The hosting of the 2010 World Cup FIFA (Fédération Internationale de Football Association) is an example of this new South Africa: a successful African state hosting a major international event. Tito Mboweni, former governor of the South African Reserve Bank (SARB), said that preparations for the World Cup came at a time of strong economic growth (Mboweni, 2007). The persistent adherence to prudent macroeconomic policies by the authorities had resulted in the country's solid economic performance in recent years and strengthened its capacity to host the games. This rhetoric portrays South Africa as a new and active participant on the world stage, a status aided by the prudent and long-sighted actions of the SARB, which created a stable macroeconomic environment. South Africa was an international success story and this achievement is linked to good economic policy.

This article contends that South African political economic leaders are in a struggle to put in place a master narrative of the economy, a supranational identification of common socioeconomic problems and goals. The SARB has put forward a dominant narrative—the need to reintegrate the economy into a rapidly changing global financial environment after the long period of apartheid isolation (Van der Merwe, 1997). The last two decades have seen constant efforts by the SARB and by the African National Congress (ANC) government to bring the South African economy in line with global financial requirements. The Congress of South African Trade Unions (COSATU) publicly condemns the neoliberal choices that accompany this goal, claiming that these policies mount to "a capitalist onslaught on the working class" (Vavi, 2010b, para.7). For COSATU's general secretary, Zwelinzima Vavi, there is a pressing need "to give a concise class understanding of post-apartheid South Africa and the nature of global capitalism" (Vavi 2010b, para.8). Vavi said that South Africa was in a crisis (Marrian, 2010). Price stability, carried out through the SARB's monetary policy, have to play a subordinate role to national developmental goals of creating jobs and eradicating poverty. If necessary, the government should tax the super-rich and use these funds to meet these targets.

The SARB plays a critical role of communicating its macroeconomic policies to the general public and of undermining alternatives, such as COSATU's, that question their decisions. To do this, the Bank tells 'monetary stories.' Central banks are not usually associated with narrative storytelling, or with nation building; yet, recent research demonstrates that monetary policy is an outgrowth of a master narrative and produces, in turn, the context in which the economy takes place. In a continuation of the FIFA story, the SARB represents itself as a team, one amongst other national teams. In this case, the analogy is with sport: the reserve bank is a team, like the rugby, cricket, and football teams, who are all working towards the common goal of making South Africa strong and internationally relevant:

> We have a busy sporting year ahead of us, with the current cricket world cup games on the go, and the rugby World Cup finals just around the corner. In monetary policy decision making, we rely somewhat on our forecasts for inflation. My current central forecast is that both the cricket and rugby teams are going to do well this year... Allow me to wish Mr White and the Springboks all the best in their endeavours in the rugby World Cup finals in France. We are fully behind you and believe that you have what it takes to bring the cup home. You dare not disappoint the people of South Africa (Mboweni, 2007, p. 5).

Mboweni presents Jake White's role as coach of the rugby team and his own as governor of the Bank, as being similar: they both have to reach targets.

> One common aspect centres around the target that both of us have. For Mr White it is to win matches and tournaments, while in my case it is to ensure that inflation remains within the target range (Mboweni, 2007, p. 1).

Mboweni uses the excitement of national sports and the feelings of patriotism associated with the successes of national teams to anchor the Bank's goals of inflation targeting.

> Of course, when the world cup finals begin in 2010 we will be keen spectators and supporters of Bafana Bafana [the South African national soccer team], but there is not much we can do to directly impact on the fortunes of the team. I will leave that in the capable hands of Mr Carlos Parreira and his team. We have to keep our eyes on a different ball and a different goal. Through this exciting growth phase that we are experiencing, monetary policy has to ensure that inflation is kept under control (Mboweni, 2007, p. 4).

Master narratives such as these are standard practice in the creation and maintenance of images of states as they promulgate frameworks through which people are led to make meanings of themselves, of their lives, of their identities, and of their social relationships. But these monetary stories by the central bank reflect a pressing need to ingrain and settle these parameters into the national imagination of South Africa and what it means to be a citizen of this country. People are implicitly asked to let go of the former vision of a post-apartheid South Africa of social and economic justice that carried the ANC to power, and work and live within a revised economic agenda of free markets, global competition, and individual responsibilities.

COSATU claims that the SARB does not give a damn about what happens to the economy and job creation, and wants the SARB nationalised because it is an asset of our people and not of shareholders (COSATU, June 25, 2009).

COSATU publicly engages with the SARB and with the minister of finance about policy direction. When the 2010 national budget came out, COSATU said that it had expected monetary policy to be changed to target employment directly and primarily, as pointed out in the election manifesto of the ANC and in the various meetings of the [Tripartite] Alliance (Mail & Guardian, 2010). This is a political debate and this article looks at the *political* role of central banks in a world characterised by decentralised and deregulated finance. The case of South Africa demonstrates well a broader theoretical discussion on the role of central banking in the global financial sytem.

Literature indicates that central banks have changed their relationship with the general public over the last two decades (Blinder, Ehrmann, Fratzscher, De Haan, & Jansen, 2008; Davies & Green, 2010; Hall, 2008; Holmes, 2009). These institutions have adopted new communication techniques that seek to anchor macroeconomic goals within society. These changes need to be understood within the broader context of the current global financial order. This is the subject of the first section, which overviews the world financial system and the roles of governance played by credit rating agencies and by central banks. This is followed by analysis of the changes in structural power bought about as central banks are made institutionally independent from political pressure within their countries and freed to follow regulations elaborated by international financial institutions. Following this, focus is given to theory on central bank communication methods and how they 'perform' the economy through the telling of monetary stories. Of particular interest to this article are central bank narratives within countries undergoing extensive social, political, and economic transitions. South Africa experienced a transition to democracy, which put a black majority government in place. Yet the decision by the South African political and economic elite to direct the economy towards global neoliberal goals radically alters the former vision of a developmental and redistributive state. The ongoing public debates about the choices open to South Africa are at the heart of this struggle to manage the national economy and instill a dominant narrative within the national imagination.

## Decentralised and privatised global finance

In the last 150 years three international financial systems have existed: the gold standard, the Bretton Woods Agreement, and free-floating currencies with no set anchor for monetary value (Broz & Frieden, 2001). Financial systems consist of (i) exchange rate arrangements; (ii) capital flows; and (iii) a collection of institutions, rules, and conventions that govern their operations. Each system produces specific relations with domestic financial markets. The gold standard commanded monetary policies of devaluation when the currency exceeded its set value in gold; Bretton Woods permitted more embedded liberal welfare policies for western countries through international financial institutions, which simultaneously undermined these policies in postcolonial countries; and the shift towards decentralisation and deregulation in 1971 compelled domestic markets to adjust to the effects of mobile capital operating between multiple financial centres worldwide. These centres exert varying degrees of influence over the global production of and access to credit (Germain, 1997).This organisation is characterised by a lack of one nexus of control—even as we recognise the ongoing dominance of Wall Street—rendering the system more complex and requiring us to pay careful attention to institutional arrangements (Porter, 2005). Two constellations of power[1] have emerged as strategic institutional arrangements central to this global governance of finance: credit rating agencies and central banks. These constellations are key infrastructures in the performance of the economy.

### First constellation of power: Credit rating agencies

Credit and bond rating agencies such as Moody's, Standard & Poor's, and Fitch produce comparative readings of investment opportunities and risks which put value on corporate and public debt worldwide (Sinclair, 2005). Credit rating is a form of institutional financial coordination that promotes the interests of investors through the production of investment data. Rating agencies essentially give value to both public and private debt by making judgements about the risk and the opportunities involved in various investment destinies. Like central banks, rating agencies are a centralising force as they act as a crucial nerve centre in the world financial order, "a nexus of neoliberal control that is exercised through emitting judgements about the economic performance of states and corporations" (Sinclair, 2005, p. 68).

Credit ratings are not imposed on governments but governments seek them as means of attracting capital and of assuring financial investors that their money is safe in the country (Sinclair, 2005, p. 10). The South African government invites foreign investors to this 'dream of a business destination,' which combines their ideals: the stability of a developed nation, the opportunity of a vibrant emerging market and a climate that fosters growth. "It's time, [the government reminds investors], to take a closer look at South Africa" (South Africa Info, 2010, para.1). Trevor Manuel, former minister of finance, states that in South Africa "we've taken some very tough decisions to provide a climate for certainty. The Constitution, the legal framework, the macroeconomic framework, all add up to certainty and predictability. South Africa has created a climate that investors need" (South Africa Info, 2010). These 'very tough decisions' resonate well with rating agencies; Standard & Poor's set South Africa's long term rating at BBB+ and foreign currency issue rating at A+ (South Africa Info, 2009). The National Treasury points out that "the affirmation of South Africa's rating reflects confidence in our credit position and future policy direction, thanks in large part to a record of prudent execution of macroeconomic policies" (South Africa Info, 2009, para. 3). The country's financial systems are presented as being sophisticated and supported by robust banking regulations that rank among the top 10 globally (South Africa Info, 2008).

These ratings reflect investor opinion on national policies as is made clear in the following excerpt from Moody's November 2009 reading of South Africa:

> There is also increased risk that easier fiscal policy, with emphasis on the social

---

1. Taken from Timothy J. Sinclair's book, *The New Masters of Capital* (2005).

safety net, will become entrenched due to the greater influence of the labor unions in government. Moreover, the growing impatience of the population for the government to deliver on promises of improved social services and housing, jobs, and better education, among other demands, could make it difficult to rein in spending increases as currently envisioned over the medium to long term (Cailleteau, Lindow, & Orchard, personal communication, April 15, 2010).

Social and political disturbances or unrest play against favourable credit ratings but they are offset by the state's stable management of the macroeconomic environment through central bank management. Moody's goes on to say that:

> The economy's growth potential is likely to shrink in a less supportive global environment…this would mean that pressure from within the government alliance for unaffordable and distortive fiscal and monetary policies will need to be resisted, despite frustration with the slow pace of progress on the jobs front (Cailleteau, Lindow, & Orchard, personal communication, April 15, 2010).

Here we clearly see Moody's argument against any accommodation by the ANC of left-wing members of the government's Tripartite Alliance[2]: the South African Communist Party (SACP) and the Congress of South African Trade Unions (COSATU). The relevance of looking at credit rating agencies when studying central bank action resides in understanding the degree to which banks need to obtain good ratings from the agencies for national and subnational debts. Agencies give good ratings when the monetary policies put in place by central banks reduce risk for foreign investors and when the political climate is stable, that is, when it will not threaten the rates of profit or the possibility of withdrawing money from the country once the investment is over. Central banks therefore undertake to influence and direct markets and public behaviour in line with these rating agencies' standards and goals.

## Second constellation of power: Central banks

A network of central banks links populations, states, national economies, and global financial arrangements within a transnational regime of financial governance. The ultimate objective of central banks has always been monetary and financial stability (White, 2005). This stability is assured through regulatory standards that are internationally negotiated and domestically applied. This goal has become more difficult to achieve as global capital moves freely across borders. The paradox is that the decentralised and deregulated global financial system depends increasingly on the regulated and centralised domestic control of central banks. National economies are stabilised through monetary policy and act as an anchor of value for global capital.

---

2. When political organizations were unbanned by the apartheid government in 1990, the African National Congress, South African Communist Party and COSATU agreed to work together as a Revolutionary Alliance (Tripartite Alliance). The 6th National Congress (of COSATU in 1997) resolved that the Alliance remains the only vehicle capable of bringing about fundamental transformation in South Africa (COSATU, 2009).

The power of central banks to implement their vision through national policies resides in historic relations of collaboration and coordination between central banks, dating from around 1930 when the Bank of International Settlements (BIS) was founded. The BIS is the world's oldest international financial institution and remains the principal locus for central bank cooperation and governance. Helleiner (1994) identifies this cooperation as a movement towards what Peter Haas (1992) calls an *epistemic community*, or networks of knowledge-based experts. Haas notes that epistemic communities play a key role in articulating complex problems and in helping states identify their interests, frame public debates, and put forward specific policy solutions. Importantly, epistemic communities have their own vision of reality built through a historic consent on how the world works.

This knowledge-based network, known as the Basel Community (White, 2005), has developed a vision of 'correct' beliefs through iteration of beliefs, practice, and experience. This vision is strengthened through the common education received by central bank governors and senior members of the banks. Interbank cooperation is fostered through the hundreds of meetings that take place every year involving central bank governors and specialists (communication experts, auditors, security experts, economists, etc.). This has resulted in convergence to a mutually accepted interpretation of the world and identification of the most appropriate solutions to financial problems. It is this shared understanding of reality that shores up the current global financial order.

Central banks therefore 'belong' both to their individual countries, where they are at the centre of national monetary and fiscal control, and to this international community of central bankers, which promotes and supports the implementation of their shared vision of the global political economy. The BIS secretariat explains it as follows: the central bank, an organisation with a public mandate, belongs to the government in a broad sense—as do the legislative, executive, and judicial branches—and acts in interplay with other governmental bodies within a country's governance structure (Oritani, 2010). Yet, central bank independence from government and political pressure is now considered a requisite element of global financial architecture. Central banks and governments clearly recognise their interdependence in the national arenas but these patterns of coordination between central banks and governments have changed with the demise of the Bretton Woods financial order. The fiat money system that succeeded the breakdown of Bretton Woods saw widereaching institutional reforms as central banks moved to assure financial stability worldwide and price stability domestically. Central bank independence was prompted by previous failures of anti-inflation policies and a belief that independence from political pressure would help secure lower inflation in the future (Crowe & Meade, 2007). The belief is that bank independence reduces the possibility of policy swings that can arise when monetary policies are determined by political parties representing special interests (Oritani, 2010, p. 41).

The 1990s saw a wave of new legislation securing this legislative independence in new banking acts and revised constitutions. The Maastricht Treaty and the creation of the European Union clearly set out the legal independence of the new European Central Bank (ECB) and its members, the central banks of Europe. This independence from direct political pressure is guaranteed by Article 107 of the Treaty, which reads that "no member of the ECB shall seek or take instructions from Community institutions or bodies, from any government of a Member State or from any other body" (European Union, 1992, p. 17). This wave of legal changes in central banking has been particularly noted in developing and emerging market economies (Crowe & Meade, 2007). Countries of the former Soviet Union, for example, saw their constitutional laws rewritten and a new independence given to their central banks. African countries have generally moved to more market-based financial systems with greater autonomy and accountability applying to central banks (Mboweni, 2004). The transition to a post-apartheid state and the rewriting of the South African Constitution were perfect opportunities to grant the SARB legal independence. Subsection 224 (2) of the South African Constitution states that "the South African Reserve Bank, in pursuit of its primary object, must perform its functions independently and without fear, favour or prejudice..." (Constitution of the Republic of South Africa, 1996, p. 1331 [28]). The SARB's monetary policy committee (MPC) clarifies that it makes monetary policy decisions independently of its shareholders and the government. Constituted by the executive directors (the governor and the three deputy governors) and the professional members of the SARB, the MPC has the mandate to elaborate and implement the monetary policy framework for the country. Although the Reserve Bank has complete instrumental independence, Mboweni adds that it is of course accountable to the citizens of South Africa (Mboweni, 2004). Accountability is indeed a key issue. The Constitution stipulates that the Reserve Bank must be in regular consultation with the cabinet member responsible for national financial matters (Constitution of the Republic of South Africa, 1996, p. 1331[28] ). Apart from this condition of regular meetings with the minister of finance, there is little legal provision to make Bank responsive to political demands and citizen discontent about economic policy. The Constitution acts, rather, as a shield that protects the committee from 'external' pressure.

## Discourses of power: Central banks as narrators

Literature indicates that central banks have changed their relationships with financial markets and the general public over the last two decades through the development and use of new communication techniques (Blinder et al., 2008; Hall, 2008; Holmes, 2009). Before the 1990s, central banks were shrouded in mystery—it was believed that they should be—and decisions were made behind closed doors (Blinder et al., 2008). Blinder et al. (2008, p. 25) point out that central banks are now making their decisions known, widely available, and transparent in the belief that if their actions are more predictable to markets, markets will react in expected ways to monetary policy. This communication can be understood broadly as the provision of information by the central bank to the public regarding such matters as the objectives of monetary policy, the monetary policy strategy, the economic outlook, and the outlook for future policy decisions (Blinder et al. (2008, p. 10). For example, the making public of the minutes from a central bank's monetary policy committee meetings along with the release of a central bank's inflation reports appear to move financial markets significantly in the direction desired by the banks (p. 34). Communication strategies are considered essential elements, for instance, in anchoring the long-run inflation levels by announcing a numerical inflation target and making it widely known to the general public. The markets and the public integrate this information and adapt their behaviour in reaction to anticipated changes, thereby enacting the desired result. These changes have been referred to as a communication revolution and are powerful components of every central bank's toolkit.

Blinder et al. (2008, p. 5) point out that no consensus has emerged on what communication policies constitute best practice for central banks. Practices, in fact, differ substantially and are evolving continuously according to state histories, practices, and internal logics. This echoes current literature on the state (Hansen & Stepputat, 2001), which points out that while there are commonalities in state, governance, and the language of 'stateness', no institution, policy paper, or universalised regime is 'the same' everywhere. Keeping in mind this caveat, it remains possible to identify common analytical frameworks within which emerging central banking practices are embedded. Using the analytical framework of cultural anthropology, Douglas Holmes (2009, p. 383) builds on Blinder et al.'s observations of central bank communication by linking them to John Maynard Keynes. According to Holmes, Keynes identified the power of central banks in his *A Tract on Monetary Reform* (Keynes, 1923). Keynes saw these financial institutions as possessing great regulatory power, pacing the activity in the economy as a whole, as virtually all transactions are in one way or another contingent on financial mediation (Holmes, 2009, p. 388). This power is subject to intense public scrutiny and to very little formal accountability (p. 387). The challenge, Keynes identified, was to tame the 'animal spirits' of economic actors when they act with little regard for monetary authorities or not in the interest of the larger group. Expectations needed to be disciplined with persuasive narratives and Keynes was concerned with developing a language for money and monetary policy (p. 390). The goal was to find a language that could make economic phenomena into meaningful public discourse and thereby, into instruments of intervention (p. 391).

Working within Keynes' intellectual tradition, Holmes applies Michel Callon's (2007) insights on performative theory—that economic theory is the means for creating economic phenomena and regulating economic behaviour rather than being merely the tools for representing or analysing them—to Blinder et al.'s research on central bank communication strategies. Callon's performative thesis argues that words perform the decisive function of creating countless contexts that frame data series, statistical measures, and econometric projections. Economic theory is therefore the means for creating economic phenomena and regulating economic behaviour rather than a simple tool for representing the economy as object. Building on this theory, Holmes introduces the notion of an *"economy of words"* as the means and medium through which this kind of creative labour is articulated and enacted (2009, p. 384; italics added).

An *economy of words* is the process by which central banks linguistically model economic phenomena operating at the limits of calculation and measurement. In other words, central banks name and render observable economic phenomena that are largely outside of common knowledge and thus, make known complex economic phenomena through simplified economic parameters. Well known symbols, such as interest rates and inflation targets, act as parameters for general social behaviour while a wider range of more complex monetary and financial tools create the broader context for the operations of financial markets. The underlying principle is that successful monetary policy is not so much a matter of control of monetary tools, such as overnight interest rates, but rather about managing expectations and future action through communication. Towards the end of the last century, central bankers came to adopt an experimental ethos of communication performed in situ (Holmes, 2009, p. 386). Initiated by the Reserve Bank of New Zealand, central banks worked out the means for modelling linguistically and communicatively economic phenomena (p. 411). Narratives, or monetary stories, informed by a continuous stream of data and analyses, articulated in a measured and consistent fashion, became the *modus operandi* for central banks (p. 385). This practice represents the most decisive and convincing demonstration of Callon's performative theory (p. 383). Words create the economy simultaneously as a communicative field and as an empirical fact. What does the central bank's communication achieve? Holmes claims that the answer is both simple and profound (p. 403). The public's expectations will cleave over time to monetary policy targets, such as permissible levels of inflation, which are integrated in their future behaviour. People, in other words, will adapt their expectations and actions to fit into the parameters set out by the central bank, such as propose d changes in the rate of interest.

Monetary storytelling is occurring actively in contemporary South Africa. As a frequent visitor to South Africa over the last few years, I am constantly surprised by the weighty and constant presence of the central bank in the media. The central bank is a very eloquent, visible, and particularly powerful actor in public debates and is foremost in the creation and maintenance of the country's macroeconomic narrative. My impression is that the Reserve Bank's governor has as much, if not more, influence than the governing party.

## South Africa

The historical trajectory of South Africa's political economy has been largely determined by its role as world gold producer and its place within the British Empire. The South African Reserve Bank has been closely tied to the western international financial system for nearly one hundred years. This was so even during the years of apartheid when the country became member of the Bank of International Settlements in 1971 and the central bank finance d the apartheid government's debt on foreign markets. The establishment of the South African central bank needs to be understood within this broader context of historic global financial ties.

A hundred years ago, domestic monetary policy was shaped by imperial banks operating in South Africa under the directions of the Bank of England

(Ally, 1994). This gradually changed as Britain found it increasingly difficult to compete with the other leading European industrial countries and the United States' rising financial power during the inter-war period of 1919 to 1939. Britain's monopolistic relationship with gold producers in South Africa had been central to maintaining its former position at the centre of the global financial system. But Jan Smuts, prime minister of the Union of South Africa, had come under criticism from Nationalists for allowing imperial Britain's interests to override South Africa's independence, especially in regards to local currency requirements, dependent on overseas production in England (p. 76). At the same time, the Chamber of Mines pushed to have more control over the gold refinery process and wanted to install a refinery within South Africa instead of shipping all its unprocessed metal to London where it fell under the control of the Bank of England. The Chamber of Mines argued that a local refinery would lead to important savings for the industry and to greater control as to whom to sell the gold to. Of interest to the Chamber was the interest shown by the United States of America who saw an advantage in breaking the British monopoly and dealing directly with South African gold suppliers. Political opposition in South Africa against the country's subordination to Britain's imperial interests finally created enough leverage to establish two key national institutions: a gold refinery and a national mint (p. 84). These moves to independence were facilitated by the challenging economic context facing post-war Britain and its limited resources in managing these crises.

Calls for a South African central bank were buttressed in the aftermath of the First World War when the British government unpegged its currency to the US dollar by coming off the gold standard and letting the British pound float. As the South African pound was linked to the sterling, it was also devalued against the dollar, plunging the country into recession. Merit was seen in breaking with the British sterling and establishing new banking norms and a state bank within the country. While this goal was at the fore of nationalist sentiment, the creation of a South African central bank was actually made possible by the Bank of England's decision to encourage the spread of central banks worldwide (Ally, 1994, p. 88). This decision built on a political economic re-evaluation of Britain's relative global strength and its place and power within the changing economic and financial world context. Britain's informal financial system, developed under its global dominance, had shrunk as it faced the economic consequences of the war and increasing rivalry from New York as financial centre (p. 89). The Bank of England saw the establishment of national central banks as a means of pursuing its influence over global finance. It reasoned that in the changed environment a more formal international monetary system would separate national political pressures and governments' interests from financial control and monetary stability, and help secure direct British influence through a worldwide banking system. Britain had consistently endeavoured to separate the interests of the mining industry from that of the Union government, wishing to secure its privileged relationship to gold producers (p. 81). The national 1919 Gold Conference of mining companies (which met to address the problems encountered with the marketing of South Africa's gold production) pinpointed the need to introduce a uniform bank act that could protect against the inflation of the currency, maintain the price of gold, and offer greater degree of national power (p. 90). A Select Committee of Parliament followed on the Gold Conference's recommendation to establish a central bank. Jan Smuts invited Henry Strakosch, managing director of the Union Corporation—a holding company with extensive foreign investments in South African gold mines—to the country for consultation and advice on improving the national banking system (Ally, 1994, p. 87). Strakosch, in collaboration with the Union Corporation's treasury, drafted the original Bill of the Currency and Banking Act of 1920, ensuring that management of the future reserve bank would not be under government control; rather he proposed setting up a central bank with private funds obtained through shareholders (p. 90). The independence of the central bank from the governing party was unusual at the time of its establishment; it is more in line with current global reforms that separate democratically-elected representatives from monetary control. The South African Reserve Bank opened its doors for business for the first time on 30 June 1921. The Bank was a paradoxical mix of British imperial interests with nationalist goals of greater independence from British rule and the identification of the need of a central bank under the control of local government.

This mix of powerful mining companies, international finance, and the central bank continue to shape the political economy of the country. Habib and Padayachee (2000) note that the 1989 Bank Act renewed historic alliances between the state and powerful business as the state prepared for its transition to liberal democracy. A group of powerful conglomerates involved in mining, finance, and energy worked to ensure that the new black-majority government would create a macroeconomic context that would facilitate the globalisation of their activities (p. 260). A pivotal aspect of this move to secure the desired macroeconomic context was to grant greater autonomy to the SARB (p. 248). Enshrined in the 1996 Constitution, the political economic structure witnessed a return to the original vision of independent global financial power within the domestic economy. This arrangement between the SARB, the government and the business elite underpins the political economy of contemporary South Africa.

## Monetary stories in the New South Africa

Sixteen years after the first democratic elections there has been little change in the overall level of income inequality. South Africa has overtaken Brazil as the world's most unequal country as its Gini coefficient index—which shows the level of income inequality—increases to 0.679 (Craven, 2009). In spite of this dismal record, the SARB continues to move the country towards full compliance with the global neoliberal regime of deregulated finance. This means working to orientate human expectations and actions towards the desired neoliberal macroeconomic goals of privatised public services, greater individual responsibility for human welfare, and new opportunities for financial investment. While the ANC is fully supportive of this orientation, social groups and trade unions are voicing their opposition. Social movements are holding the government to its former electoral promises of social and economic redress for the poor majority. This tension is manifest within the Tripartite Alliance government where COSATU publicly opposes the central bank's conservative monetary policies.[3]

The following excerpts from an article in the *Mail & Guardian* newspaper, published February 2010 (Mapenzauswa, 2010), make evident this public debate over monetary policy, poverty, and economic growth between COSATU, on the one hand, and the SARB and Minster of Finance Pravin Gordhan, on the other hand:

> The ANC's labour union and communist allies want an overhaul of monetary policy, saying the central bank has pursued its inflation targeting mandate blindly at the expense of economic growth. (2010, para. 4).
>
> Unions have proposed that the 3% to 6% target for consumer inflation be scrapped or widened, or that the central bank's mandate to be broadened to take into account economic growth and job creation (2010, para. 6).
>
> I wish to confirm that the Reserve Bank will continue to pursue a target for CPI inflation of 3% to 6%, Gordhan [the minister of finance] said (2010, para. 7).
>
> Ongoing assessment, discussion and commentary about our monetary policy by analysts, interested members of the public, interest groups and the broader research community is constructive for the emergence of a social consensus in this area over the longer-term, he [Gordhan] said (2010, para. 9).
>
> In apparent reference to calls [by COSATU] to nationalise the central bank, Gordhan reiterated that South Africa's Constitution stipulated the institution should pursue its mandate independently and without fear, favour or prejudice (2010, para. 10).
>
> The role of the Reserve Bank in maintaining financial stability would also be enhanced, Gordhan said. He warned that South Africa's present inflation levels were higher than those of its trading partners, lowering its competitiveness (2010, para. 14).

The SARB has the task of grounding its economic narrative in a country undergoing significant social and political transformations and upheavals. In contrast to well established liberal market democracies where the distribution of power within the political economic structure is largely accepted by the population, the SARB needs to make sure that its narrative is seen as unquestionable, as the undisputed truth, regardless of deepening tensions between private financial interests, on the one hand, and escalating poverty and pockets of exclusion, on the other.

When the new governor of the central bank, Gill Marcus, took up her functions in November 2009, Pravin Gordhan sent her a letter in which he reiterated that credible monetary policy holds a central place in South Africa

---

3. This tension extends equally to the South African Communist Party (SACP) who criticizes some of the ANC's policies as anti-poor; however the focus here is on COSATU who engages publicly and regularly with the ANC executive and the SARB on issues of monetary policy.

as it endeavours to attract foreign investment and stimulate growth (Gordhan, 2010, p. 2). In this letter, he emphasised that communication with the public needed to be improved so as to increase the effectiveness of the central bank in achieving its mandate of low inflation and greater economic growth. This letter is an effective media communication that confirms the direction of the SARB in line with the broader global financial regime and the ideological links between the ANC and the SARB as the change in the governor of the central bank was carried out. The letter aimed at reassuring financial markets that the transition to the new governor of the central bank would not interrupt the same conservative monetary policies in place since the ANC came to power. It was also a message to social actors, such as labour unions and grassroots activists, that there would be no change in monetary policy and no question of nationalising the central bank. COSATU National Spokesperson Patrick Craven asks:

> The Freedom Charter called for the people to share in the country's wealth. How can we achieve that when the country's most important financial institution is not under any democratic control by, or accountability to, the people (Craven, 2010, para. 4).

This idea was qualified as "nuts" by Governor Marcus (South African Press Association, 2010, para. 1). These calls to nationalise the SARB have been accompanied by simultaneous demands by private shareholders of the Bank to obtain a market value for their shares in the event of nationalisation. The present 2010 South African Reserve Bank Amendment Bill aims to confront both challenges to the SARB's independence.[4]

These debates are examples of frequent ideological confrontations in the public arena between left-wing members—the SACP and COSATU of the Tripartite Alliance Government—and the minister of finance, and the SARB. What the Reserve Bank and the ANC national government are endeavouring is to effectively sideline calls from the leftwing members for nationalisation of the central bank, for an easing in monetary policy towards lower rates of interest, for less Bank preoccupation with the inflation target of three to six percent, and for greater emphasis on expansionary macroeconomic policies and job creation. Yet ANC support of the central bank's economic policies appears to stand in direct contradiction to declarations made by former President Jacob Zuma:

> The ANC, a disciplined force of the left, accepted the electoral mandate which came primarily from the workers and the poor, with a commitment to take further the struggle for a better life for all. The ANC must now use its victory and control of State power to improve the quality of life of the poor and marginalised (Zuma, 2009, para. 10-11).

There is a division in the economic discourse used by the Minister of Finance and the SARB, on the one hand, and the revolutionary rhetoric of the ANC executive, on the other. This can be explained by a desire to maintain the image of social and economic justice being performed through the president and his

---

4. The Bill aims to stop shareholders from circumventing the current act's limitation on shares per shareholder to 10 000 and to define clear criteria for the disqualification of persons from serving on the board of the Reserve Bank.

office. The president brings together the nation; he is the concerned father that listens to all the problems. Debates are thus carried out between the central bank, the finance minister, and the members of the Tripartite Alliance, leaving the president aside.

These mediatised debates are a double edged sword; I believe that they actually help anchor the central bank's goals in important ways. COSATU and the SACP are historic and powerful social bodies that act as social and political media rods for the SARB's narrative. Being called upon by these actors to justify its monetary policies, the SARB is brought into the public realm and the rather obscure institution is made known and 'real' through exchange with these well known social actors. By engaging with them, the central bank becomes more visible to the wider public and its *economy of words* is disseminated. What's more, these debates permit the SARB to establish more direct and influential links with the country's citizens as COSATU and SACP directly inform their members—workers, social groups, and activists—of the Reserve Bank, its role, and its economic goals. Holmes' (2009) work on the Reserve Bank of New Zealand points to these innovations used by central banks for securing the implementation of monetary policy. His hypothesis is that central bank communications *are* the instruments of policy themselves, *they* make the economy. In this sense, South Africa's central bank is creating the context, or the dominant narrative, of the national economy through ongoing debates with COSATU. The current political economic power structures ensure that there is no real threat to the SARB's independence—neither to its vision nor to its power to implement policies. This explains the willingness with which it engages in these public dialogues. In so doing, its vision is actually embedded within the public realm and validated. The dialogues, in other words, create this particular *economy of words*.

The SARB uses special occasions for storytelling that permit it to tie its policies to powerful national symbols. In a remarkable speech given in 2009 at the Annual Steve Biko Memorial Lecture, Mboweni, then governor of the South African Reserve Bank, stated:

> To break a bit with tradition, the thrust of my address tonight will be on economic issues. In particular, I will share a few observations and thoughts on selected macroeconomic developments in South Africa in the past 15 years. From 9 November 2009 I will no longer be allowed to comment on monetary policy. As the outgoing governor, however, I will take advantage of this platform to remind you of a few truths, one being that no central bank worth its salt can ever tolerate high inflation. Price stability may not be a sufficient condition but I maintain that it is a necessary condition for a solid foundation for sustainable growth and prosperity (Mboweni, 2009, p. 2).

> I would like to believe that Steve Biko would have been gratified by the fairly contained pace of inflation over the past 15 years, knowing the dire consequences of inflation for the poor—those who are usually least able to hedge against inflation—in particular. Since 1994 average headline inflation has amounted to approximately 6.5 per cent per annum. Over the preceding 15 years, 1979 to 1994, it had averaged almost 14 per cent per annum. Inflation has been uneven over the

period, though, induced typically by significant changes in key exogenous drivers of inflation, such as oil prices (p. 3).

Secondly, the recent upsurge in strike action has led to some commentators describing the wave as a "winter of discontent". In this regard, I would like to comment on some worrying trends in the settlements reached. Wage settlements above the projected rate of inflation and in excess of productivity gains tend to undermine the fight against high inflation. They lead to labour cost increases way above those of trade competitors and, therefore, loss of competitiveness (p. 3)

It is astonishing that the central bank is invited to address the public at this particular event. The fact that the SARB is there speaks in all probability to its desire to make these kinds of links between its policies and national symbols. Mboweni's discourse itself is striking for several reasons. Firstly, it clearly demonstrates the way the central bank produces a narrative of the economy using influential national images linked to the history of South Africa and its struggle against apartheid. To link Biko, known for his elaboration of a pro-black radical doctrine and his death at the hands of state interrogators, to inflation targeting seems to be a wild attempt to validate divisive economic policies with a man who would almost certainly have contested these very policies. COSATU's position on the SARB's conservative monetary policy framework is more indicative of a position that Biko would have likely taken, that of focusing on the developmental needs of the country where the unemployment rate and inequality gap are amongst the highest in the world (Dlamini, 2010). Yet, the central bank attempts to authenticate its controversial monetary policy by making this powerful historic personage speak in its favour.

Secondly, this reference to Biko transforms the failure of state development in terms of poverty reduction and service provision into a narrative of policy success and state accomplishment. The central bank congratulates itself for having obtained better macroeconomic goals than those achieved under the previous apartheid administration. Since 1994 average headline inflation has amounted to approximately 6.5 percent per annum. Over the preceding 15 years, 1979 to 1994, inflation had averaged almost 14 per cent per annum (Mboweni, 2009). The SARB uses the dimension of time—before the transition of 1994 and the current post-apartheid period—to shed a favourable light on its current performance. It portrays the current South Africa state as putting good governance practices in place and respecting its macroeconomic engagements, in a much better way than had done the apartheid state. This is ironic because the Reserve Bank was an integral part of the South African apartheid state's political economic structure. But by using this difference in time, it differentiates itself from the apartheid past, showing that the country has turned a new economic page with satisfactory results.

Thirdly, Biko's well known line, 'that the most potent weapon in the hands of the oppressor is the mind of the oppressed', (Biko & Stubbs, 1978) resonates strangely with the central bank's desire to direct human economic action through communication. Biko's link between the ideational and material life takes on a new twist as the governor calls upon Biko's persona to validate the Reserve Bank's macroeconomic policies. The man who is being called upon to speak on behalf of contested policies is the very person who spoke about the need for the oppressed to free their minds from political manipulation. In other words, Biko is being used to authenticate monetary policies that depend on reflexive subjects. Central banks recognise that the ideational—influencing and directing people's ideas and expectations about their socioeconomic lives—will create the desired national economy through managing human expectations and their action.

## Conclusion

The SARB and the ANC executive have a vision of South Africa as a full member of the deregulated and decentralized global financial order. These political economic leaders are putting in place a master narrative of the economy; a supranational identification of the country as an economic power participating in a globalised world. There is social tension as the visions associated with the overthrow of colonial power and the election of the first black-majority government are put aside by the state to ensure compliance with the interests of capital and the global financial system. People are implicitly asked to let go of the former vision of a post-apartheid South Africa of social and economic justice and to work and live within a revised economic agenda of free markets, global competition, and liberal freedoms and individual responsibilities. This direction undermines the former vision of social and economic justice that accompanied the ANC to power. Social groups contest this route. In particular, COSATU challenges the central bank on its monetary policies and calls the ANC executive to respect its former commitments of improving lives through shared wealth and social justice. The national strike of public workers, carried out by COSATU just a month before the ANC's national general council (NGC) in 2010, is an indication of the deepening rift within the government Tripartite Alliance. The strike demonstrates the state's difficulty in outlaying a more unified vision of the political economy of the country. COSATU is calling for a wage increase for the public sector workers and the SARB responds that wage increases in the public sector are inflationary (Donnelly, 2010). This tension has not been resolved and South Africa is at a defining moment in this struggle for a master narrative of the national economy and, consequently, of society.

The challenge facing the SARB is the struggle to *settle* the revised economic orientation away from one of redistribution to one based on neoliberal principles. In other words, the SARB needs to get South Africans on board as it moves the national economy and the human action that makes it, towards global financial and economic norms and standards. This challenge is met, amongst other methods, through the role that the SARB has adopted in defining the parameters of acceptable economic action within the country. These socioeconomic boundaries are drawn by using and adapting new communication techniques developed by central banks over the last two decades. Words create the economy as a communicative field and as an empirical fact (Holmes, 2009). In this context, the language of macroeconomic fundamentals adopted by the SARB and the ANC government is presented as the defining order of permissible economic and social action for people living in South Africa. Monetary storytelling reinforces the message that the SARB's policies are part of the country—what being South African is all about—and, therefore, the definitive bench mark for economic choices. The SARB reinforces these stories by linking them to powerful national symbols such as sport and historic figures of apartheid resistance. In this context, the question is how will the SARB make sure that domestic inflation is maintained within the target range of three to six percent and that foreign investors are not scared off by political unrest. The 'political unrest' also draws on the FIFA success to point out that "The World Cup has demonstrated to the working class and the poor that indeed the state has the fiscal muscle to spend on developmental projects. We have seen what is possible with unity and decisive leadership. When we demand better education, healthcare, jobs and housing we will now have the World Cup experience as a reference point" (Vavi, 2010a).

# References

Ally, R. (1994). *Gold and empire: The Bank of England and South Africa's gold producers, 1886-1926*. Johannesburg: Witwatersrand University Press.
Biko, S., & Stubbs, A. (1978). *I write what I like*. London: Bowerdean Press.
Blinder, A. S., Ehrmann, M., Fratzscher, M., De Haan, J., & Jansen, D. (2008, May). *Central bank communication and monetary policy: A survey of theory and evidence* (Working Paper No. 898). Frankfurt, Germany: European Central Bank. Retrieved January 1, 2009, from,
http://www.ecb. int/pub/pdf/scpwps/ecbwp898.pdf
Broz, J. L., & Frieden, J. A. (2001). The political economy of international monetary relations. *Annual Review of Political Science, 4*(1), 317-343.
Cailleteau, Pierre, Lindow, Kristin, & Orchard, Kenneth. (2009). *Credit Opinion: South Africa, Government of*. New York/ London: Moody's Investor Services.
Callon, M. (2007). What does it mean to say that economics is performative? In D. MacKenzie, F. Muniesa & L. Siu (Eds.), *Do economists make markets?: On the performativity of economics* (pp. 311-357). Princeton, NJ: Princeton University Press.
Constitution of the Republic of South Africa. (1996). Retrieved from http://www.info.gov.za/documents/constitution/1996/a108-96.pdf
COSATU. (2009). *Tripartite Alliance*. Retrieved August 30, 2010, from http://www.cosatu.org.za/show.php?include=docs/intropages/2009/webcont0805a.html &ID= 2 0 5 1 &cat=About
COSATU. (2009, June 25). Reserve Bank 'doesn't care a damn'. *Mail & Guardian*. Retrieved August 20, 2009, from http://www.mg.co.za/article/2009-06-25-cosatu-reserve-bank-doesnt-care-a-damn
Craven, P. (2009). *COSATU condemns world-record inequality*. Retrieved October 3, 2009, from http://www.cosatu.org.za/show.php?include=docs/pr/2009/pr1001d.html&ID =2458&cat=COSATU%20Today
Craven, P. (2010). *Nationalise the reserve bank – COSATU*. Retrieved June

8, 2010, from http://www.politicsweb.co.za/politicsweb/view/politicsweb/en/page71654?oid= 157454&sn=Detail
Crowe, C., & Meade, E. E. (2007). The evolution of central bank governance around the world. *Journal of Economic Perspectives,* 21(4), 69-90.
Davies, H., & Green, D. (2010). *Banking on the future: The fall and rise of central banking.* Princeton, NJ: Princeton University Press.
Dlamini, S. (2010). *Speech to the COSATU Western Cape Provincial Congress by COSATU President, Sidumo Dlamini.* Retrieved February 26, 2010, from http://www.cosatu.org.za/show.php?include=docs/sp/2009/sp 0718.html&ID=1766&cat=Media%20Centre
Donnelly, L. (2010, 10 September). Let them eat taxes. *Mail & Guardian.* Retrieved September 10, 2010, from http://www.mg.co.za/article/2010-09-10-let-them-eat-taxes
European Union. (1992). *The Maastricht Treaty.* Retrieved November 4, 2009, from http://www.eurotreaties.com/maastrichtec.pdf
Germain, R. D. (1997). *The international organization of credit: States and global finance in the world-economy.* Cambridge: Cambridge University Press.
Gordhan, P. (2010). *Clarification of the Reserve Bank's mandate.* Retrieved February 16, 2010, from http://www.reservebank. co.za/internet/Publication.nsf/LADV/24D185F00B5E0608422576CE004861 EF/$File/ClarificationOfBanksMandate3p.pdf
Haas, P. (1992). Introduction: Epistemic communities and international policy coordination. *International Organization,* 46(1), 1-35.
Habib, A., & Padayachee, V. (2000). Economic policy and power relations in South Africa's transition to democracy. *World Development,* 28(2), 245-263.
Hall, R. B. (2008). *Central banking as global governance: Constructive financial credibility.* Cambridge: Cambridge University Press.
Hansen, T. B., & Stepputat, F. (Eds.). (2001). *States of imagination: Ethnographic explorations of the postcolonial state.* Durham, NC: Duke University Press.
Helleiner, E. (1994). *States and the reemergence of global finance: From Bretton Woods to the 1990s.* Ithaca, NY: Cornell University Press.
Holmes, D. (2009). Economy of words. *Cultural Anthropology,* 24(3), 381-419.
Keynes, J. M. (1923). *A tract on monetary reform.* London: Macmillan.
Mail & Guardian. (2010). *COSATU steps up fight on inflation policy.* Retrieved September 2, 2010, from http://www.mg.co.za/article/2010-02-18-cosatu-steps-up-fight-on-inflation-policy
Mapenzauswa, S. (2010, February 17). Inflation target to stay, no rand pegging. *Mail & Guardian.* Retrieved January 1, 2010, from http://www.mg.co.za/article/2010-02-17-inflation-target-to-stay-no-rand-pegging
Marrian, N. (2010, September 15). Tax super rich, says COSATU. *Cape Times,* pp. 1.
Mboweni, T.T. (2004). *The global economy and central banking in Africa.* Lecture presented to the National Bank of Belgium, Brussels, Belgium. Retrieved January 2, 2010, from http://www.bis.org/review/r041117d.pdf
Mboweni, T.T. (2007, March 20). *The benefits of being a good host: The FIFA World Cup and the South African economy.* Lecture presented to the

Corporatesport Directors' Dinner, Sandton Sun Hotel, Johannesburg, South Africa. Retrieved April 12, 2010, from http://www.bis.org/review/r070322c.pdf

Mboweni, T.T. (2009, September 10). *Reflections on some economic and social developments in South Africa in the past 15 years.* Paper presented at the Tenth Annual Steve Biko Memorial Lecture, University of Cape Town, Cape Town, South Africa. Retrieved January 1, 2010, from http://www.reservebank.co.za/internet/Publication.nsf/LADV/EBC6A3F194B451904225762D004BE59A/$File/Biko+lecture 1.pdf

Oritani, Y. (2010). *Public governance of central banks: An approach from new institutional economics.* (BIS Working Paper No. 299). Basel, Switzerland: Bank of International Settlements. Retrieved from http://www.bis.org/publ/work299.pdf?noframes=1

Porter, T. (2005). *Globalization and finance.* Cambridge: Polity.

Constitution of the Republic of South Africa, (1996). Retrieved January 1, 2010, from http://www.info.gov.za/documents/constitution/1996/a108-96.pdf

Sinclair, T. J. (2005). *The New Masters of Capital: American bond rating agencies and the politics of creditworthiness.* Ithaca, NY: Cornell University Press.

South Africa Info. (2008). *South Africa: Economy overview.* Retrieved June 9, 2010, from http://www.southafrica.info/business/economy/econoverview.htm

South Africa Info. (2009). *South Africa's credit ratings affirmed.* Retrieved June 9, 2010, from http://www.southafrica.info/business/economy/rating-220609.htm

South Africa Info. (2010). *Alive with investment possibility.* Retrieved August 30, 2010, from http://www.southafrica.info/business/investing/vignette.htm

South African Press Association. (2010). *Marcus on nationalisation, SARB reserves.* Retrieved April 12, 2010, from http://www.polity.org.za/article/marcus-on-nationalisation-sarb-reserves-2010-02-24

Van der Merwe, E. J. (1997). *Monetary policy operating procedures in South Africa.* (BIS Policy Paper No. 5). Basel, Switzerland: Bank for International Settlements. Retrieved January 1, 2010, from http://www.bis.org/publ/plcy05.htm

Vavi, Z. (2010a). *After the World Cup—how can we build on our success? Address to Cape Teachers' Professional Association, 15 July 2010.* Retrieved September 15, 2010, from http://www.cosatu.org.za/show.php?include=docs/pr/2010/pr0716e.html&ID =3 6 09&cat=COSATU%20Today

Vavi, Z. (2010b). *Speech to the South African Communist Party 89th anniversary rally, 1 August 2010.* Retrieved September 11, 2010, from http://www.cosatu.org.za/show.php?include=docs/pr/2010/pr0802a.html&ID=3685&cat=COSATU%20Today

White, W. R. (2005). *Past and future of central banking cooperation: Opening remarks.* Basel, Switzerland: Bank of International Settlements. Retrieved January 1, 2010, from http://www.bis.org/publ/bppdf/bispap27.pdf

Zuma, J. (2009). *Consolidating working class power in defence of decent work and for socialism.* Opeaning address to the COSATU 10 th National

Congress, Gallagher, Midrand. Retrieved June 13, 2010, from http://www.cosatu.org.za/docs/cosatu2day/2009/sp 0921.html

# The neoliberal turn in the SADC: Regional integration and disintegration

Jessica Evans

The SADC vision is one of a common future, within a regional community that will ensure economic well-being, improvement of the standards of living and quality of life, freedom and social justice, peace and security for the peoples of Southern Africa. This shared vision is anchored on the common values and principles and the historical and cultural affinities that exist amongst the peoples of Southern Africa. (SADC, 2010, p. 1)

On August 17, 1992, in Windhoek, Namibia, the Southern African Development Coordination Conference (SADCC) was transformed into the Southern African Development Community (SADCC; Lee, 2003, p. 47). The transformation of the SADCC into the SADC was a watershed mark in the geopolitical dynamics of the region, reflecting a closing to the era of Cold War proxy wars on the continent, an anticipated end to the Total Strategy[1] and apartheid state in South Africa, and optimism about the potential of regional cooperation and development among the newly liberated states. With these geopolitical transformations at hand, the SADCC, which had emphasized regional economic cooperation and coordination with a primary goal of reducing dependence on apartheid South Africa, would inevitably have to undergo some critical structural and policy changes due to the inclusion of a democratic South Africa. Transformed into the SADC, this new regional body ostensibly reflected a change in South Africa's posture towards the region, anticipated by Nelson Mandela's early awareness of "the need for peaceful cooperation for *mutual benefit* if the region's future is to be secure" (Simon, 1998, p. 4). According to Hentz, the new SADC programme was a prototype of developmental regional integration and cooperation (2005, p. 33).Yet, it would appear that, to date, there have been very few meaningful projects and policies developed within the SADC that have actually promoted "mutual benefit" and "development" (see for example Taylor, 2003 and Tsie, 1996). Rather, the SADC has increasingly embraced a free market approach to integration along the lines of neoliberal orthodoxy, exacerbating the existing asymmetries and inequalities. Thus, the developmental content of the SADC has fallen into

---

1. The Total Strategy refers to the South African apartheid state's attempt to defend its racially inscribed capitalism through an ideological positioning against the "total onslaught" of Marxism among liberated African states. This was to be achieved through a stick-and-carrot combination of diplomacy and ideological legitimation via national-level compromises with key Black constituents and regional "cooperation" (which largely would have amounted to increasing regional economic dependence on South Africa), as well as heavily militarized tactics of destabilization against liberated Black-African states (Davies & O'Meara, 1984).

disrepute, leading critics to the conclusion that it is developmental only in name (Hentz, 2005, p. 33).

The shift within SADC's priorities and ideological posture must be understood with reference to the coinciding shifts in the global economy following the end of the Cold War and the consolidation of neoliberalism as a global agenda, and the regional geopolitical transformations that followed the end of South Africa's apartheid state. Shifts in the composition and tools of the global political economy were instrumental in transforming the formal agenda of regionalism in Southern Africa. In turn, the adoption of neoliberal orthodoxy has engendered multiple microregional processes that have complicated the prospects for the successful consolidation of a regional imaginary. An examination of the competing regional processes instigated by the neoliberal turn is, therefore, instructive in identifying the disjuncture and contradiction that have become endemic to SADC regionalism.

In this article, I argue that the exogenous pressures of the global political economy, which have shaped contemporary SADC regionalism, have produced informal, bottom-up regional forces, which, when left outside of the formal regional consideration (either intentionally or unintentionally), have the potential of fostering regional disintegration rather than integration.

I use a case study of the role of informal cross-border traders and circular migrants in the SADC, with particular focus on the response of South Africa as a regional centre for informal cross-border trade and circular migration. On the one hand, as a result of the region-wide adoption of neoliberal orthodoxy through international influence and structural adjustment programs in many states, a hollowing and weakening of the state's ability to provide for its population, massive public sector retrenchment, wage *freezes*, and unemployment have ensued, causing a substantial reliance of the region's population on informal sector livelihood strategies (Tripp, 2001, p. 1). Increasingly, these informal sector livelihood strategies are premised on informal cross-border trade and migration, particularly into South Africa, a practice that has been facilitated by the opening of borders to formal trade and capital flows under neoliberal restructuring (Williams & Carr, 2006, p. 3). In response to increasing in-migration, South Africa has sought to stem the cross-border movement of informal traders through a reassertion of state sovereignty and the border with heavy policing measures and an exclusionary migration policy (Pederby, 2001, p. 16). The reassertion of the border has had the effect of freezing regional relations and detracting from the construction of regional identity by further entrenching notions of difference and otherness, contributing to rising levels of xenophobia (p. 29). This, then, would seem to run counter to the self-proclaimed logic of regionalism by the SADC and contradict South Africa's supposed commitment to and support of integration as a means of promoting equitable regional development and peace, as repeatedly and publicly proclaimed by former President Thabo Mbeki (Taylor, 2003, p. 311). My intent in this article is to use South Africa as a case study to highlight the problem of neoliberal regionalism in the SADC. The SADC's movement to a neoliberal integration policy has created a set of informal microregional processes which, if met by an unresponsive or restrictive policy environment, have the potential of further fragmenting the region and detracting from the overall goals of peace, growth, and equitable development.

The remainder of this article is organized as follows. First, I situate the current problem, as it pertains to regionalism, within the tradition of the new regionalism(s) approach (NRA). The NRA school of thought is derivative of critical international political economy, and as such emphasizes the importance of situating regionalism(s) as a factor in the overall structure and forces at play in the international political economy. This is particularly useful for the argument being advanced here, as the very problems of SADC regionalism being addressed are in dialogue with the larger processes of global restructuring under neoliberal hegemony.

Second, I demonstrate how shifts in the structure and character of the international political economy have influenced a con comitant shift in SADC regionalism, namely that of a shift to neoliberal orthodoxy. To this end, I examine how issues of structure and agency have contributed to this shift.

Third, I review how this shift in agenda has impacted SADC regionalism with reference to an increase in informal cross-border trade and migration as an emergent dimension of informal micro-regionalism(s) and the subsequent reaction of South Africa in evoking an exclusionary statist stance on migration policies, thus hampering and fragmenting regional relations (Mulaudzi, 2009, p. 49).

Last, I demonstrate how these processes are products of and responses to global neoliberal hegemony, so as to reveal the propensity towards disintegration that the SADC faces.

## The NRA and critical international political economy

Traditional integration theory began from an ontological presumption of states as the fixed locus of power in the international system, negotiating between themselves optimal economic interstate relations. Within the context of the Cold War and assumptions of global structural fixity, regionalism was characterized as an introverted process of protectionism coordinated at a supranational level, with the depth and breadth of interstate organization being the determining factors of successful integration (Söderbaum, 2004a, p. 21). However, from the mid-1980s onwards, a "new regionalism" has emerged in the context of "comprehensive structural transformation of the global system" (Hettne & Söderbaum, 2000, p. 457). This new regionalism is characterized by a multiplicity of complex and dynamic processes involving state and non-state actors engaged in transnational networks and is taking form as the result of emerging global, regional, national, and local social forces (Söderbaum, 2004a, p. 50).

As a result of the post-Cold War consolidation of neoliberal hegemony and accelerated processes of social, political, and economic globalization, it is impossible to isolate one level of analysis as dominant, as the level of importance and nature of interactions between the various levels can change, contingent upon a particular process' spatio-temporal situation (Hettne & Söderbaum, 2000, p. 457). To this end, the study of new regionalism(s) is most comfortably and appropriately situated within the tradition of critical international political economy. As Söderbaum noted.

> Critical international political economy (IPE) provides a useful analytical perspective for this endeavour, because it transcends state-centric ontology and rationalist epistemology and is concerned with structural and social change; historical power structures, emphasizing contradictions in them; and change and transformation expressed in normative terms…. [It] does not take states as givens, but neither does it wish them away, which is important in accounting for the changing governance structures in today's global political economy. (2004b, p. 419)

As critical international political economy emphasizes an examination of the historical contingency of the global structural conditions that influence and define the parameters of political-economic behaviour, processes of regionalism must be understood within the context of post-Cold War structural transformations in the global political economy and how these transformations have shifted the composition and character of regionalism(s) and the particular composition of the state-society complex in the contemporary global order. In so doing, the study of new regionalism(s) allows for a consideration of how regions are socially constructed and thereby politically contestable. The project of the NRA, rather than fixating on regional organizations and state actors, is to describe the processes by which a geographical area is transformed into an active political subject and how various actors are constituted in these processes as active agents capable of articulating collective interests within the emerging regional and global order (Hettne & Söderbaum, 2001, p. 461).

Aside from the global or exogenous emphases of the NRA, there is a concomitant analytical shift to the endogenous forces of regionalism. Regionness is a pivotal concept for the NRA analyses of the endogenous forces of region formation. Regionness is to "define the position of a particular region in terms of regional cohesion, which can be seen as a long-term historical process, changing over time from coercion… to voluntary cooperation" (Hettne, 2005, p. 551). Regionness as a concept allows one to understand how a variety of formal and informal social, political, and economic actors interpret the idea of the region and to what extent these multiple interpretations of region find congruence or contradiction with each other (Söderbaum, 2004a, p. 47).

The notion of regionness is perhaps the most salient feature of the NRA that bridges the exogenous and endogenous forces of regionalization. Although the exogenous forces of global order bear influence on the formal macroregional project (often state-led and institutionally defined), these very influences are also responsible for what the NRA sees as the unbundling of the state through neoliberal globalization. As Taylor noted,

> Macro-regions involve a monumental expansion in the proportion of a regional market, while at the same time diminishing the authority of political units…[B]ecause of their scale, macro-regions are most likely to generate the greatest tensions and contradictions, and are least susceptible to the construction of any form of regionness. (2003, p. 315)

This unbundling makes the state but one actor among a plurality of formal and informal regional actors (Söderbaum, 2004a, p. 50). Networks formed by these informal actors may include, but are not limited to, transnational corporations, ethnic business networks, civil society organizations, private armies, and the informal border politics of small-scale trade, bartering, smuggling, and crime. These informal networks reflect microregional processes that are more beholden to "real processes on the ground and constitute the interface between top-down and bottom-up regional processes (Söderbaum & Taylor, 2003, p. 3). At times, these formal and informal actors of regionalization act in opposition to each other, while at other times, myriad partnerships may exist between the formal, state actors, and informal actors (Söderbaum, 2004a, p. 51). To this end, the formal and informal modalities of regionalization must be analyzed within the same theoretical framework rather than arbitrarily separated. Multiple regional processes are occurring at multiple scales at a given place and point in time.

Simon expressed similar theoretical viewpoints as the NRA when he noted that it would be faulty to assume a single future for development and regionalism in Southern Africa. Rather, he maintained, it is important to consider regional processes as diverse and plural with divergent and convergent futures (Simon, 1998, p. 4). The neoliberal turn of regionalism in the SADC, as a factor in larger global restructuring processes, will impact different spaces in an asymmetrical and variegated fashion (Taylor, 2003, p. 314). Rather than producing a totalizing tendency towards homogenization, as proponents of (neoliberal) globalization claim, the unfettered movements of capital will produce uneven geographical developments, reflected in the "different ways in which different social groups have materially embedded their modes of sociality into the web of life" (Harvey, 2006, p. 77). As the regional centre of capital, South Africa's outward expansion of (often speculative) capital projects into Southern Africa as a means of dispersing its apartheid inheritance of crises of accumulation has had tremendous impact upon the myriad microregional processes emerging within the SADC (Bond, 2000, p. 49). These microregional responses manifest as Polanyian-type responses of societal self-protection to uneven geographical developments producing both convergent and divergent regional imaginaries (Harvey, 2006, p. 114). Within the SADC, highlighting these plural tendencies of regionalism may help to identify the sources of contemporary xenophobia, while also revealing spaces for emergent contestation to neoliberal order.

## From SADCC to SADC: Global transformation and the neoliberal turn

The SADCC was established in 1980 by a core group of liberated Southern African states, Angola, Botswana, Lesotho, Malawi, Mozambique, Swaziland, Tanzania, Zambia, and Zimbabwe (Lee, 2003, p. 45). Given the geopolitical context of South Africa and the Total Strategy, the priorities of the SADCC were to reduce dependent relations in general, though particularly upon South Africa, and foster regional cooperation and development among liberated states through a deliberate and politically strategic coordination of donor funding (Sidaway & Gibb, 1998, p. 166). Market integration, as contemporary regionalism was being practised, was not an objective of the SADCC (Hentz, 2005, p. 28). This was largely due to the fact that the economies of Southern Africa lacked the requisite diversification (as most states remained primary product exporters), comparative advantage, and infrastructure to facilitate any meaningful economic integration (Lee, 2003, p. 47). For these reasons, regional cooperation and development were seen as a necessary precursor to market integration.[2]

The SADC was established in 1992 following the end of the Cold War and the proclaimed victory of the West. At this time the African National Congress (ANC) was negotiating its ascension of power in South Africa. For the SADCC, the implications of these geopolitical transformations was a contraction in the options for donor assistance outside of Western states and international financial institutions, where, during the Cold War and during the reign of apartheid, such alternatives had been available (Tsie, 1996, 78). The SADCC and its member states needed to acquiesce in order to stay afloat; alone, they simply did not have the resources to continue. Additionally, with the ending of apartheid, the SADCC could no longer position itself in opposition to South Africa, and thus needed to prepare for inclusion in the regional body.

Although these geopolitical transformations were significant, many of the fundamental structural conditions remained the same in Southern Africa. Most economies remained weak and undiversified and the region lacked the requisite infrastructure and comparative advantage to make market integration successful (Lee, 2003, p. 47). Perhaps most important, South Africa remained (and does to this day) the most industrialized state in the region, leading popular media and scholars alike to assert that SADC members were likely more dependent upon South Africa than they had ever been (Sidaway & Gibb, 1998, p. 166).

The role of external actors in influencing the shift in SADC regionalism, in accordance with the global structural transformation that occurred in the 1990s, is significant because the SADC and its member states have been largely dependent on foreign assistance and debt relief. Importantly, massive external debt in Southern Africa has been a significant factor in tying the region, politically and economically, to the West. Between 1986 and 1990, African countries paid back more to the International Monetary Fund (IMF) than they received in new assistance (Tsie, 1996, p. 76). This, in addition to the global recession of the 1980s, provoked a serious debt crisis in Southern Africa. The neoliberal policies pursued by many governments of advanced capitalist societies during the global recession had the effect of further indebting Southern African states. Dollar-denominated debt, set against consistently depreciating national currencies, rendered Southern Africa largely unable to detach itself from the external political control of the West, as it continued to be reliant on foreign aid and debt relief (Tsie, 1996, p. 77).

The SADC itself is almost entirely reliant on external support. According to Lee, approximately 86% of the SADC's funding is derived from Western governments and international financial institutions (2003, p. 48). This

---

2. See Seidman (1989) for a detailed analysis of the structural conditions that formed the basis for SADCC's emphasis on economic coordination and cooperation rather than integration, and some of the alternative strategies being tabled at this time.

continued trend of foreign dependency, coupled with a lack of feasible alternatives, has situated the region in a highly vulnerable and susceptible position. Given space constraints, it is not possible to provide a comprehensive overview of the specific arrangements and agencies involved in this externally imposed transformation, but I highlight below a few key moments in the transformation with regard to the SADC region and its member states primary donor community: the IMF, the World Bank, the European Union, and the United States.

First, the World Bank and the IMF, while previously sceptical of supporting regionalism in Southern Africa, instead favouring separate functional programmes and state-specific liberalization strategies, began to shift tactical strategies during the 1990s. The IMF and World Bank have since come to embrace open regionalism as a means of overcoming the fragmented opening of the region to the world economy, seeking to create "a sub-regional unified, open economic space for the free movement of goods, services, capital and people [and] move away from unsuccessful import substitution strategies" (Söderbaum, 2004a, p. 92).

Second, the European Union has been a key actor in promoting the new SADC regionalism, as well as in shifting the World Bank and IMF's regard for regionalism. According to Söderbaum, it was the EU that attempted to draw attention to the negative spillover effects of uncoordinated structural adjustment programmes, which was instrumental in changing the World Bank's and IMF's attitude towards regionalism (2004a, p. 94). The EU emphasized that regionalism does not have to be an alternative to global market integration, but can be congruent with it, claiming that "successful integration requires a market-friendly economic environment [and] openness to third countries" (Söderbaum, 2004a, p. 95).

Third, beginning in 1996, there has been a reorientation in American policy towards the SADC, which has shifted engagement with aid to a relationship more focused on trade (Lee, 2003, p. 48). The United States' African Growth Organization provides incentives in the form of debt relief, loan guarantees, business partnerships, and access to American markets, conditional upon the SADC's conformity to the norms of democratization, liberalization, and privatization (Söderbaum, 2004a, p. 93). The United States Agency for International Development's special Initiative for Southern Africa claims Southern Africa is a "promising" region. The objective of the initiative is to open markets and exports so as to promote a focus on growth-oriented reforms and the reintegration of South Africa into the regional economy on mutually beneficial terms (Söderbaum, 2004a, p. 93).

The brief overview above demonstrates how crucial external forces have approached aid and trade partnerships with the SADC using a markedly neoliberal strategy. However, South Africa and Botswana stand out as anomalies in this scenario. They did not cede to externally dictated structural adjustment programmes, but nevertheless undertook structural adjustment voluntarily "under the threat of losing international credit-worthiness" (Bond, 2003, p. 67). Importantly, South Africa, as the regional hegemon, has been instrumental in both embodying and conveying the hegemonic norms of neoliberalism on a national and regional scale.

When the ANC came into power in 1994, it received wide popular and electoral support, and was regarded as an alliance of Black nationalists with socialist unions and radical social movements, seeking radical social, economic, and political change (Peet, 2002, p. 54). As such, the ANC's initial and formal economic policy was growth through redistribution. Not long after the fall of apartheid, however, the ANC gradually began to shift gears, adopting stringent fiscal and macroeconomic policies with an aim of promoting redistribution through growth. Although South Africa has received foreign debt relief and assistance, most notably the 1993 $850 million IMF Compensatory and Contingency Financing Facility, it has been unique in that it was not subject to the structural adjustment policies under which almost every other SADC member state undertook neoliberal restructuring (p. 73).

Rather, the ANC government undertook a self-imposed structural adjustment in the form of its 1996 Growth, Equity and Redistribution (GEAR) policy, a macroeconomic policy package that was decidedly "Thatcherite" in its orientation, as Thabo Mbeki once publicly announced (Bond, 2000, p. 82). Critical of wage and service expenditure, the ANC through GEAR sought a regressive tax on consumption, increased liberalization of exchange controls, wage freezes, supply-side incentives to promote investment and export competitiveness, and a restructuring of state assets through privatization and joint public–private ventures (Bond, 2000, p. 80). Although conceived of domestically, giving it the air of a homegrown macroeconomic policy, GEAR was mostly the product of ideological pressure from the international financial institutions (most notably the World Bank) as well as the complex of domestic interfaces between elites and key constituencies (Bond, 2000, p. 189).

As the ANC was negotiating the liberation of South Africa in the 1990s, its well-known socialist leanings had begun to concern the West. Previously a strategic regional bastion of liberal and Western norms, the newly independent South Africa could potentially become a counterhegemonic node in the South. Notably, Bond argued, the ability of South Africa's Left and progressive forces to distance themselves from international financial institution borrowing was identified as a key threat by the World Bank (2000, p. 155). To this end, the early 1990s saw an increased scrutiny of South Africa by the World Bank and the IMF, whereby the World Bank courted leftist ANC members under the pretences of "trust-building" exercises and advisory roles (Peet, 2002, p. 73). Gumede described in detail these courting sessions:

> During 1992 and 1993 several ANC staffers, some of whom had no economic qualifications at all, took part in abbreviated executive training programmes at foreign business schools, investment banks, economic policy think tanks and the World Bank, where they were "fed a steady diet of neoliberal ideas." It was a dizzying experience. Never before had a government-in-waiting been so seduced by the international community. Both the World Bank and IMF sought to influence the ANC's economic policy, frequently warning against pursuing 'unorthodox' policies. (2005, p. 73)

Notably, the incumbent ANC minister of finance, Trevor Manuel, had been sponsored by the World Bank and IMF for training in orthodox international economics, and Prime Minister Nelson Mandela and his successor Thabo Mbeki were in frequent discussion with international financial institution elites and prominent Western policy advisors. The 1994 Reconstruction and Development Programme and the subsequent, highly reformatted GEAR were reviewed by a constellation of such elites and advisors of the West and the international financial institutions, including former advisor to the United States' Democratic Party, Stan Greenberg, who became the ANC-appointed policy advisor (Gumede, 2005, p. 76).

However, to reduce the ANC's transition to mere ideological courtship, as outlined above, would be far too simplistic and would ignore the complexities of interwoven agency and vulnerability that plagued the ANC. The apartheid state's political economy had been predicated on an accumulation strategy fuelled by the exploitation of cheap Black labour for mineral extraction and the production of luxury goods. This racially inscribed accumulation strategy, however, failed to match mass production with mass consumption, leading to an acute crisis of overaccumulation, a legacy with which the ANC had to contend (Bond, 2000, p. 5).

On the level of acting elites, inviting the World Bank to take on assessment and advisory roles was viewed as a necessary measure for dealing with South Africa's capital crisis while keeping the bank at arm's length. In building a macroeconomic policy that was, ostensibly, to enable the avoidance of debt crises through liberalization, privatization, financialization, and the regional dispersion of overaccumulated capital, leading ANC architects of GEAR sought to decrease the potential conditions that would necessitate accepting an international financial institution loan, which would be conditionally attached to the more stringent macroeconomic structural adjustment packages (Bond, 2000, p. 10, p. 190). Through a combination of international ideological pressure and the ANC's vulnerable position in the emergent post-Cold War global order, South Africa undertook voluntary alignment with the Washington Consensus and global neoliberal hegemony. Former communist and ANC negotiator Mac Maharaj, speaking to the ideological corner into which the ANC was backed, claimed, "We could not go it alone. Countries that did this, such as Sweden, had the space to do so with the Cold War still raging and the world being bipolar. The ANC came to power at the end of the Cold War in a unipolar world. We had no room to manoeuvre" (Gumede, 2005, p. 76). By the time GEAR was tabled in 1996, Mandela and Mbeki both contended that in order for a Black government to be taken seriously and gain respect in the West, it needed to toe the line of orthodoxy (Gumede, 2005, p. 73).

In the context of a changing global order in the post-Cold War environment, the SADCC faced tremendous external and internal pressure to conform the content of its regionalism to the norms and expectations of the now unipolar global order. The SADCC was thus transformed into the SADC and came to embrace neoliberal orthodoxy and market integration as the means for regional development, promising redistribution, development, and poverty alleviation through growth. This shift was affected by the role of international financial institutions and key Western donor states in both directly and indirectly imposing the hegemonic norms of economic orientation onto individual states and the SADC as a whole. Along with the impact of international financial institutions and Western donors in reframing the SADC agenda, the role of South Africa has also been pivotal. To be sure, although the adoption of neoliberal orthodoxy via GEAR seemed to anticipate how South Africa would come to envision its regional relations, this line of explanation is not unproblematic. Hentz, for example, has argued that the evolution of South Africa's approach to regionalism has been the result of the ANC's negotiating a "complex political matrix'" between domestic labour and business interests (2005, p. 44).

## Cross-border movements and regional (dis)integration in SADC

Southern Africa is a region imbued with deeply historical migration patterns. Throughout the 20th century, patterns of labour migration were, possibly, the single most important factor connecting the various colonies and countries into a regional labour market (Crush et al., 2005, 1). It is not an exaggeration to state that the political economy of Southern Africa, during this time, could only be understood with reference to labour migration (Andersson, 2006, p. 375).

The South African migrant labour system was the most prolific and far-reaching model, recruiting migrants to work in the mining and commercial agriculture sectors from nearly every other country in the region, throughout the 20th century. Figures for South Africa's contract labour migration range from 99,950 in 1920, to as high as 233,808 in 1960, tapering off in the 1990s at 192,044 (Crush et al, 2005, p. 3). The South African model of contract migrant labour became a model for the region, later adopted by Botswana, Namibia, Swaziland, Zambia, and Zimbabwe (p. 4). Although the contract labour system was adopted elsewhere throughout the region, the patterns and benefits to be accrued from such a system remained largely skewed in favour of South Africa and its momentum towards industrialization. South Africa's ambitions of becoming a secondary producer and escaping what seemed to have been the fates of many other African countries, marginalized in the global economy as primary producers, necessitated the creation of economic linkages with neighbouring countries (West, 1990, p. 117). The reality of the Southern African region has been effectively predicated on these historical patterns of labour migration.

Though migration has historically characterized Southern Africa, the nature and composition of migration in the contemporary post-apartheid era is also fundamentally altered. Mobile populations remain a fundamental component of the region's political-economy, though the late 20th and early 21st centuries have witnessed an increasing informalization of migrants. Apartheid's accumulation strategy, premised largely on cheap and exploitable Black migrant labour in the extraction of natural resources and production of luxury goods, had produced an acute crisis of overaccumulation (Bond, 2000, p. 5). In order to deal with this crisis, the ANC government undertook a number of political and economic measures such as the formal promotion of domestic job creation and labour standards in South Africa, and a strategy of moving overaccumulated capital into infrastructural and speculative financial ventures, which concomitantly led to a significant reduction in the need for unskilled contract labour migrants (Adepoju, 2001, p. 45; Andersson, 2006, p. 377; Bond, 2000, p. 49; Crush et al, 2005, p. 6). As a result of this reduction, the primacy of contract labour in the region's political economy has been increasingly supplanted by the informal sector, which is nevertheless largely contingent on mobile populations such as circular migrants and informal cross-border traders (Iheduru, 2003, p. 48; Boas, 2003, p. 34). Whereas, previously, a large proportion of migrant populations (though highly exploited) followed a formalized process, contemporary migration patterns in the region are increasingly placed outside of the para meters of supranational institutional consideration. This points to a marked disconnect between formal regionalism in practice and the realities of transnational linkages on the ground.

Having traced the shift in the SADC, and its member states', policies from growth through redistribution to redistribution through growth, in this final section I demonstrate how the neoliberal turn has created internal antagonisms through bottom-up regional pressures and a subsequent reassertion of the state at the border. Rising unemployment rates, wage freezes, and massive public sector retrenchment, coupled with the opening of borders to flows of trade and capital, have created the conditions for a significant expansion of the informal sector economy, increasingly characterized by cross-border movements (Tripp, 2001, p. 1). Recent SADC reports have said that over 45% of the total population within the SADC region lives on less than $1 per day, demonstrating the need of almost half the regional population for a social safety net of some sort (SADC, 2008, p. 1). In the absence of such social safety nets in much of the region, the informal sector and informal cross-border trade and migration have grown and become pivotal sites of livelihood strategies in the liberalizing the SADC. Popular estimates now assert that informal cross-border trade constitutes approximately 30 to 40 per cent of the value of SADC's formal regional trade, though because of its clandestine nature, the bottom line is largely unknown (Johnson-Nunez, 2009, p. 11). These growing cross-border movements are a significant factor of regionalizaton and represent what Söderbaum and Taylor have labelled informal micro-regionalism(s), the result of a disconnect between the formal project of regionalism through the SADC and the actual lived practices and perceptions of regional linkages on the ground (2003, p. 3). To the extent that these formal and informal processes contradict rather than support each other, the prospects of consolidating regionness are weakened.

In the process of growing formal and informal interstate linkages, there has been an increased emphasis on the securitzation of the border and migration policies in the SADC. Although the borders of states are becoming more porous to the movement of trade and capital, and thus to people as well, there have been significant attempts to reify the political border through exclusionary and often discriminatory migration policies in order to shut down the movement of peoples (Crush et al., 2006, p. 31). Yet, significant research has identified informal cross-border traders and migrants as an integral mechanism for promoting regional integration. The activities undertaken by informal cross-border traders and circular migrants serve to dismantle the structure of trade dominance biased toward the former colonial nations and instead strengthen intra-SADC trade by physically demonstrating the existence of a common market by bringing the concept of regional economic integration down to the individual level. (Johnson-Nunez, 2009, p. 31)

Furthermore, in a study of Zimbabwe's female cross-border traders, Muzvidziwa noted the propensity of their activities to necessitate and contribute to the creation of a trans-border culture that transcends nationality and ethnic differences by emphasizing commonality through economic interdependence and cooperation (2001, p. 72). The SADC programme of action claims to seek political, social, and economic development through the building of regional ties, a common values system and collective regional identity (Mulaudzi, 2009, p. 50). Yet the SADC's inability and unwillingness to provide a safe and facilitative environment for these microregional processes, which have the potential to lay the grounds for the realization of such objectives, has promoted regional disintegration rather than integration.

The case of South Africa can be used to illustrate these internal antagonisms for a number of reasons. Because South Africa is the major industrial centre of the SADC, it functions as the centripetal force of the region. The asymmetrical patterns of growth within the region, exacerbated by a region-wide adoption of neoliberalism, have largely accrued to South Africa, making it a primary destination for informal cross-border movements and trade. Official government figures as of May 2010 cite a South Africa-SADC trade surplus of nearly R2.3 billion (Department of Trade and Industry, 2010). Unevenly developed markets, largely derived from South Africa's export dominance in the region, have resulted in significant price differences and differing availability of commodities, providing the economic incentive and rationale for undertaking cross-border trade activities (Johnson-Nunez, 2009, p. 12). Coupled with growing region-wide unemployment, the relative strength of the South African economy has made it a centripetal force in the region, attracting informal cross-border traders and circular migrants, who use formal and informal routes of entry into the country (Akokpari, 1999, p. 4).

Second, the widespread failures of neoliberalism to promote redistribution through growth, both regionally and in individual states, can be seen as a root cause of the evocation of restrictionist immigration policies. Although South Africa has fared better at the macroeconomic level under regional liberalization, the implementation of domestic liberalization through the GEAR policy has, nevertheless, resulted in massive internal unemployment and drastic cuts to social services and public sector wage freezes and retrenchment (Mulaudzi, 2009, p. 56). The South African state's inability to meet the needs of its national population has been a significant impetus for scapegoating informal cross-border migrants and traders, accusing them of undermining the national population's access to the South African economy and social services. Rather than addressing the systemic deficiencies of GEAR for alleviating national poverty and raising standards of living, South African officials deflect critical attention by accusing "illegal" foreigners of being impediments to the successful implementation of GEAR. Informal cross-border traders and migrants are accused of subverting (declining) formal employment opportunities and legislation for nationals by agreeing to work at lower unregulated wages, crowding out the informal sector economic livelihoods of nationals by setting up in South African urban markets, and draining the capacity of (already paltry) public services (Pederby, 2001, p. 24).

In response to in-migration, South Africa has established an extremely restrictionist immigration policy reminiscent of the apartheid era, centred on a draconian approach to border and heartland policing and attempts to control and halt both legal and undocumented migration (Pederby, 2001, p. 16). South Africa's exclusionary immigration policies can be seen as an attempt to restore state legitimacy in the "last bastion of sovereignty" under neoliberalism (the domain of security), where it otherwise lacks such sovereignty under austerity reforms (Söderbaum, 2004b, p. 433). To this end, a rise in xenophobia among the national population has ensued, promoting the reification of difference, rather than fostering a common regional identity and values framework. The rise of xenophobic attitudes can be evidenced in the number of violent eruptions that have occurred in South Africa against foreigners, in general, and informal economic operators, in particular. Incidences of xenophobic attacks in South Africa have been resurgent since shortly after the democratic transition. The ongoing incidences of xenophobia have ranged from the riots against street vendors in Johannesburg in 1997; to the two-week-long xenophobic attacks that spread like wildfire across South Africa in May 2008, leaving 62 dead and more than 100,000 displaced; to the post-World Cup hostility, documented by threats to foreigners by citizens and public servants alike and the evictions of foreigners in order to "get rid of the *makwerekwere* [derogatory name for Black foreigners]" (Johnston, 2010). The effect of these circumstances on regionalism is a violent othering that fragments the identification and consolidation of a common regional identity and values framework (regionness), from which meaningful regional cooperation and development could otherwise emerge (Mulaudzi, 2009, p. 56).

Third, the criminalization of SADC cross-border migrants and traders has generated an illicit informal economy at the border. A host of illicit economic activities have sprung up around "assisting" informal migrants' entry into South Africa, including human smuggling, bribes paid for entry or to escape deportation, bribes paid for visas, etc. Corruption has become endemic at most South African border posts (Crush et al., 2006, p. 8). These illicit border economies are instructive as to the complex linkages between formal and informal actors, as state officials eliciting bribes at the border are intertwined with regional and transnational criminal networks of human smugglers, such as the *maguma guma*. These activities in themselves are indicative of informal micro-regionalism(s) articulated through complex state-criminal network linkages and highlight what some have argued is the increasing criminalization of the state under neoliberalism (Vigneswaran, 2008, p. 6). Additionally, these economic activities thrive on the maintenance of a stringent and exclusionary migration regime. To the extent that public officials are able to extract rents from clandestine migration, there is an informal economic incentive to subvert regional initiatives for a SADC-wide facilitation of movement and harmonization of migration policy (Vigneswaran, 2008, p. 13).

Finally, South Africa holds a significant amount of sway in terms of the types of regional arrangements that are passed through the SADC. South Africa's posture towards regional migrants has been significant in hampering the implementation of a regionally harmonized migration policy. The proposed SADC Free Movement Protocol of 1996, which was to confer the rights of employment, residence, and establishment to all SADC citizens and establish a SADC body of oversight specifically for the enforcement and implementation of the protocol, was vociferously rejected by South Africa (Williams & Carr, 2006, p. 11). The resultant Facilitation of Movement Protocol, which left the definitions of employment, residence, and establishment subject to domestic legislation, made no requirements for implementation and provided no body of oversight and enforcement, was largely the result of South African manufacture and coercion (Oucho & Crush, 2001, p. 150; Williams & Carr, 2006, p. 11). The result of this has been to render regionally governed migration policy impotent, so that migration policy remains firmly within the jurisdiction of the state. Failing a regional migration policy, the cross-border movements of peoples will continue to be couched in terms of border control, security, and exclusionary national citizenship rather than development and integration, further criminalizing foreigners and promoting regional disintegration rather than integration.

## Conclusion

To date, regionalism in the SADC has largely failed to deliver on its programme of action, to promote equitable regional development, raise the standards of living, and alleviate poverty. Understanding this failure requires moving beyond a functionalist approach that assumes structural fixity and sees interstate negotiations and institutions as the determinant factors in successful regional consolidation. As I have demonstrated here, to look at regionalism in the contemporary global political economy requires moving beyond formal interstate relations. Although functionalist analysis can provide some insight into how regional-level policies are negotiated, implemented, and enforced, it fails to consider how multiple regional processes are occurring at multiple scales, pursued by different actors towards different ends. In approaching regionalism in the SADC through the lens of the NRA, one can uncover a myriad of regional processes occurring simultaneously, promoted by both formal and informal actors.

By situating the transformation of the SADCC into the SADC within the wider transformations occurring in the global political economy, I have shown how the SADCC, which was cautious of Western economic orthodoxy and market integration as the means to region-wide development, was transformed into the SADC, which has come to embrace economic orthodoxy and austerity measures. Although the conditions that underpinned the SADCC's rationale for distinguishing itself from the Western model of integration had not changed, global pressures to conform to neoliberal hegemony affected a policy shift in the regional body's *modus operandi*. Thus, at the formal level, a particular form of regionalism has been pursued, heavily influenced by neoliberal hegemony and the interests of global capital and regional elites.

The shift to neoliberal orthodoxy within the SADC as a whole, and within individual member states, however, has in turn produced bottom-up informal regional pressures through the creation of an environment conducive to a proliferation of informal cross-border movements and trade. These informal movements and economic activities represent the livelihood strategies of the majority of the SADC population, which trickle-down growth has yet to reach. This is enabled by increasingly porous borders, rising unemployment rates that have resulted from region-wide and state-led liberalization, and the region's uneven geographical development (Bond, 2000, p. 9).

As Taylor noted, informal micro-regional processes represent the interface between elite-driven agendas and the popular reactions they elicit, making more readily identifiable the "imminent possibilities of transformative counter-movements" (2003, p. 316). As bottom-up processes, informal cross-border traders and circular migrants are more intimate with and responsive to the particular socioeconomic, labour, and cultural needs of Southern Africa's peoples (Johnson-Nunez, 2009, p. 12-13). They can, if properly facilitated, represent not just livelihood strategies, but also spatial practices that can challenge and transform the uneven geographic development of Southern Africa at the micro level, as well as foster a common identity and values framework premised on solidarity and interdependency. Yet the policy environment in the SADC (most notably South Africa) has, to date, marginalized and criminalized such integrative potentials amongst mobile populations.

South Africa, as a major destination for regional cross-border migrants and informal traders, rather than enabling greater intraregional movement to facilitate close r regional integration, has attempted to stem the flow of migrants through a criminalizing and restrictionist migration policy. This restrictionist migration policy might be seen as an attempt to reassert state legitimacy in terms of securitized borders and is otherwise effectively impotent. The criminalization of cross-border migrants and informal traders has contributed to a rise in xenophobic attitudes, thus detracting from the construction of a common regional identity and values, and provided economic incentive for the continued criminalization of migrants through a maintenance of restrictionist migration policies. Thus, the shift to market integration in the SADC has produced concomitant processes of integration and disintegration.

As the NRA emphasizes, regionalism cannot simply be reduced to interstate negotiations and trade liberalization. Cross-border migration and informal trade have been long-standing features of the Southern African political economy, becoming all the more prevalent under liberalization measures, albeit in different forms. A cogent analysis of the possibilities, limitations, and actualities of regionalism must move beyond formal economic and political measures to also take into consideration the informal manners through which regionalism(s) is constructed. In so doing, it becomes possible to identify the potential counter-forces and agents of transformation that are arising within contemporary global restructuring and taking form through articulations of cultural identity, self-organization, and self-protection (Söderbaum & Taylor, 2003, p. 16). Transformative counterforces of self-organization and self-protection, however, will not necessarily be progressive in their agendas. This point is most amply demonstrated through the reactionary articulations of xenophobia, which are emergent features of the post-liberalization SADC environment. Studying informal cross-border traders and circular migrants as microregional actors may better enable scholars and policy makers to promote the progressive, transformative, and integrative potentials therein, while identifying where such processes might elicit reactionary and disintegrative movements.

## References

Adepoju, A. (2001). Regional Organizations and Intra-Regional Migration in Sub-Saharan Africa: Challenges and Prospects. *International Migration*, 39(6), 43-59.

Akokpari, J. K. (1999). The Political Economy of Migration in Sub-Saharan Africa. *African Sociological Review*, 3(1), 1-15.

Andersson, J. A. (2006). Informal Moves, Informal Markets: International Migrants and Traders from Mzimba District, Malawi. *African Affairs*, 105(420), 375-397.

Boas, M. (2003). Weak States, Strong Regimes: Towards a 'Real' Political Economy of African Regionalization. In D. C. Bach (Ed.), *Regionalisation in Africa: Integration and Disintegration*, Bloomington: Indiana University Press.

Bond, P. (2000). *Elite Transition: From Apartheid to Neoliberalism in South Africa*. London: Pluto Press.

Bond, P. (2003). *Against Global Apartheid: South Africa Meets the World Bank, IMF and International Finance*. London: Zed Books.

Crush, J. et al. (2005). *Migration in Southern Africa*. Paper prepared for the Policy Analysis and Research Programme of the Global Commission on International Migration.

Crush, J. et al. (2006). International Migration and Good Governance in the Southern African Region. *Southern African Migration Project*, Migration Policy Brief No. 17, 1-45.

Davies, R. and O'Meara, D. (1984). The State of Analysis of the Southern African Region: Issues Raised by South African Strategy. *Review of African Political Economy*, 29, 64-76.

Department of Trade and Industry (2010). Government of the Republic of South Africa. Retrieved from http://www.dti.gov.za/econdb/raportt/rapregi.html

Gumede, W. M. (2005). *Thabo Mbeki and the Battle for the Soul of the ANC*. Cape Town: Zebra Press.

Harvey, D. (2006). *Spaces of Global Capitalism: Towards a Theory of Uneven Geographical Development*. London: Verso Press.

Hentz, J. (2005). South Africa and the Political Economy of Regional Cooperation in Southern Africa. *Journal of Modern African Studies*, 43(1), 21-51.

Hettne, B. (2005). Beyond the 'New' Regionalism. *New Political Economy*, 10(4), 543-571.

Hettne, B. and Söderbaum, F. (2000). Theorising the Rise of Regionness. *New Political Economy* 5(3), 457-473.

Iheduru, O. C. (2003). New Regionalism, States and Non-State Actors in West Africa. In D. C. Back (Ed.), *Regionalisation in Africa: Integration and Disintegration* (pp. 47-66). Bloomington: Indiana University Press.

Johnson-Nunez, R. (2009). Circular Migration and Employment in Southern Africa. *Trade and Industrial Policy Strategies (TIPS)*, Working Paper Series 2009.
Johnston, N. (2010). Xenophobia and the World Cup. *Mail and Guardian*. Retrieved from http://www.mg.co.za
Lee, M. (2003). *The Political Economy of Regionalism in Southern Africa*. Cape Town: University of Cape Town Press.
Mulaudzi, C. (2009). New Regionalism in Southern Africa: Between South African Hegemony and Globalization. *Lusotopie*, XVI(1), 47-65.
Muzvidziwa, V. (2001). Zimbabwe's Cross-Border Women Traders: Multiple Identities and Responses to New Challenges. *Journal of Contemporary African Studies*, 19(1), 67-80.
Oucho, J. and Crush, J. (2001). Contra-Free Movement: South Africa and the SADC Migration Protocols. *Africa Today*, 48(3), 139-158.
Pederby, S. (2001). Imagining Immigration: Inclusive Identities and Exclusive Policies in Post-1994 South Africa. *Africa Today*, 48(3), 15-32.
Peet, R. (2002). Ideology, Discourse, and the Geography of Hegemony: From Socialist to Neoliberal Development in Post-Apartheid South Africa. *Antipode*, (34)1, 54-83.
SADC (2008). *SADC Region Poverty Profile*. Retrieved from http://www.sadc.int/conference/content/english/CC%20Summaries/The%20SADC%20Region%20Poverty%20Profile%20SUMMARY.pdf
SADC (2010). SADC Vision Statement. Retrieved from http://www.sadc.int/
Seidman, A. (1989). Towards Ending IMF-ism in Southern Africa: An Alternative Development Strategy. *Journal of Modern African Studies*, 27(1), 1-22.
Sidaway, J. and Gibb, R. (1998). SADC, COMESA, SACU: Contradictory Formats of Regional Integration. In D. Simon (Ed.), *South Africa in Southern Africa: Reconfiguring the Region*. Athens: Ohio University Press.
Simon, D. (1998). Shedding the Past, Shaping the Future. In D. Simon (Ed.), *South Africa in Southern Africa: Reconfiguring the Region* (pp. 1-18). Athens: Ohio University Press.
Söderbaum. F. (2004a). *The Political Economy of Regionalism: The Case of Southern Africa*. New York: Palgrave Macmillan.
Söderbaum, F. (2004b). Modes of Regional Governance in Africa: Neoliberalism, Sovereignty Boosting, and Shadow Networks. *Global Governance*, 10, 419-436.
Söderbaum, F. and Taylor, I. (2003). Regionalism and Uneven Development in Southern Africa. In F. Söderbaum and I. Taylor (Eds.), *Regionalism and Uneven Development in Southern Africa: the Case of the Maputo Development Corridor* (pp. 1-18). Aldershot: Ashgate.
Taylor, I. (2003). Globalization and Regionalization in Africa:
Reactions to Attempts at Neoliberal Regionalism. *Review of International Political Economy*, 10(2), 310-330.
Tsie, B. (1996). States and Markets in the Southern African Development Community (SADC): Beyond the Neoliberal Paradigm. *Journal of Southern African Studies*, 22(1), 75-98.
Tripp, A. (2001). Non-Formal Institutions, Informal Economies, and the Politics

of Inclusion. *Discussion Paper No.2001/108, World Institute for Development Economics Research*, United Nations University.

Vigneswaran, D. (2008). Zimbabwean Migration and the Informal Economies of Immigration Control. *Paper presented at the Political Economies of Displacement in Post-2000 Zimbabwe*. Johannesburg: Wits University Campus.

Williams, V. and Carr, L. (2006). The Draft Protocol on the Facilitation of Movement of Persons in SADC: Implications for State Parties. *Southern African Migration Project, Migration Policy Brief* No.18, 1-21.

West, W.G. (1990). Region Formation under Crisis Conditions:

South vs Southern Africa in the Interwar Period. *Journal of Southern African Studies*, 16(1), 112-138.

# Indian hair, the after-temple-life: Class, gender and race representations of the African American woman in the human hair industry

Nadège Compaore

The penultimate paragraph of an online marketing campaign for Virgin Remy Indian hair reads as follows:[1]

> Polished Natural Relaxed Straight *Virgin Remy Indian* Hair provides the finished Silky *straight look* of newly informal African American hair without rival or peerless in shine, texture, luster, body and movement that will demand the attention of any multitude! Gathered directly from the *temples of India*, this *rare* natural hair texture is in *high demand globally* for its soft texture showing an affinity to that of silky straight relaxed *African American hair* (eIndianHair.com, para.9; my emphasis).

In many respects, the above content is telling of the "production"[2] process, the targeted clientele, the intended use, as well as the key racial and spatial dimensions involved in the marketing of "Virgin Remy Indian Hair"[3] as a commercial product. Furthermore, when examining the name of the product, the distinctive trait of the hair (the fact that it is *human* hair) appears silenced at the benefit of the racial and geographic attributes of the hair (the fact that it is *Indian*). As such, the attribute "Indian" can be seen to be an implied brand, thus carrying a weight equal to that of the terms "Virgin" and "Remy".[4]

This paper follows Virgin Indian Remy hair from its production in India to its global distribution, with a focus on its marketing, distribution and use in the United States (US). The focus on the US is justified by the storyline in the above advertisement, which identifies Virgin Indian hair as having an 'affinity to that of silky straight relaxed *African American hair*' (eIndianHair.com, para.9; my

---

1. Note that 'informal hair' is used in the following paragraph as a synonym of 'relaxed hair', perhaps erroneously so, given the usual meanings of "informal" outside the hair context. Relaxed hair refers to chemically treated hair that transforms naturally curly hair into straight hair. The other common term for relaxed hair is permed hair.
2. Since the paper deals with human hair rather than manufactured synthetic hair, production simply refers to where the hair originates, how it is collected, sewn (so as to be used for extensions or weaves), and packaged for distribution.
3. "Virgin Remy Indian hair", "Virgin Remy hair", "Virgin Indian hair", "Indian hair", "Remy hair", will be used interchangeably in this paper. These terms will also be used to connote the human hair in general.
4. Virgin hair simply refers to unprocessed (chemically) hair, but this term will be problematized later on in the paper, as it pertains to the notion of "Virgin Indian" hair that is not mixed hair from other races. Remy hair refers to hair cut or shaved for sale, which still has 'the cuticles on, and in the same direction to keep the hair soft, long lasting, and tangle free (Hair & Cuticle Inc., 2008).

emphasis). In this context where the US as an importing country is privileged among other regions, and given that the advertisement implicitly stresses stereotypical attributes of female hair textures, as well as a tacit focus on Black women,[5] the paper seeks to situate and discuss the class, gender and race representations of African American women, within the marketing, distribution and use of Remy Indian hair. Specifically, the paper questions what such representations of African American women mean *vis-à-vis* Indian women who "produce" Virgin Remy hair; and what they mean *vis-à-vis* men. Furthermore, the paper is particularly interested with *self-representations* of African American women *vis-à-vis* the use of Indian hair, and seeks to understand what these self-representations mean *vis-à-vis* the identity of Black women in the US. Indeed, this investigation seeks to uncover useful tools for locating and unpacking discourses and practices for and against the use of human hair within African American women's self-representations. Specifically, the study seeks to emphasize the race, gender, and class dimensions of the global impact of marketing human hair, and to thus uncover the multiple power relationships involved in the human hair industry. Ultimately, a close analysis of these self-representations can serve to justify the need for exploring two important issue areas. First, it will provide the basis for a clearer understanding of fundamental constructions of "blackness" within the Black American community, which can be located within global production chains such as the human hair industry. Second, it will provide a needed appreciation of the mechanisms through which representations of Black American women in Hollywood and in the American music industry impact on the beauty ideals and the self-representations of Black women in Africa, the Caribbean, Europe and Latin America. In other words, as a study which aims to expound the linkages between body politics (in this case hair politics) and identity politics in African American communities, this paper also positions itself as trigger for future analyses on the political economy of the human hair industry globally. To be sure, although this is not the focus here, the paper hopes to provoke debates on the linkages between the human hair industry and enduring structural conditions of poverty and subordination within and across Black American communities and Black communities worldwide.

Anchored within Chandra Talpade Mohanty's (2003) anti-colonial and anti-capitalist feminist project, this paper identifies key self-representations within the human hair debate in the African American community as centered on a dichotomization of "natural" "Afro" hair *versus* "non-natural", "White-like" "straight" hair. In this context, the empirical and theoretical examination of the use of human hair extensions as a means to "straight" hair is pertinent for locating narratives and counter-narratives of the connections between hair politics and identity politics within the African American community. Mohanty's anti-colonial and anti-capitalist feminist discourse is useful for decolonizing feminist discourses from representations of the "other" as simplistic homogeneous entities that are either authentic or not, legitimate or not, oppressed or not. Furthermore, recognizing the importance of wider capitalist structures in shaping power relations between different groups around class, gender, and racial dimensions is crucial to this analysis.

---

5. In addition to referring to African American hair in their advertisement, the pictures on the website of eIndianHair.com solely depict women, and mostly Black women.

The paper suggests that dominant discourses of resistance by some black feminists against the use of human hair by African American women problematically apprehend African American women as a homogeneous and singular category that can be captured in space and time. Rather, this essay advances that there is no hairstyle that is authentically "black", "natural", and as such, exclusively legitimate for African American women. The discussion aims to show the importance of engaging with multiple meanings of "blackness",[6] as a means to productively examine hair and identity politics locally within the American context, but also globally. The focus on the global speaks to the importance of capitalist power structures that construct and perpetuate a specific politics of hair and identity. The rest of the analysis is presented in a threefold discussion. In the first section, the paper opens up with a critical examination of the assumptions that guide the production, marketing, and "consumption"[7] of Virgin Remy Indian hair. The second section discusses power relations at the intersections of class, gender, and race, with regards to the production and consumption of Virgin Remy Indian hair locally (within India and within the US), and globally (in particular between India and the US). Building from the previous sections, the third section tackles the core theoretical concern of this paper, and addresses the significance of African American women's self-representations within various discourses on, and practices of human hair extensions.

## Selling Indian, constructing *the* African American woman

### The Indian preference

Via internet, phone, regular mail, or international delivery services, individuals or groups worldwide can purchase any type of Virgin Indian Remy hair (straight, wavy, curly, etc.), using cash or a major credit card.[8] Before being accessible to people everywhere, from Kingston Jamaica to Kingston Ontario, Indian Remy hair as the name conveys, originates in India. While there are other types of Remy hair on the market such as Chinese, Brazilian, Malaysian and Russian hair (Dream Girls, 2007: para.2), Indian hair remains the preferred type of human hair in the US market, and so despite it being the most expensive kind (Good hair, 2009). It is important to question why there is a privileging of Indian hair in the African American human hair market; what explains the increasing demand of Indian hair in the US in particular; and how the supply mechanisms of Indian hair has sustained this demand.

An investigation by journalist Swapna Majumdar (2006: para.12-13) shows that while the Chinese demand for Indian hair has steadily risen over the years,

---

6. This proposition reacts specifically to bell hooks' (1992) discussion of "blackness", whereby blackness is implicitly understood as a "singular universal" (Mohanty, 2003).
7. As in the disclaimer regarding the "production" process, consumption here simply refers to the use of human hair by individuals, for hairstyling purposes.
8. Indeed, all the online sites examined in this paper and which advertise and sell Virgin Remy Indian hair offer the aforementioned means of payment.

(whereby China has maintained the lead as India's number one hair exporter),[9] US imports of Indian hair have also grown significantly, with $82 million worth of hair exported to the US in the 2004-2005 fiscal year. One is right to ask why, given that the quality of human hair is primarily determined by whether it is remy (cuticles on, and in the same direction) and virgin (unprocessed), preference is given to Remy Indian (rather than Remy from other races) in the African American community. Some distributing companies advance that the affinity between Indian hair texture and that of *relaxed* African American hair is what makes Indian hair the preferred choice of African American women (eIndianHair.com: para.9). Others claim that 'Indian Remy hair is the most popular type for most African Americans because it naturally matches *their own hair texture* so well' (Remy Hair Talk, 2009: para.1; my emphasis). However, the difference between "natural" African American hair texture and "relaxed" African American hair texture is significant. Indeed, going from one to the other requires intense chemical treatment. Thus, this disparity in explanations from otherwise analogous marketing campaigns justifies that doubt be cast upon the so-called affinity between Indian hair and African American hair as a selling factor. Furthermore, basing African American women's preference for Indian hair among others is an undoubtedly clever marketing move, as it justifies a continued supply for Indian hair based on the supposed demand for it by the African American community. In this sense, the marketing story is conveniently made to correspond to basic neoliberal accounts of the market, according to which *demand determines supply*.

In order to further problematize the above aforementioned marketing accounts for the privileging of Indian hair in the US hair market, this analysis suggests that the marketing of Indian hair heavily determines its demand rather than a simple demand and supply mechanism . That is, Indian hair has been constructed as more desirable than other types of hair, without such a characteristic having actually been tested. Indeed, apart from the above explanations, there has been no concrete evidence from the examined distribution companies. Thus, although the term "virgin" in the human hair industry has come to signify unprocessed hair, one may view the "virginity" of Indian hair (recall the name of the product as "Virgin Remy Indian hair") to be implicitly constructed and marketed on racial lines. As seen above, Remy Indian hair is privileged in the US market relative to other types such as Brazilian, Chinese, and Russian hair for instance. It may be argued that rather than resulting from its necessary affinity with African American hair,[10] Indian hair is the preference of African American women because it has been made so through marketing that emphasized a racial hierarchization of hair, with Indian hair placed at the top of the hierarchy. In other words, Indian hair has been constructed as "rare" (eIndianHair.com, para.9), exotic, and better than European or Chinese hair. The Merriam-Webster (2011) online dictionary defines "rare" as either 'marked by unusual quality, merit or appeal' or 'seldom occurring or found'. Given that the *unusual appeal* of Indian hair sharing

---

9. Note that China exports Indian hair in order to resell it eventually worldwide (Majumdar, 2006: para.13).
10. The "affinity" explanation is also especially dubious given that African Americans (both men and women) have many different types of hair textures, yet the marketing campaign assumes "African American hair" to be a coherent and singular kind of hair.

an affinity with African American hair has thus far been contested in this paper, one is left with the second meaning of rare as 'seldom occurring or found'. In relative terms however, one need not conduct intensive research to be aware that the Indian population is much higher than that of Russia or Brazil for instance, rendering the seldom factor untenable. As such, it is difficult to sustain a justification for the privileged status of Indian hair, especially as it remains the most expensive kind as discussed above. It is no surprise therefore that some of the distribution and export sites resort to the fact that Indian Remy hair, unlike Chinese, European or Brazilian hair, is collected in Hindu temples as a selling point—or should we say an "exotic" factor upon which to build an image of rarity (see eIndianHair.com; Human Hairs Impex, 2007). In addition to the homogenization of African American hair, the various marketing campaigns construct a homogenized view of all Indian Remy hair as a coherent category of hair that is always better than all non-Indian hair. One would have a hard time believing however that each Indian woman's hair is always more desirable than the hair of other races, including the African American community. The discourses that underpin the marketing of Indian hair are therefore homogenizing on three levels: 1—viewing African American hair as homogeneous; 2—viewing Indian Remy hair as a homogeneous category, and 3—viewing all non-Indian hair (such as African American, European or Chinese) as less desirable groups of hair relative to Indian hair. Finally, and very illustrative of the above discussion on the virginity of Indian hair as readable on racial lines, is China's exports of Indian hair, with the purpose of mixing the latter with Chinese hair, so as to ultimately resell it at a lower cost (Majumdar, 2006: para.11). In this sense, the fact that clients assume Indian hair to be of superior quality relative to other types of hair automatically justifies the lower price that one is expected to pay if Indian hair is mixed with any other kind of hair; this testifies to the successful hierarchization of hair within the human hair industry.

## Marketing to African American women: "Made" in India or "Made" for the US?

That Virgin Indian Remy hair has successfully gained preferential treatment among the African American community is now evident. The final part of this first section seeks to illuminate the fact that in the marketing process, the production stage (dominated by Indian men and women) is profoundly disconnected from the consumption stage (dominated by African American women). The rationale behind this discussion is that such disconnect may aid in understanding why the purchase of actual Indian hair by African American women appears less problematized by this group of women (as individuals and as a community), than their use of the hair.

In the documentary *Good Hair* (2009), which analyzes the various traditions and trends in "Black" hairstyles, interview questions posed to women who purchased human hair (more often than not, Indian hair), revolved around why they used human hair, the affordability of the hair, as well as the social and political implications of their practices for their social, political, and economic status in the US. In short, the fact that the hair came from the shaven heads of actual Indian women who donated their hair to deities was never directly discussed with interviewees, nor were the choices and working conditions of those who worked on the hair (washing, drying, sewing it in manufactures nationwide and worldwide). To be sure, the documentary *Good Hair* did raise awareness of the production process, but separated its discussion of the production process from its coverage on the use of Indian hair by African American women. One may argue that this divide serves to explain why throughout the film, fond "consumers" of Indian hair (mostly African American singers and Hollywood personalities) do not show awareness or concern of the issues and actors involved in the production process.

This situation is also problematically reflected in the marketing campaigns of the sample of US-focused and (perhaps even more problematically so) of non-US focused distribution companies examined in this paper. By US-focused companies, this paper refers to those companies whose marketing campaigns are principally but not exclusively targeted to African American women (as in the opening paragraph of this essay). Note that in the sample of the nine online marketing/distribution companies examined in this essay, three are Indian-based Import-Export companies (Human Hairs Impex, 2007; Gupta Group, 2009; The Indian Remy Hair, 2007), one is a Toronto-based Canadian company (Hair & Cuticle Inc., 2008), while the remaining five are American-based (Dream Girls Hair, 2007; eIndianHair.com; International Hair Company, 2010; Remy Hair Talk, 2009; Remy Hair Today, 2008). With this brief inventory in mind, it is telling that beyond mentioning the temple-collected hair and the washing, sorting, and sewing of the hair by Indian women on or off site, none of these companies render visible the choices, conditions, actors and structures involved in the production of Virgin Remy hair. For instance, Remy Talk summarizes the steps from producing to distributing Virgin Indian Remy hair in the following manner:

> Indian hair comes from various temples in many different parts of India, and is sold at auction to companies all over the world.[11] In turn, these companies wash and sort the hair for use in many different forms including putting it on wefts, in wigs, in creating various pieces, and much more (Remy Hair Talk, 2009, para.1).

As such, Virgin Remy Indian hair is made to be free of any power struggles, reflecting a classless, genderless, raceless image. For instance, how does the hair get to the various Hindu temples, and why? Are hair donors voluntary? Forced? Remunerated? Are they aware of what happens to their hair after they leave the temple? What are the class, gender, and race dimensions at play? Is the hair collection institutionalized or informal? Who benefits and who loses? Apart from the knowledge provided by some sites which explain that the hair is donated to the temple based on Hindu religious beliefs, potential clients who visit any of the aforementioned sites will conveniently purchase their chosen style of Virgin Remy without any further concerns for issues that may be involved in the production phase of the hair in India. As such, past the

---

11. As the Indian-based Import-Export companies point out, these companies can also be found inside India, such as the Chennai-based Gupta Enterprises (Gupta Group, 2009; Human Hairs Impex, 2007).

name of the product (Virgin Indian Remy hair), it may be forgotten that the hair physically originates in India and used to belong to someone else. What appears important in these websites is the commercialization of the product, hence the heavy emphasis on its marketing, as assessed in the earlier part of this section. Thus, disconnected from any grounds on which to potentially problematize the product that they are being encouraged to purchase, eager clients such as African American women seeking to model their looks according to Hollywoodian standards of beauty, are able to concentrate on the image and life-style that is being sold to them. With the glamorous head shots of Hollywood celebrities such as Halle Berry and Kelly Rowland (respectively on the top left and top right hand corner of eIndianHair.com's webpage titled "Straight Indian Hair"), the focus is solely and without a doubt, on appealing to the potential buyer, in this case African American women. When local workers are mentioned, it is again solely to reassure the customer that the company only deals with "skilled workers" (The Indian Remy Hair, 2007: para.3). Therefore, in this consumer-focused and producer-blind marketing process, the fact that Virgin Indian Remy hair is produced for the US market is more visible than the fact that it is produced in India. Ultimately, this discussion serves to further problematize an implicit homogenization of African American women, by highlighting a marketing process that assumes that all African American women interested in Indian Remy hair are attracted to the Hollywood lifestyle.

## Power relations in the human hair industry

For an unconventional business such as the trade of human hair, extant academic scholarship on the topic is scarce. Indeed, Black feminist scholarship and other scholarship on hair politics tend to remain centered around the issues of hair in general (Banks, 2000), hair relaxing and synthetic hair, (hooks, 1992; Banks, 2000), and so even when they acknowledge the use of human hair (Banks, 2000). As such, the rest of this section will draw heavily from the 2009 documentary film directed by Jeff Stilson, and narrated by comedian Chris Rock on the one hand, as well as from the work of journalist Swapna Majumdar reporting for the Women's eNews (2006). This phase of the paper seeks to situate the various power relations locally and globally, *vis-à-vis* the market mechanisms underpinning the trade of Virgin Remy Indian hair. To do so, one must first understand the actors and structures at play in the production process.

Although their roles remain invisible on the web pages of the various distribution companies examined so far, temples play a very active role in the Indian human hair business. From collecting tonsured hair to auctioning it, Majumdar shows that temples are formidable administrative organizations that contain a panoply of actors of different kind (2006). Devotees who go to Hindu temples to offer their hair to their deity have their heads tonsured by temple barbers. The occupation of barber is largely held by male barbers, although there has been an increasing amount of female barbers, given the increased levels of tonsure due to a rising population (Majumdar, 2006: 19). Once the hair is tonsured, temple workers garner it into bags, in preparation for auctions. Temple administrators deal with the logistics and finances relating to the auctioning of hair, by advertising auction notices on the temple's official website, and holding scheduled auctions (Majumdar, 2006). Temples were said to have collected at one point in time in the early 2000s, an average of about $1 million for 3 million kilos of hair sold (Majumdar, 2006: para.18); with increased demand, this number is expected to have increased. While these workers are remunerated with unequal salaries, the devotees who offer their hair as a sacrifice to show gratitude to their deity are simply not remunerated, and would probably refuse any monetary payment. In effect, most do not seem to realize that the hair is auctioned off all over India and abroad. The answer of a newly-tonsured woman to whether she expects to see the hair on someone else's head is telling of this reality: "God likes hair too much"[12] (Good Hair, 2009). The level of trust that this devotee as an individual places in her religious institution constitutes a highly significant power structure. This kind of power relations will not be explored further in this paper, but is useful in terms of stressing that class, gender and race are but a chosen focus in the present analysis. It also serves to stress that while one may be tempted in understanding the stages in which the hair is collected as a succession of events, the various power relations that are constantly negotiated and played within the temple, as well as between the temple and outside entrepreneurs is so complex and multi-layered that it would be faulty to understand the process as linear. It is worth indicating that while both men and women offer their hair in sacrifice to their deity, women's hair is the kind that is used for weaves and extensions, whereas men's hair is usually used for 'coat linings and to extract L-Cystein (…)' (Majumdar, 2006: para.7).

It is only after this very complex process that the successfully auctioned hair can be sent off to a manufacturing site where workers sort out, wash, and tie the hair into wefts. Remy Indian hair is the most sought-after category of hair as per Majumdar's findings, with this type of hair selling for as much as $160 per kilogram (2006: para.8). Exporters confirm that Hollywood is the biggest consumer of human hair (Majumdar, 2006: para.14), which explains why Chris Rock comically dubs LA "the weave[13] capital of the world" (Good Hair, 2009). If one is to believe the fact that the Black Hair industry is a $9 billion industry, with 60 to 70% of that industry being made of the human weave hair alone (Good Hair, 2009), then there is need to further problematize why those at the very core of the production of weave hair (the Indian women who donate their hair to their Gods, the Indian men and women who work in the temples to collect the hair, and all those who work on manufacturing sites inside and outside India) do not share the bigger portion of the benefits in this global industry. However, it is imperative to insist that one not look at this issue as one of poorer Indian "producers" of human hair *versus* rich American "consumers" of human hair. Indeed, to do so would be to trivialize the important structural foundations that underpin the various power relations at play, and which resist any homogenization of the different groups of actors involved in the human hair industry.

12. The implication is that God likes hair too much to give it away.
13. A weave is 'synthetic or natural hair that is braided, sewn, bonded (i.e. glued), or woven into already existing hair (Banks, 2000: 173). Weaves are the most common way through which human hair is used. In this paper, weaves strictly refer to human hair weaves.

## A structure versus agency debate

*Good Hair* juxtaposes on the one hand the work of Indian women who "produce" human hair, with the pleasurable use of the produced hair by African American women on the other hand. Indeed, the poverty that characterizes the conditions in which Indian women must work to process the human hair (*Good Hair*, 2009) takes a more poignant meaning when contrasted with the opulence that defines the lives of Hollywood celebrities who made up a large number of the film's interviewees.

However, one should be careful so as not to simply retain a representation of poor Indian women contrasted to rich African American women. For instance, Majumdar (2006: para. 1-2) points out that Bollywood actress and Miss India 1976 "offered her waist-length locks at the 1,200-year-old Sri Venkateswara Temple in Tirupati (…) to thank its deity for granting her a private wish (…)". In a parallel vein, many customers who buy human hair in the US are working class[14] women ranging from hairdressers to teachers and students, who believe that they must wear human hair to enhance their looks (*Good Hair*, 2009). Ironically, one may link these two groups of women on religious grounds, given that, as one male interviewee believes, 'the weave culture is a culture of indoctrination' (*Good Hair*, 2009). Without going further into that debate, it is clear that women of all classes in India (from poor women working in the manufacture to sort out collected hair to rich women like Nafisa Ali who donate their hair to deities), as well as women of all classes in the US (as per the above brief discussion) participate in sustaining the market of Indian human hair, willingly or not. In other words, the transnational power relations between Indian and African American women involved in the human hair industry goes beyond a mere rich women *versus* poor women issue.

Rather than a simple dichotomization of the actors involved, I suggest that women in India and women in the US confront power relations that are shaped by the local and global structures that regulate their actions. As such, in terms of local structures – although for instance Nafisa Ali did not plan for her hair to be auctioned off to an unknown buyer—the Indian state's policies, which make the hair trade a legal one in India, does not guarantee any measures against the practices of Hindu temples in India[15] auctioning off hair, nor do temples forbid it. In turn, such local policies and rules work to the advantage of the African American woman who is interested in buying Indian human hair, thus providing African American women with a sense of entitlement to hair that does not belong to them. Local power structures may work in similar ways in the United States, and can be found for example in expectations created by the music industry. The case of Melissa Ford, a renowned "video girl" whose career involves appearances in numerous hip-hop and R&B music videos, is

---

14. We recognize here that a definition of "working class" is a subject of debate and may have conceptual limitations. I use it here rather loosely, recognizing it may encompass the unemployed, students, and people who might otherwise see themselves as "middle-class", or who may in some definitions be considered "petty-bourgeoisie".
15. The Indian government has a council on hair. The council was represented in Majumdar's report by its representative, the regional director of the time (2006: para. 13).

a telling example. Indeed, Ford proudly asserted that she changes her weave monthly, and does not know what she would do "if she did not have the kind of money that [she does]" to afford it; she reports spending between $3,000 to $5,000 monthly just for the purchase of the weave (*Good Hair*, 2009). Although Ms. Ford's statements suggest independent choices of hairstyles, it is clear that the privileging of Black women with extra-long wavy or straight hair in the Black American music industry constrains her to keep using human hair in order to fit the demands of the music industry and remain competitive, thus maintaining a degree of longevity in her career. Therefore, one is presented with another case of local[16] powerful structural forces that are able to subordinate the independence of individual actors.

Furthermore, global capitalist structures that allow individual entrepreneurs, companies and other institutions to pay workers such as Indian temple barbers a meagre $68 a month[17] (Majumdar, 2006: para. 21), while simultaneously allowing importing countries such as the United States to pay $1.50 for a strand of hair that expensive beauty salons may then weave into extensions or wigs that can sell for between $1,500 and $3,000' (Majumdar, 2006: para. 5), participate in justifying and perpetuating unequal power relations within and between the aforementioned actors. To be sure, these actors are diverse and the power relations discussed can be captured both within and between class, race and gender dimensions. The actors in consideration in this paper include global capitalist entrepreneurs, Indian citizens who offer their hair in sacrifice and Indian workers in the human hair business, female American celebrities and working class American women, decision-makers in the entertainment business, American and Indian states who shape and control the policies that regulate the import and export of human hair. The next section looks at the gender dimensions of such structurally-founded power relations.

## Gendered and Racial Power Relations

In order to examine gendered power relations in the US, it is important to recognize that the subject of hair is fundamentally linked to that of sexuality. A quick look at the pictures of the women displayed on the various websites show very glamorous, sexually alluring women. The marketing on these websites often appeal to the heteronormativity of hair politics in the African American community. This is especially pronounced in the movie *Good Hair*, whereby most questions to men and women imply that human hair weaves are designed to sexually attract the opposite sex. Thus, actress Nia Long speaks of "weave sex", only addressing heterosexual sex, where the man has to abide by the rules of weave sex determined by the woman (i.e. no weave touching, as this might temper with the expensively acquired weave). Melissa Ford for her part cautions that "men have to be patient" while the weave is being done, as this may take up to eight hours; and an African American male interviewee goes as far as to

16. Note that although the United States is the leader in terms of shaping practices in the R&B and hip-hop music industry, this industry is truly global in its nature and functioning, and goes well beyond the boundaries of America. Therefore, this example speaks to the importance of global power structures.
17. About 100 female barbers are said to cater to approximately 4,500 to 20,000 female devotees a day.

commodify African American women: "the price of maintaining [an African American] woman is like real estate in new York City, it's skyrocketing" (Good Hair, 2009). It is important to note that there appears to be a consensus among the men and women interviewed, who view the weave as a means to appeal to the opposite sex, and view men as the expected providers of the means to purchase the weave, should the women not be able to afford the price

These gendered relations lead to a layered racial and gendered power relations involving African American women, African American men, and White women in the US. I suggest that this is so, given two conditions. First, the sentiment among African American men that they "cannot afford a [African American] woman because of their hair", or that rules that emanate from the use of human hair such as "weave sex" make matters too complicated for them (Good Hair, 2009). Second, the fact that in the US, Black women's sexuality 'has been constructed in a binary opposition to that of white women' (Hammonds, 1997: 170). These two conditions thus explain why when men in a barber shop are asked whether they think White women were easier to deal with than African American women (sexually), many strongly answered "yes" *(Good Hair,* 2009). Paradoxically, the question may be whether the "straight" White-like look that the weave provides is a means for African American women to appropriate a White woman's body in order to reclaim the interest of African American men.

## Self-representations: Flair and identity politics

When invoking the term "body", we tend to think at first of its materiality –its composition as flesh and bone, its outline and contours, its outgrowth of nail and hair. But the body, as we well know, is never simply matter, for it is never divorced from perception and interpretation (Peterson, 2001: ix).

This analysis fully embraces Peterson's understanding of the body not only as material substance, but also as a site of *perception and interpretation*. Who perceives and interprets, to what purpose, and what are the wider implications of such perceptions and interpretations on the body? In seeking to tackle these questions within the present topic, this section posits African American hair types as reflective of, and impacting on various perceptions and interpretations of "the Black female body".[18]

### "Straight" hair versus "Natural Hair": Internalized or internal racism?

The title of the first chapter of bell hooks'[19] book *Black Looks*, is unambiguously telling of its agenda: Loving Blackness as Political Resistance (1992:1). In this

---

18. The expression is borrowed from the title of the 2001 edited book by Michael Bennett and Vanessa D. Dickerson "Recovering the Black Female Body: Self-Representations by African American Women".
19. The paper will maintain the name of this author in lowercase letters, to reflect the author's wish; hooks' rationale for this is that what matters most is the "substance of books, not who I am" (William, 2006: para.1).

chapter, hooks denounces the perpetuation of white supremacy reinforced daily by Black people through images in the mass media; she calls this phenomenon "internalized racism" (hooks, 1992: 1). Hooks (1992: 2) argues that unless Black people are free from 'hegemonic modes of seeing, thinking, and being', they cannot liberate or decolonize themselves, nor can they contribute to non-Blacks removing their colonizing gaze. In order to make further sense of how Black people practice internalized racism, how these mechanisms develop and how they are sustained, hooks (1992: 6-7) critically examines images in the mass media, which she calls the "spectatorship" of "images of race and representation". It is in this context that hooks examines the fixation of the music industry on hair, specifically that of African American women. She contends that highly sexualized images of Tina Turner and Diana Ross sporting White-like long hair are designed to represent these singers as desirable to White males (hooks, 1992: 70-71).

hooks' call for resisting such internalized racism may at first sight, be echoed with Mohanty's call for an anti-colonial feminist discourse and praxis, whereby colonization is defined as "almost invariably imply[ing] a relation of structural domination and a suppression—often violent—of the heterogeneity of the subject(s) in question" (Mohanty, 2003: 18). In this sense, this paper would align with hooks that a representation of the Black female body in the mass media is one where light-skinned Black women with "straight" long hair are favoured (Turner and Ross for instance), and where images of dark-skinned "nappy-haired" women are suppressed. Thus, the homogenization and objectification of African American women would reflect a colonization of the Black female body through a regulation of their hairstyle. As such, the promotion of a product such as Virgin Indian Remy hair can be seen as serving to discipline the Black female body. To be sure, wearing weaves made of Indian hair would thus represent an attempt to suppress the heterogeneity of "natural" hair textures and styles in the African American community, and an attempt to force African American women into sporting White-like "straight" hair. These observations echo longstanding concerns regarding popular expressions in the American Black community such as "good hair". "Good hair" is defined as "hair that is naturally straighter in texture. However, "good" hair can be quite curly but not tightly coiled or curled such as nappy hair" (Banks, 2000: 172). In this definition, the binary that opposes "good hair" (straight and White-like) to "bad hair" (nappy and African-like) is evident. These are all discursive representations that would support hooks' argument of internalized racism.

Nevertheless, this type of criticism risks repeating the problems that it seeks to address, on two accounts. First, one may argue that seeking to socialize African American Women so that they all are "Happy to be Nappy"[20] (hooks and Raschka, 1999), is an attempt to discipline the Black female body into following a specific path, that of what may be called "the nappy way". Second, assuming that all African American women would have relatively nappy hair at once essentializes and homogenizes their bodies into a single coherent group, when many African American women (much like Black women in other continents) naturally do not have "nappy" hair. As such, this kind of assumptions can bring not internalized racism, but *internal* racism within the Black community, where

---

20. The title of a children's book that hooks co-authored with Chris Raschka as the illustrator.

those who do not have "nappy" hair are implicitly assumed to be relatively "less Black" than the nappy-haired individuals, and become ipso facto a lesser discussed group. It can therefore be argued that dichotomizing the hair debate into "nappy/natural/liberated" hair *versus* "straight/non-natural/colonized" hair duplicates the very problematic that such a debate initially sought to redress, namely the dichotomy between "good" *versus* "bad hair".

"I am not my hair"

Inspired by bell hooks' insistence to keep her name in lowercase letters so that readers focus on the substance of her books rather than focusing on who she is (William, 2006: para.1), one can seek to negotiate a differentiation between hair and identity. Indeed, many African American women have already offered counter-discourses to criticisms of "internalized racism", in order to assert their capability to wear any kind of hairstyle—including weaves made of Virgin Remy Indian hair—without compromising their racial identity as African American women. In this vein, singer India Arie's popular song powerfully entitled "I am not my hair" (released in 2006), is the illustration *par excellence* of such counter-discourses. Her chorus (A-Z Lyrics, 2011: para.3) sums it best:

> I am not my hair
> I am not this skin
> I am not your expectations, no no
> I am not my hair
> I am not this skin
> I am a soul that lives within

Echoing Arie's lyrics, and commenting on her own use of weaves made of human hair, rapper Eve maintains that "I am not my hair ... It's just like putting on clothes" (*Good Hair*, 2009). Thus, these women bring their voices, resisting labels of not being "natural" or "Afro" enough, instead claiming their hair as a mere adornment that does not impact on their identity. While the rationale behind discourses and practices such as India Arie's can be justified as resistance mechanisms to the homogenization that may emerge from essentializing and disciplining constructions of Black American women as "natural" "nappy" women, it would be a mistake to agree with these resisting voices that one's identity can be totally divorced from one's body. Rather, one's hair is apprehended as a reflection of one's body, and in Peterson's definition, it is subject to perception and interpretation. As was suggested at the beginning of this section, such perceptions and interpretations are best understood in a plural sense. By this stage, it is clear that both the body being apprehended and the body doing the apprehending perceive and interpret, respectively self-representing and representing the apprehended body. This explains the focus of the analysis so far not just on representations but also on self-representations.

To claim that "I am not my hair" denies the fact that the body is inescapably perceived and interpreted by oneself and by others. This would be an untenable position, as it would assume that one's body exists in isolation from other bodies. Rather, this paper suggests that in order to refrain from homogenizing and essentializing discourses and practices (in short from colonizing methods), counter-discourses should acknowledge the possibility of multiple meanings. With this premise, one can transform the risks of hooks' proposition of "loving blackness" from a proposition that may lead to colonizing practices into one that is brings productive debates. To do so, "blackness" cannot be understood as a singular, but rather as expressing multiple meanings, which would therefore transcend essentialist discourses. However, to accept the possibility of a plurality of meanings involves the acceptance of the fact that there is always a perception and an interpretation for a meaning to be expressed. Hence, I, as a subject that accepts the existence of other subjects, can no longer say that "I am not my hair", but I may assert that I can be apprehended as more than one kind of hair, and still be apprehended as a *legitimate* subjectivity that is continuously in the making.

I can be more than one kind of hair

To acknowledge the legitimacy of multiple meanings is to also acknowledge the importance of language in creating or suppressing possibilities. As such, one should consciously recognize that the way in which one uses language can fundamentally be colonizing or emancipatory. Here, Mohanty's concern over homogenizing discourses and practices can be tied with Katie King's concern with "the politics of naming", and can help unpack the implications behind the term "blackness" or "African American hair" for instance. In King's 2002 piece entitled "Lesbianisms, Feminisms, and Global Gay Formations", she argues that using the term "lesbian" in singular may suggest that there is only one way of being a "lesbian" (and quite often, the hegemonic Western way). Yet, a lesbian may mean different things to different people (King, 2002). For some, it cannot be temporal, while for others, it is essentially in fact, a transition (King, 2002). Similarly, the term "blackness" can be used in many registers. However, blackness in hooks' understanding is intended to define a certain way of being an African American. For women for instance, this may be based on whether they wear long straight hair—keeping in mind that some Black women may have naturally long hair straight hair, or whether they happily sport nappy hair—if they happen to be naturally "nappy-haired" indeed.

In essence, this section argues that the implication that someone "can wear their race wrong" (Rooks, 2001) is highly problematic. Indeed, unless there is an openness about what blackness may be, and an acceptance of the possibility that it can be the "happy nappy" or the weave-on Remy Indian hair for instance, the debate risks creating new hegemonies. To be sure, this argument does not deny the many issues that stem from the human hair industry, and which have been discussed above. Rather, it contends that the denunciation of these issues should not create other ones or duplicate the challenges it is trying to address. For instance, movements such as "the Black Power" in the 1960s that aimed to reclaim pride in "Afrohair" and that expressed their mottos through expressions such as "black is beautiful", "dark but beautiful", can be alienating to light-skinned African Americans who are "are obliged to "prove" their blackness", given an assumption within the African American community that lighter-skinned African Americans feel superior to others" (Shohat, 1997: 203). It can be convincingly argued that similar alienating effects would target African American women who choose to wear Virgin Indian hair, within an environment that constructs such hair-styles as "un-black" or "un-African". This implies the understanding that African American Wom*en* (rather than the implicit conceptualization of the African American Wom*an*) are plural subjectivities, and that their individual transformations need to be engaged with, rather than arbitrarily suppressed. In this respect, Shohat (1997: 204) evokes the work of Kobena Mercer who points out that "natural hair" in the African American diasporic context is "not itself African; it is a syncretic construct. Afro-diasporic hair styles, from the Afro to dreadlocks are not emulations of "real" African styles but rather neologistic projections of diasporic identity." The terms *syncretic* and *neologistic* are particularly important here, as they speak to the fact that the black female body, like other bodies, cannot be isolated in space or time, as it is continuously changing at the contact of other bodies. In this sense, Rooks' (2001: 283) attempt at a "sense-making dialogue" between African American bodies who claim the right to adorn their bodies with different hairstyles, and African American bodies who seek to retain their hair as is, represents a productive beginning at initiating a plural, engaging, and constructive representations of African American women.

## Concluding remarks

In the preceding analysis, I have argued that the so-called "authentic" or "natural" African American woman must be able to be bound in time, and "untouched" by outside bodies in order to be indeed, "natural". This, it is clear, is not possible. Therefore, one must instead recognize the possibility of multiple subjectivities, and be willing to openly engage with these subjectivities in a constructive manner. Furthermore, attempts at counter-discourses on the use of human hair by African American women risk turning into exceptionalist and essentializing discourses, as they myopically focus on local conditions—on the US for example, thus failing to understand in what ways alternative discourses and practices can negotiate new productive spaces and meanings. As far as concerns the industry of Indian hair specifically, a productive avenue that can begin to shape new discourses and new understandings of the linkages between local and global politics of hair and identity will be one that will identify and engage a common agenda across class, gender, and racial dimensions. Thus, engaging with debates surrounding the cultural appropriation of "black" hairstyles globally (such as dreadlocks, cornrows, braids), can serve as a productive way to assess what "black" hairstyles mean for other groups that come into contact with the multiple meanings of black cultures, and what such appropriations mean for the appropriation of other cultural practices by black communities—through the weave world for instance. Through such a productive engagement, one can begin to subsequently engage with the implications of various cultures of "blackness"—as represented through the use of human hair for instance—for the socio-political and economic conditions of

Black communities, and for the agency of individuals and groups within Black communities. Only by opening up new spaces and meanings in this manner, can one open up the possibility of discourses and practices of "a politics of engagement rather than a politics of transcendence" (Mohanty, 2003: 122), the consequence of which will be truly decolonizing and anti-capitalist.

In closing, the paper proposes a shift in focus that will consider the importance of locating African American women's experiences such as their discourses and practices *vis-à-vis* the use of Virgin Remy Indian hair (and human hair in general), within wider global capitalist power structures. In other words, understanding African American hair and identity politics as part of a global puzzle is a *sine qua non* to a more productive discussion of the sociopolitical and economic underpinnings and implications of the debate undertaken in this paper. Shohat (1997: 208) illuminates this point best when she states that 'the global nature of the colonizing process and the global reach of the contemporary media virtually oblige the cultural critic to move beyond the restrictive framework of the nation-state.

# References

Books and book chapters

Banks, Ingrid. 2000. *Hair matters: Beauty, Power, and Black Women's Consciousness*. New York: New York University Press

Hammonds, Evelyn M. 1997. "Toward a Genealogy of Black Female Sexuality: The Problematic of Silence," in M. Jacqui Alexander and Chandra Mohanty (eds.), *Feminist Genealogies, Colonial Legacies, Democratic Futures*, New York: Routledge, 170-182

hooks, bell. 1992. *Black looks: race and representation*. Toronto: Between The Lines

hooks, bell, and Chris Raschka. 1999. *Happy to be Nappy*. New York: Hyperion Books for Children

King, Katie. 2002. "'There Are No Lesbians Heré: Lesbianisms, Feminisms, and Global Gay Formations," in Arnaldo Cruz-Malavé and Martin F. Manalansan IV, (eds.), *queer globalizations: citizenship and the afterlife of colonialism*, New York: New York University Press, 33-48

Mohanty, Chandra Talpade. 2003. *Feminism Without Borders: Decolonizing Theory, Practicing Solidarity*, Durham: Duke University Press

Peterson, Carla. 2001. "Foreword: Eccentric Bodies," in Michael Bennett and Vanessa D. Dickerson (eds.), *Recovering the Black Female Body: Self-Representations by African American Women*, New Brunswick: Rutgers University Press, ix-xvi

Rooks, Noliwe. 2001. "Wearing Your Race Wrong: Hair, Drama, and a Politics of Representation for African American Women at Play on a Battlefield," in Michael Bennett and Vanessa D. Dickerson (eds.), *Recovering the Black*

*Female Body: Self-Representations by African American Women*, New Brunswick: Rutgers University Press, 279-295

Shohat, Ella. 1997. "Post-Third-Worldist Culture: Gender, Nation, and the Cinema," in M. Jacqui Alexander and Chandra Mohanty (eds.), *Feminist Genealogies, Colonial Legacies, Democratic Futures*, New York: Routledge, 183-209

Films

*Good Hair*. Dir. Jeff Stilson. Perf. Chris Rock. HBO Films., 2009. DVD.

Web sources

A-Z Lyrics. (2011). *India.Arie Lyrics: I Am Not My Hair*. Retrieved on March 20, 2011 from http://www.azlyrics.com/lyrics/indiaarie/iamnotmyhair.html

Dream Girls Hair. (2007) *Remy Human Hair_Definition*. Retrieved on March 20, 2011 from http://www.dghair.com/remy-human-hair.htm

eIndianHair.com. (Undated). *Virgin Remy Hair*. Retrieved on March 20, 2011 from http://www.eindianhair.com/virgin_remy_hair.htm

— (Undated). *Place Your Order Today*. Retrieved on March 20, 2011 from http://www.eindianhair.com/order.htm

Gupta Group. (2009). *About Us*. Retrieved on March 20, 2011 from http://www.guptagroup.com/about%20us.html

— (2009). *Activities*. Retrieved on March 20, 2011 from http://www.guptagroup.com/activities.html

Hair & Cuticle Inc. (2008). *Home: Welcome to Hair & Cuticle Inc*. Retrieved on March 20, 2011 from http://www.cuticlehair.ca/

Human Hairs Impex. (2007). *Process*. Retrieved on March 20, 2011 from http://www.humanhairsimpex.com/Process.htm

— (2007). *About Us*. Retrieved on March 22, 2011 from http://www.humanhairsimpex.com/index.htm

International Hair Company. (2010). *Gorgeous Virgin Indian Remy Hair!* Retrieved on March 27, 2011 from http://www.inhairco.com/virginremy.html#Remy%20wavy

Majumdar, Swapna. Women's eNews. (July 9, 2006). *Indian Temples: Do Brisk Business in Women's Hair*. Retrieved on March 12, 2011 from http://www.womensenews.org/story/business/060709/indian-temples-do-brisk-business-womens-hair

Merriam-Webster. (2011). Definition of RARE. Retrieved on March 19, 2011 from http://www.merriam-webster.com/dictionary/rare?show=0&t=1302037906

Remy Hair Talk. (2009). *Indian Remy hair Extensions!* Retrieved on March 19, 2011 from http://www.ibremyhairextensions.com/

Remy Hair Today. (2008). *Remy Hair Today*. Retrieved on March 20, 2011 from http://www.remyhairtoday.com/index2.html

The Indian Remy Hair. (2007). *Indian Natural Remy Hair*. Retrieved on March 27, 2011 from http://www.theindianremyhair.com/contact.html

Williams, Heather. The Sandspur. (February 10, 2006). *bell hooks Speaks Up*. Retrieved on March 20, 2011 from http://media.www.thesandspur.org/media/storage/paper623/news/2006/02/10/News/Bell-Hooks.Speaks.Up-1602355.shtml?norewrite200609102135&sourcedomain=www.thesandspur.org

# The role of radio and mobile phones in conflict situations: The case of the 2008 Zimbabwe elections and xenophobic attacks in Cape Town

Wallace Chuma

## Background to the study

Between March and June 2008, two violent events that are the focus of this paper unfolded in Zimbabwe and South Africa, both resulting in loss of life and forcing mass displacement. The first was the March 2008 'harmonised' general election in Zimbabwe, which was preceded by profound levels of violence, most of which was state-orchestrated as the ruling Zanu-PF party struggled to retain its hold on power. The March election did not produce an outright winner for president, prompting a run-off in June that same year, during which the violence escalated further. According to Human Rights Watch (2012), nearly 200 people were killed in the violence, while 36,000 were displaced.[1] The second violent event happened in South Africa, where black South Africans targeted foreign Africans living in the country, in a wave of both sporadic and highly coordinated at-tacks that lasted just over a month. The attacks claimed the lives of 62 people and displaced an estimated 35,000 (*Mail & Guardian*, 31 May 2008).[2]

In both cases, the violence was both lived and mediated. Within the broader public spheres in both countries, the televised, often harrowing images of violent death and destruction made for hotly contested readings and interpretations. However, within the private spheres of ordinary citizens caught up in the violence, the appropriation of the media was tied to the need to survive (or the compulsion to inflict pain on the 'other', in the case of the perpetrators).

Radio and new information and communication technologies (ICTs)—especially mobile phones—are by far the most pervasive media available to most Africans today. Although the area of radio and ICTs for development in Africa has attracted a growing body of research (see DeBruijn, Nyamnjoh, and Brinkman, 2009; Bosch, 2011; Gunner, Ligaga and Moyo, 2012), there has not been adequate research attention on the uses of radio and ICTs in conflict situations, or the appropriation of the convergence capabilities of new media to enhance reporting by traditional media such as radio. This makes the present case studies on Zimbabwe and South Africa all the more interesting.

---

1. See: http://www.hrw.org/news/2011/03/08/zimbabwe-no-justice-rampant-killings-torture. Accessed 23 July 2012.
2. See: "Toll from xenophobic attacks rises." http://www.mg.co.za/article/2008-05-31-toll-from-xenophobic-attacks-rises). Accessed 10 September 2013.

## Scope and objectives of the research

The main focus of the research was to explore how victims of repression and violence appropriated radio and new media in conflict situations, as well as how radio stations themselves appropriated new media for purposes of enhancing their coverage of life-threatening situations in the two countries. With regard to individuals, a purposive sampling procedure was used in both cases to identify the interviewees, who were subjected to in-depth interviews. Six radio stations were initially selected for research, and these included Cape Town-based community radio stations (Bush Radio, Radio Tygerberg and Radio Zibonele), as well as three 'pirate' radio stations that broadcast into Zimbabwe via shortwave and the Internet. These included Radio Voice of the People (VOP; based in South Africa), SW Radio (based in the UK) and Voice of America (VOA, Studio Seven; based in Washington). During the research process, however, Radio Zibonele could not be included because management representatives at the station were not available to be interviewed.

The study sought to, *inter alia*, explore the uses of ICTs by the selected radio stations and the different ways in which men and women access and participate in the use of these technologies, within the communities under study. The research also sought to establish the linkages, if any, between the use of radio and mobiles.

The general objective was therefore to begin to explore the roles that both old and new media play in changing African communities, especially in the ways in which citizens negotiate their day-to-day struggles, and particularly in conflict situations. Beyond the comparative analysis of the case studies, the overarching aim was ultimately to contribute to the body of knowledge on how radio and ICTs could be used in disaster mitigation and conflict resolution in the African context.

With regard to radio stations, the study sought to elicit information on how they framed the 2008 conflicts in both cases, whether and the extent to which they appropriated ICTs (such as the Internet, social media platforms and mobile phones) to enhance their reporting of the conflict, and also to document the lessons learnt from the experience of covering the two events. The interviews with ordinary citizens in both Zimbabwe and South Africa were aimed at establishing the roles that the mobile phone in particular and ICTs in general played in their lives during the conflicts, and the role of community and 'pirate' radio as their sources of information during that period. The study also sought to establish whether there were variations in the uses of radio and ICTs among citizens in both cases, based on variables such as gender and age. Based on collected data, the study ultimately also sought to identify the constraints and opportunities in the use of radio and ICTs by Africans in conflict situations. This is important for, among other things, future policy making.

## Literature review and conceptual framework

The role of radio and new media in Africa has attracted considerable scholarly attention, especially following the introduction of multiparty politics on the continent in the early 1990s. Among other things, researchers have been interested in understanding the role of both radio and new media in promoting democracy and development (see Ronning, 1995; Nyamnjoh, 2005). Even the role of radio in conflict situations has also attracted some attention, especially in the aftermath of the 1994 genocide in Rwanda, where sections of the media, including radio and newspapers, gave editorial support to the conflict (Gourevitch, 1998; Thompson, 2007).

The articulation of the role of the media in both democracy and development is in many instances informed by Jurgen Habermas's notion of the public sphere (see Bosch, 2011). The public sphere concept generally relates to a media system that provides accessible space for the articulation of 'rational-critical' discussion and debate by the citizenry. Such debate and discussion is considered an essential ingredient of both democracy and development. Habermas used the concept in his seminal inquiry into the rise and decline of a bourgeois participatory democracy centred on critical-rational debate. He defined the public sphere as:

> ... the sphere of private people come together as a public; they soon claimed the public sphere regulated from above against the public authorities themselves, to engage them in a debate over the general rules governing relations in the basically privatised but publicly relevant sphere of commodity exchange and social labour. The medium of this political confrontation was peculiar and without historical precedent: people's public use of their reason (1992:27).

Coffee shops, salons and other public places were the sites for this debate, whose participants gradually constituted a countervailing force to the authoritarian state of early modern Europe. The bourgeois public sphere offered space in which citizens had access to deliberate about their common affairs and articulate broader social interests, and hence became an institutionalised arena of discursive interaction. Although the concept has been criticised for, among other things, assuming the existence of a universal and all-inclusive public sphere (and therefore being ahistorical), it continues to be used as an analytic category to measure the extent to which the media act as platforms for public participation. In relation to the role of radio in African societies, the concept remains useful, not least because radio is the de facto mass medium in Africa, given its pervasiveness.

In addition to conceptualising the role of the media in relation to the public sphere, the media are also considered to perform other roles including being watchdogs to power, being sources of information, education and entertainment, voices of the voiceless, and so forth. These roles are most commonly assumed in liberal-pluralist approaches to the media (see Curran, 2005).

The above articulations of the role of the media in society, though very important, locate that role within 'normal' or peaceful situations. Given the nature of this study, it is important to also reflect on debate on the role of the media—both old and new—in the context of conflict situations. Probably the most cited reference in this regard is the work of Norwegian scholar Johan Galtung on the subject of what is commonly known as 'war' and 'peace' journalism. Galtung has been highly critical of dominant media representations of conflicts that glamourise war, focus on the dualism of victory and defeat, and are biased in favour of 'official' sources. He advanced the model of "peace journalism," the key components of which included the following: peace-orientation, i.e., humanizing all sides and placing emphasis on the destructive effects of violence and the importance of achieving peace; exploring untruths on both sides; and focusing on solutions rather than victory or defeat (Galtung, 1998). Although the model attracted its fair share of criticism for conceptual and practical weaknesses—such as lack of clarity on the methodology of peace journalism—(see, for example, Shinar, 2009), it remains useful in helping explore the role of media in conflict situations in Africa.

With respect to the appropriation of media (including new media) by citizens caught up in conflict, this study is also informed by the currently thin body of research on the subject in Africa and elsewhere. As Eytan Gilboa (2009) observes, despite the critical significance of the roles played by new media in conflict and conflict resolution, this area "has been relatively ignored, neglected by both scholars and practitioners" (p. 88). The paucity of research and analysis in this area, he argues, "may be attributed to the difficulties inherent in multidisciplinary research and the absence of adequate tools, models, and frameworks for analysis" (p.89). In his articulation of a framework for analysing the role of media in conflict resolution, Gilboa points to the critical role that the Internet and mobile phone play both in conflict situations and in conflict resolution.

In his exploration of the uses of mobile phones in post-conflict Liberia, Michael L. Best (2011), noted: "In Liberia people cling to their mobile phones as tools for security and safety. They use phones to combat crime, sexual violence, and to help in medical emergencies" (p. 25). Besides being lifestyle tools, mobile phones in conflict or insecure situations in Africa were also lifeline instruments, argues Best. In March 2012, the Liberian police, with the support of the private sector in that country, gave free mobile phones to a group of women in the small town of Weala—one of the most affected by the civil war and where violence against women continued to be rampant—with the instruction to use them to alert the police (via a toll-free number) when any type of security problem was brewing, including domestic violence and other types of violence against women and girls in the area. As a result of this intervention, instances of domestic violence dropped significantly.[3] In light of the foregoing, it is important to note that with the proliferation of new information and communication technologies, some of the roles associated with traditional, institutionalised media are no longer just their preserve.

The Internet, for example, offers a panoply of communicative possibilities which dwarf the mostly linear and time-and-space-bound features of traditional media. Mobile telephony, which is the second area of focus of this paper, continues to attract significant research attention because of its phenomenal growth in Africa and elsewhere, as well as its increasing embeddedness to both old and new communication technologies. In sub-Saharan Africa, mobile

---

3. See UN report: "From conflict resolution to prevention: connecting Peace Huts to the police in Liberia." (http://www.unwomen.org/2012/09/from-conflict-resolution-to-prevention-connecting-peace-hut-to-the-police-in-liberia/)

phones have grown so rapidly that between 2000 and 2008, access to them grew from 1 in 50 Africans to over 60 percent (De Bruijn, Nyamnjoh & Brinkman, 2009). In South Africa, access to mobile phones is now well over 80 percent, and is growing.

In many parts of Africa, as Aker and Mbiti (2010: 208) note, mobile phones "have represented the first modern telecommunications infrastructure of any kind" given that the fixed telephone service never went as far as the most remote parts of the continent. The rapid increase in mobile phone coverage has been possible thanks to massive investment in the industry by both local and multinational players, sometimes against considerable odds in the early days. Although the costs of access, both in terms of the mobile phone device and airtime vary from country to country, the past decade has generally seen a lowering of costs across the board, resulting in greater uptake. The fact that there is a huge market for used mobile phones as well as cheap imitation models imported from China makes it far easier to acquire a working phone in Africa. So rapid has the growth in mobile phones been in Africa that some scholars have referred to them as 'the new talking drums of Africa', in reference to the traditional African drum which was the key communicative tool in mostly precolonial Africa (see De Bruijn, Nyamnjoh & Brinkman, 2009).

Although research on mobile phones has covered a range of areas such as access, costs, policies among others, this article is interested mostly in research that explores the ways in which citizens and marginalised communities appropriate new media (including mobile phones) for self-expression and for subverting power, especially in authoritarian political contexts. Moyo (2010), for example, explores the manner in which Zimbabwean citizens in the diaspora appropriated new media—blogs, news websites and 'pirate radio'—to counter state propaganda churned out via the mainstream state-controlled media. The political and economic crisis in Zimbabwe, which began in earnest in 2000, resulted in the closure of democratic space for many citizens who did not support the ruling party, Zanu-PF (see, Raftopoulos and Savage, 2005; Campbell, 2003; Nyarota, 2006). The closure of privately-owned newspapers by the state made hundreds of journalists and other media workers jobless, and many of them left the country. From their bases in the diaspora, some of the citizens started online news websites, weblogs and 'pirate radio' stations which provided alternative and oppositional narratives of the crisis, countering the state's version of events. These developments attracted and continue to attract scholarly attention (see Mano and Willems, 2008; Chuma, 2008, 2010).

The use of new media to subvert power has not been confined to Zimbabweans in the diaspora. Within Zimbabwe itself, citizens engaged with mobile phones and illegal 'pirate radio' to communicate amongst themselves and with the outside world as violence and electoral fraud took centre stage during the 2008 elections (Chuma, 2008; Moyo, 2010). Short message services (SMS) were shared amongst voters—especially opposition voters—with information ranging from safe voting sites to preliminary results for different constituencies. During the xenophobic attacks in Cape Town, foreign nationals also used SMS to warn each other of violent hotspots. Victims also called in on talk show radio programmes to relate their ordeals.

It is clear from the foregoing that citizens appropriate new media to suit their particular circumstances, and any credible approach to the study of usage should take this into account. This article assumes as its point of entry the critical view that the appropriation of technologies, both old and new, takes place in a wider socioeconomic and political context which shapes it, even as technology shapes the same social milieu (Croteau & Hoynes, 2003). In both cases under study, the usage of both radio and mobile phones during conflict is considered not just as a one-off phenomenon, but as one shaped by broader political, economic and social circumstances in the two contexts.

## Methodology

Given the nature of the inquiry at hand, this study applied a combination of qualitative and quantitative approaches, though with a strong qualitative/ interpretive bias. An analysis of 'uses' or 'appropriations' of media by citizens lends itself to more than just figures and quantifiable highlights of instances of use. It requires an examination of the contexts in which such use is occurring, including both personal and social contexts.

As highlighted earlier in this article, the principal method used in the research in both cases was in-depth interviewing. Structured interviews were held in Cape Town and Harare between August and November 2010, and involved victims of xenophobic attacks in South Africa and election-related violence in Zimbabwe. Although a random sampling procedure was applied, for convenience purposes the research team selected sites where most violence took place in the two contexts. In Cape Town, interviews were held in the 'townships' where most of the violence occurred in 2008, namely Khayelitsha, Langa and Du Noon. In Zimbabwe, given that the violence was a national phenomenon, and was largely targeted at opposition Movement for Democratic Change (MDC) and other civil society activists, the researchers chose Harare and Masvingo as sites of interviews and arranged most of the contacts through the MDC and civil society groups. The interviews comprised both open and closed-ended questions, including brief biographical details of the respondents (such as age and gender), their location in 2008, how they were affected by the event in question, their patterns of use of radio and mobiles, etc. Fifty interviews were held in each of the two case studies, for a total of one hundred. The research teams in both cases were subject to initial training that included ethical guidelines in researching human subjects.

In addition to interviews with individuals, the research team also interviewed editorial staff at selected radio stations which were involved in programming during the conflicts in both cases. The interviews sought to establish how these stations framed the conflicts as well as the extent to which they appropriated new media such as the Internet and mobile phones to enhance their coverage of the events.

Document analysis also formed a lesser part of the methodology in this study. The close scrutiny of relevant documents on radio, mobiles and other new media was aimed at establishing the background historical, contextual as well as theoretical framework for the study. Additionally, the scrutiny of both critical and popular literature on both the elections in Zimbabwe and xenophobic attacks in Cape Town was meant to provide context to the study. Document analysis was therefore critical in order to inform the type and scope of questions raised in the interviews as well as the general thrust of the intellectual inquiry as a whole.

## Findings and discussion

### The central role of the mobile phone in the context of crisis

A key finding of this study was the centrality of the mobile phone in the lives of the interviewees in both cases, with mobiles being by far the most used source of information by victims of violence and conflict. Nearly all the interviewees (99 percent) in South Africa stated they possessed a mobile phone during the time of the conflicts in 2008 and relied on it for key information, while 80 percent in Zimbabwe confirmed the same. Although in both cases the use of phones was largely confined to making or receiving calls, as well as sending and receiving text messages, the mobile phone played a key role in keeping the victims of violence abreast of the situation around them in a context where access to information could mean life or death.

It emerged from the interviews—especially in Cape Town—that the mobile phone also occupied a key space in the day-to-day social lives of citizens before and after the crisis. It served multiple functions in their pursuit of pleasure and recognition in general, and specific functions during emergencies such as during the xenophobic attacks. Although the majority of respondents admitted to having owned rather basic phones in 2008, by the time of the interviews in 2010 they had moved on to smart, Internet-enabled phones which allowed them to spend significant amounts of their time on social networking sites, especially on Facebook. The convenience the mobile phone provided had become so naturalised that the majority of the respondents found it difficult to imagine the world before the device was introduced.

However, during the xenophobic attacks in Cape Town, the mobile phone was a key 'must-have' for the victims. A typical victim was aged between 25 and 30, male or female, who had arrived in South Africa within the last two years (from 2008), a holder of a diploma or university degree from Zimbabwe, and worked contract jobs as labourer or waiter/waitress in Cape Town. Although the extent of victimhood varied from being threatened to being injured and displaced, a common feature among all the respondents was their reliance on their phones for information: warnings on violent hotspots, directions to municipal halls or 'protection centres' that the City of Cape Town made available to accommodate the displaced immigrants, updates on whether the situation in the townships had calmed enough for them to return, and, perhaps most important, updating family and friends both in Zimbabwe and overseas on their situation. In a number of instances, the victims received financial support from family members in the United Kingdom, Australia, Canada and the United States to help then resume their disrupted lives after the attacks ceased. The mobile phone was the most convenient tool for these transactions.

The use of mobile phones was somehow less pervasive in Zimbabwe (80 percent of respondents) during the 2008 elections. This was partly because the country was in the middle of a severe economic crisis at the time and mobile phones were still fairly expensive gadgets for many people. The critical shortage of SIM cards at the time also meant that even those with handsets could not get connected. Further, it emerged from the interviews that the generally bad network coverage by the three service providers in the country (Econet, Telecel and CellOne) resulted in limited access to mobile communication. However, among the respondents who made regular use of the phone—especially Harare residents—it was an extremely important resource in the context of horrific state-sponsored violence against members of the opposition. They used the phone to communicate with family and friends and warn each other of violent hotspots, communicated with their political parties and civil society groups to report on attacks, and probably most importantly, opposition election agents filed election results from the local voting sites to the national vote-counting centres as a way of preventing rigged results. In some cases, the local opposition agents took photos of the final results and uploaded them on the Internet, constantly updating citizens within and out of Zimbabwe who were keenly following the elections.

Another interesting aspect of the usage of mobile phones in Zimbabwe was the circulation of viral SMS messages among mostly opposition voters who subscribed to the activist civil society portal called kubatana.net. According to its founder Beverly Clarke, the portal sent out a total of 78 text messages to a list of subscribers between 25th March and 4th August 2008. This period covered both the harmonised elections in March and the presidential election re-run in June. According to Clarke, the list of subscribers grew phenomenally from 1040 in March to 4200 by August, largely because of the popularity and relevance of the messages they sent out. She wrote:[4]

> The list of subscribers almost doubled in the two weeks following the 29th March election, and then doubled again in the months between the harmonised election and the presidential election run off. This growth was largely due to word of mouth—one person receiving our SMS updates, sharing them with a friend or colleague, and this person contacting us to subscribe as well... information in these text messages included reminders to go and vote, clarification about the voting process, House of Assembly and Senate results, inspiration, hope, requests for feedback, announcements of events, offers to share relevant information by post and email, and suggestions for citizen activism.

A sample of the messages sent out shows a variety of interesting details relevant to the election. For example, on the morning of the election, on 29th March, the following SMS was sent out: "Kubatana! Some poll stations asking foreign born for renunciation certificates. This is NOT a requirement, Call Zim Lawyers to assist-091278995/04251468." This was a very critical message because Zimbabwean law does not allow dual citizenship and authorities could easily stop especially foreign-born Whites (suspected by the government to be opposition supporters) from voting on the pretext of not presenting a certificate

---

4. Personal communication with Beverly Clarke, 8th September, 2010.

renouncing their foreign citizenship. The Zimbabwe Lawyers for Human Rights, a non-profit body, offered free legal services to anybody victimised by the state during the elections. Other messages provided basic information about where to vote, the contact details of the Zimbabwe Electoral Commission encouraging citizens to phone them to complain about the delays in results, and updates on both local and global news reports.

Finally, with regard to the usage of mobile phones in both cases, it emerged that gender was, albeit in a small way, a factor in how citizens appropriated mobile phones in the context of conflict. From the interviews, it emerged that most of the men had access to and made use of mobile phones, while some women did not get to use such phones (only 20 percent of women in Zimbabwe had phones in 2008) and therefore had to rely on radio or word of mouth. For those with handsets, especially in Cape Town, they used them mainly to send "Please Call Me" messages because they did not have airtime. This is an important finding which reflects the connection between gendered structural inequalities in general and access to communication.

The role of community radio

Another interesting finding was that local/community radio could be declining in influence in contexts of high media density such as South Africa, where they have to compete with numerous other sources of information. This is a critical departure from the highly acclaimed role that community media and alternative media played as nodes of 'independent' critique and information during the Apartheid era.

The majority of respondents (80 percent) in Cape Town said they did not rely on local radio stations for information on the violence. While one could argue that this naturally makes sense given the nature of the conflict and the fact that many of the respondents were in constant movement as they sought refuge, this argument becomes difficult to sustain if one considers that most of the respondents said they actually relied on TV, national or commercial radio and mobile phones. The TV and national radio provided a global/national picture of the violence, while mobile phones were sources of more intimate information such as updates from and to family and friends affected by the violence. The most popular radio stations cited in Cape Town were national stations SAFM and Metro FM.

However, the fact that the majority of xenophobic attack victims did not rely on community radio for news does not take away the fact that these radio stations covered the violence. Both Bush and Tygerberg radio stations deployed journalists to cover the attacks, and relied on the police, non-governmental organisations, local authorities and the accounts by victims for their stories. They also received tip-offs and updates from members of the public via SMS and phone calls. For Bush radio, the coverage was two-fold: news bulletins giving updates on latest developments, as well as its daily talk show 'Saki Sizwe' (Building the Nation). During the attacks, the show regularly hosted a guest from the Refugee Forum, a non-profit organisation that offered assistance to victims of the violence. According to station manager Adrian Louw, the majority of callers on the talk show expressed outrage at the ongoing attacks and in some cases offered valuable information such as the location of temporary housing facilities made available by the City of Cape Town for the victims. Although the talk shows were generally themed around what was happening at the time, there were also sessions that focused on the role that Africans outside South Africa played in support of the anti-Apartheid struggle. According to Louw:

> At Bush radio we also put emphasis on our history. When we were in exile during the Apartheid days, when we went to Tanzania, Zimbabwe, Zambia and many other African countries, which embraced us with open hands. So we did vox pops with the general public. We wanted to know why South Africans were turning up against the very people who had helped them in their darkest days (Interview, 29 April 2011).

Besides treating the attacks as xenophobic, Bush radio also high-lighted what Louw refers to as "economic gangsterism" as a motive for the violence in its news bulletins. This was particularly true of attacks on Somali shopkeepers, who operated shops in the 'townships' and offered competitive bargains which their local South African rivals failed to match.

The picture was significantly different in Zimbabwe, where the state still held monopoly over the airwaves during the period under review. The Zimbabwe Broadcasting Corporation (ZBC) radio and TV stations churned out propaganda news items in support of the Zanu-PF party, therefore leaving supporters of the opposition with little option but to revert to so-called 'pirate' radio stations and mobile phones. The most popular sources of information among therespondents were radio VOA and Radio VOP, both of which broadcast on short wave from outside Zimbabwe.

All the three 'pirate' stations provided comprehensive, though largely pro-opposition coverage of the elections, from the pre-election campaigns, the voting process, the violence and the results. An interesting feature of the coverage by these radio stations is that they employed a vast network of stringers across the country including the most remote parts, and these journalists filed copy using their mobile phones. All three stations had provisions whereby a stringer with a story, but no airtime would simply send a text message to a toll-free number and the station would call back and allow him or her to file the story by phone. Members of the public who witnessed violent activities or other potential story ideas also had access to toll-free numbers, and radio stations would assign a stringer closest to the scene to follow up the story. According to Gerry Jackson, station manager for SW Radio Africa, her station had the following in place during its coverage of the elections:

> We had a mobile phone in Zimbabwe where listeners could leave a text or voice message with their contact details. This information was then emailed to us and we would call the listeners back to take part in an open forum. Twitter was not applicable to the Zimbabwe (2008) poll at that time due to the lack of broadband. We sent news headlines into Zimbabwe three times a week to 30,000 (mobile phone) subscribers to this free service. Our website carried all breaking news around the election and was a vital resource for those interested in the Zimbabwe situation

at the time. We had a key role in exposing the violence. We named and shamed perpetrators via SMS and our website and SW broadcasts (Interview, 6 November 2010).

The use of 'pirate' radios was, however, fraught with real danger. In the run up to the elections, some non-profit organisations distributed free radio short wave radio sets to mostly rural-based citizens to allow them access to alternative information. However, following its loss during the March 29th election, Zanu-PF went on a violent confiscation spree, seizing these radio sets, forcing citizens to either hand them over or pretend not to have them and continue to tune into pirate radio stations in secret, mainly in the forests away from home.[5]

## Radio and the appropriation of new media

Both community radio stations in South Africa and 'pirate' radio stations in the Zimbabwe case study exploited the potential of new media to enhance coverage of the two violent situations in a fairly substantial way. This is especially so if we consider that this was in the era before popular social platforms such as Facebook and Twitter. In South Africa, interviews with radio personnel at Bush Radio and Radio Tygerberg showed that in addition to deploying journalists to the theatres of violence, they also benefitted from phone-ins and SMS updates from members of the public for their coverage of the violence. Both stations did not do live streaming at the time and did not have feedback facilities on their websites, and attribute this mainly to their limited budgets. Station managers at both stations also conceded that they did not make deliberate or special allocation of resources towards the xenophobic attack stories per se, not least because of budgetary constraints. The attacks were therefore covered just like any other criminal activities in the country. Both Bush and Tygerberg radio stations also argued that since national radio and television were giving extensive coverage to the attacks, it was futile to compete with them. Viewed against the backdrop of the highly limited use of community radio as a source of information in Cape Town by the victims, this becomes interesting in the sense that it somehow negates the normative role of community media, which are supposed to constitute local public spheres for citizens sharing the same geography or interests.

In Zimbabwe, the 'pirate' radio stations adopted a call-back approach (mentioned above) which enabled members of the public with stories to contact the station, which would call them back on their mobiles for more details, or deploy their stringers closest to the theatre of action to give coverage. The stations' websites were also regularly updated, while live streaming was possible but largely for Zimbabweans in the diaspora. Radio VOP was particularly strong when it came to updating its website and taking up feedback from readers/listeners who contacted the station to report on events unfolding in their communities, especially cases of state-orchestrated violence.[6] In fact, it can be argued that 'pirate' radio stations in Zimbabwe generally practised

---

5. Interviews in Masvingo, November 2010.
6. Interview with John Masuku, Executive Director, Radio VOP, August 2010.

both professional and citizen forms of journalism in the coverage of the 2008 elections.

There was a correlation between innovative appropriation of new media and popularity of radio stations. In other words, those radio stations that fully exploited the convergence capabilities of new media were cited by most of the respondents as their primary sources of information during the violent events. This was so particularly in Zimbabwe during the 2008 elections.

## Concluding discussion

The findings of this article—which is part of a larger study on media convergence and development in Africa—are important for one's understanding of the role of Africa's most pervasive mediums and communication tools. Although this particular article focused on the uses of radio and mobiles in the context of violent and life-threatening situations, the findings can arguably apply to 'normal', everyday situations as well. They point to the critical role that mobiles play in the daily experiences of Africans today and how that role is certain to increase as the costs of access become lower and broadband for mobiles becomes more common. They also provide important insight into the role that 'pirate' radio can play as a key source of independent information in a context of an authoritarian political establishment which prohibits free media.

The findings also suggest a number of other things. First, that radio and mobile phones remain critical avenues through which Africans send and receive information. This is important because, for policy and practical purposes, the issue of access to these vital sources of information is necessary for active citizenship. Policy-makers, especially in restricted media environments such as Zimbabwe, will need to understand that the existence of legislation curtailing free expression and limiting media ownership may negate, but will certainly not stop citizens finding alternative and creative ways of accessing and generating information. In Africa, it is important therefore to create information and media policy regimes that facilitate increased citizen access to radio and mobiles (as well as the Internet). As the study revealed, these media can play critical, even life-saving roles in the context of violence.

Second, the study shows that appropriating new media by radio stations can enhance their newsgathering processes while promoting participatory cultures and practices among listeners and audiences. The period covered by this study is five years ago, and since then a lot has happened in terms of the proliferation of new media and social media platforms. Radio stations have naturally adapted to this, albeit in varying degrees. It is important that radio stations in Africa be adept at appropriating new media to help tell their stories better as well as to attract and retain audiences. This is important not only for their roles in society, but also for their very survival. African audiences increasingly have access to a range of news sources and therefore have increased choices. Should radio stations fail to adapt to these changes, they risk being irrelevant.

Third, there is a link between gender (and class) and access to both radio and mobiles. It emerged from the study that men had more access to and exploited more facilities on the mobiles, while women had scant access to mobiles, which they largely used to send 'call back' messages. What was not clear and perhaps needs further research is whether having limited access to the full exploitation of the facilities of the mobile phone made women more vulnerable to the violence in this particular case. The gender dynamic in the use of media is an important finding for policymakers. Addressing gender imbalances in society is important for a range of reasons, including the creation of equitable access to media and promotion of active citizenship.

Fourth, the findings suggest that the traditional conceptualisation of community radio as the natural local public sphere may no longer hold true as new forms of mediated socialisation emerge, especially around the mobile phone. The increasing number of Africans owning mobile phones and using them for a variety of things means that the mobile phone is perhaps the mass medium of the future on the continent. This is because phones are no longer just used for making and receiving calls. The introduction of broadband 3G in Zimbabwe in 2010, for example, saw a significant number of users using mobiles for social networking, banking and to access the Internet. In South Africa, the recent drop in broadband prices augurs well for mobile phone users. During interviews, respondents argued that should there be a repeat of the events of 2008 in both Zimbabwe and South Africa, they would be able to exploit the multiple facilities of their mobiles even more to access and send out information relating to their situations, hence mitigating their vulnerability. Although radio, including community radio and other traditional media continue to be vital sources of information and journalism that citizens require to make informed decisions, the Internet-enhanced mobile phone allows users to access all this information on a click and further, allows users to network with the outside world beyond the institutionalised gatekeeping of traditional media.

This study set out to establish the role and uses of radio and mobiles in conflict situations in two African countries, less as a detailed comparative endeavour than an exploration of two cases as a way of identifying and documenting the lessons that can be learned. What emerges is a picture of the centrality of both old and new media in the generation and reception of critical information in the lives of citizens caught up in conflict.

## References

Aker J. C., Mbiti I. M. (2010). "Mobile Phones and Economic Development in Africa." *Journal of Economic Perspectives.* 24(3), 207232.
Best, M. L. (2011). "Mobile phones in conflict-stressed environments: Macro, meso and microanalysis" In M. Poblet (Ed.), *Mobile technologies for conflict management: Online dispute resolution, governance, participation.* Law, Governance and Technology, Series 2.
Bosch, T. (2011). "Talk radio, democracy and citizenship in (South) Africa". In Herman Wasserman (Ed.), *Popular Media, democracy and Development in Africa.* London: Routledge.
Campbell, H. (2003). Reclaiming Zimbabwe: The Exhaustion of the Patriarchal Model of Liberation. Cape Town: David Philip.

Chuma, W. (2008). "Mediating 2000 elections in Zimbabwe: Competing 'journalisms' in a society at crossroads". In *Ecquid Novi*, 29(1), 21-41.

Chuma, W. (2010). "Reforming the media in Zimbabwe: Critical reflections". In Dumisani Moyo & Wallace Chuma (Eds.), *Media Policy in a Changing Southern Africa: Critical reflections on media reforms in the global age.* Pretoria: Unisa Press.

Curran, J. (2005). "Mediations of Democracy". In Curran, J. & Gurevitch, M., (Eds.), *Mass Media and Society.* London: Hodder Arnold. Fourth Edition.

Croteau D, Hoynes W. (2003). (3rd Ed.). *Media/Society: Industries, Images, and Audiences.* Thousand Oaks: Pine Forge Press.

DeBruijn M, Nyamnjoh FB and Brinkman I (2009). *Mobile Phones: The New Talking Drums of Everyday Africa.* Bameda and Leiden: Langaa & African Studies Centre.

Galtung, J. (1998). "Peace Journalism: What, why, who, how, when, where". Paper presented at the Workshop "What are journalists for?". TRANSCEND. Taplow Court, UK. 3-6 September.

Gilboa, E. (2009). 'Media and conflict resolution: A framework for analysis". *Marquette Law Review,* (93)1, 87-110.

Gourevitch, P. (1998). We wish to inform you that tomorrow we will be killed with our families: Stories from Rwanda. New York: Picador USA.

Gunner, L, Ligaga, D & Moyo, D. (Eds.). (2012). *Radio in Africa: Publics, Cultures, Communities.* Johannesburg: Wits University Press.

Habermas, J. (1992). The Structural Transformation of The Public Sphere: An Inquiry into a Category of Bourgeois Society. Cambridge, MA: MIT Press.

Human Rights Watch (2008), "Perpetual Fear: Impunity and Cycles of Violence in Zimbabwe". Report released in Johannesburg, on 8th March 2008.

Lynch, J. & McGoldrick A. (2005). *Peace Journalism.* Stroud: Hawthorne Press.

Mano, W and Willems, W. (2008). 'Emerging communities; emerging media: The case of a Zimbabwean nurse in the British Big Brother show". *Critical Arts: A Journal of South-North cultural and media studies,* 22(1), 101-128.

McGoldriçç A. (2006). "War Journalism and 'Objectivity'". *Communication and Conflict Online,* (5)2, 1-7.

Moyo, D. (2010). "The new media as monitors of Democracy: Mobile phones and Zimbabwés 2008 election". *Communicare: Journal for Communication Sciences in Southern Africa,* 29 (September 2010), 7185.

Nyamnjoh, F. (2005). Africa's media: Democracy and the Politics of Belonging. Pretoria: Unisa Press.

Nyarota, G. (2006). Against the Grain: Memoirs of a Zimbabwean Newsman. Cape Town: Zebra Press.

Raftopoulos, B. & Savage, T. (Eds.). (2004). *Zimbabwe: Injustice and Political Reconciliation.* Cape Town: Institute for Justice and Reconciliation.

Ronning, H. (1995). "Democratisation Processes in Southern Africa and the Role of the Media". In Waldahl, R. (Ed.), *Perspectives on Media, Culture and Democracy in Zimbabwe.* Oslo: Dept. of Media and Communication.

Shinar, D. (2009). "Can peace journalism make progress? The coverage of the 2006 Lebanon War in Canadian and Israeli media". *The International Communication Gazette,* 71(6), 451-471.

Thompson, A. (2007). *The Media and the Rwanda Genocide*. London: Pluto Press.

# The story of Cape Town's two marches: Personal reflections on going home

Stephanie Urdang

**March 30 1960**: 30,000 Africans march on Cape Town from the African townships on the outskirts of the city, a distance of over eight miles. They head for Parliament but detour to the Police headquarters at Caledonian Square when they hear that the army has surrounded it. It is a call to end the pass laws, to end apartheid. This march took place nine days after the notorious Sharpeville massacre.

**September 13, 1989**: 30,000 South Africans of all races march on Cape Town, from St. George's Cathedral to the Cape Town Parade, a Peace March. It is a call to end the unbridled state violence, to end apartheid.

The first contributed to my leaving South Africa. The second contributed to ability to return to the country I never ceased to consider home.

It is early March 2011 and I am back in Cape Town, back "home", for three months to work on the book I am writing about the confluence of forces that demolished apartheid. Day by day I get to know the city I grew up in, the city I left in my early twenties. With no specific agenda than to absorb postapartheid Cape Town, I do something different each day. A few days after I arrive, I enter the newly opened exhibition space in the crypt of St. George's Cathedral, the Cathedral of Archbishop Desmond Tutu.

I stop before a floor to ceiling blown up photograph that captures the 1989 march. At the head are religious leaders, Christian and Muslim, providing gravitas to the event. There are other prominent leaders that represent a swath across South Africa's political and economic life—trade union, the Mayor of Cape Town, business leaders, community leaders, academics. The march was sparked by the recent killing of 23 people in Cape Town's black segregated townships in the aftermath of yet another violent response by the South African police to the resistance that was at its height throughout the country.

I am moved, emotions wrenching as I stare into the dense mass of thousands upon thousands of Capetonians, black, white, men, women, young, old, in business suits with ties, in shirt sleeves and t-shirts, serious faces, smiling faces, somber faces, glowing faces Christians, Muslims, Jews, nonbelievers. Faces of a people who know they are winning although they could not know that just five months later Nelson Mandela would be released. The ANC would be unbanned and the stage set for democratic elections.

As I stare the memory of another march numbering 30,000, 29 years earlier, flashes into my mind when country-wide anti-pass protests were organized in African townships all over South Africa. It was when, on March 21 1960 69 peaceful demonstrators were killed in what has become known as the Sharpeville Massacre. Nine days later 30,000 protestors set off from the African townships on the edge of the city for an eight-mile silent march into the center of Cape Town.

The pass laws forced all Africans living in urban areas to carry pass books in the land of their birth to prove that they had permits to be there. These laws defined every movement and aspect of their lives. Relegating them to no more than units of labor, they provided a draconian means of controlling and directing a cheap—*very* cheap—labor force. The pass laws were one of the main pillars of apartheid and the fuel for a vibrant South African economy. In 1952, four years after the apartheid government came to power, the laws were extended to include all male Africans over the age of 18 regardless of whether they lived in the towns or the rural areas; four years later African women were lassoed into the law.

The call went out: Leave your passes at home, present yourself to your local police station and be arrested. Township after African township throughout South Africa responded. In Sharpeville, calm and cheerful protesters sent jitters down the spines of the skittish police, young and inexperienced. They fired wildly into the crowd. Most of the victims were shot in the back while trying to flee, including ten children, some on the backs of their mothers. The killings caused reverberations around the world, bringing with it unprecedented shock and horror at the extent of the brutality of the apartheid regime, which the world had largely managed to tolerate and ignore. The Johannesburg stock exchange went into a tail spin to be saved by a consortium of US banks.

The protests had been confined to the areas proscribed for Africans. Such demonstrations could be contained by the local police. Not so Cape Town. The specter of 30,000 Africans walking deliberately and silently out of the townships of Nyanga, Langa and Gugulethu scared the bejeebies out of the white government.

At the head was Philip Kgosana, looking even younger than his 23 years. Kgosana, one of the few Africans admitted to the University of Cape Town lived in the all-male substandard barracks

built for grossly underpaid 'migrants' (foreigners in their own country) as 'temporary' (they were in fact permanent) housing whose wives and children were not permitted to accompany them. Becoming steeped in their stories of suffering and witnessing their living conditions, Kgosana dropped out of university to work as a political activist.

At the head of 30,000 strikers crammed into the narrow streets of Cape Town, Kgosana demanded a meeting with the Minister of Justice to present their demands. The police spokesman agreed to a meeting later that afternoon on condition that Kgosana tell the marchers to return home. Fearful that the police would begin to fire and cause life-threatening havoc he knew he had no choice but to ask the protestors to turn around and retrace their steps.

When Kgosana arrived at the designated time, it was not the Minister of Justice who was waiting for him but police reinforcements. He was arrested. After nine months in jail he was released on bail. He fled his country and went into exile. (He is now, like many exiles, back home.)

I was in my last year of high school the day of the march. Our school went into virtual lock down. All five hundred students were instructed to go to the auditorium where we listened as the ominous words of the principal explained the threat outside. Fear rippled through the boys and girls sitting crosslegged on the wooden floor. I caught it full force. My father's law practice, in keeping with his left politics, was not in the center of the town where most white lawyers attended the needs of white clients, but in Athlone, a socalled 'Coloured' area, where he and the young black lawyers he mentored attended the legal needs of a black community. I feared for his safety.

Later my mother, sister and I waited anxiously for his return. I was struck by my father's uncommonly quick and light step, lacking any of his usual end-of--day draggy tiredness. He was positively glowing. No sooner had the news of the march spread to him in his law office, than he was in his car driving to a vantage point to view the extraordinary phenomenon.

*"This is the beginning of the end!"* he announced at the dinner table. *"The government cannot deny what has happened today. The passes have to go."* Unlike my principal, my father saw no threat. What he saw was a disciplined and a determined mass of African workers taking up the struggle, flexing their collective muscle to protest the scurrilous pass system, warning the oppressive ruling class that they were ready to take on the revolution. The workers had risen. There could be no turning back. Or so, on that day, he fervently believed.

He underestimated the might of the apartheid machine.

A State of Emergency was declared that afternoon, presaging a severe clampdown on political activism and activists for decades to come. In short succession the Unlawful Organizations Act was passed, which declared the African National Congress and the Pan Africanist Congress illegal; the Terrorism Act was passed, which allowed for indefinite detention without trial; the Communism Act was more stringently enforced. Thousands fled into exile. Thousands were arrested and tried, meted out harsh sentences; or detained without trial and often tortured. Others were banned and/or placed under house arrest. The tyrannical state was bent on crushing any resistance and for a while it succeeded. For the next eight or nine years, the revolution was in the doldrums and South Africa experienced a hiatus in open political activity.

I recently found online black and white white grainy photographs of the 1960 march that were banned from publication in South Africa at the time. African men, I discern no women, packed tight as they walk silently into the center of the city to add their protest to the antipass campaign. Looking at the power captured in these photos and reflecting on what followed to crush it I am reminded why I am not a face in the crowd in the photos of the 1989 march. For me as a young white South African caught in these hiatus years, I could no longer tolerate the brutality of the South African regime, nor could I continue to live under perpetual privilege. I could see no alternative but to leave.

Twenty-nine-and-a-half years would separate the two marches and almost thirty years before the combination of forces—the end of Portuguese colonialism, heightened armed struggle, intensification of internal resistance, and international success in isolating the apartheid regime—would render the walls of apartheid so porous they would topple down. By the time the pass laws had been repealed four years earlier in 1986, 20 million Africans had been arrested and charged, and then either imprisoned, fined or 'deported' to the so-called Bantustans, the cornerstone of apartheid policy which assigned

13 percent of the most nonarable territory of South Africa as ethnicallybased "homelands" for the 80 percent African majority.

It was only after I emigrated to the United States in 1967, that another march caught my imagination and attention. On August 9, 1956 African women marched on Pretoria, the seat of the apartheid government, to protest the expansion of the pass laws to include African women. Their call to the Prime Minister Strijdom became a rallying cry beyond South Africa: "Now you have touched the women, Strijdom! *You have struck a rock!*

As a new feminist, involved in the vibrant women's movement, I could appreciate how the march was a catalyst for challenging the prevailing stereotype in South Africa—and beyond—that women were tied to their families and disinterested in politics. It sparked my interest and I began to learn about the strong role of women throughout the anti-apartheid struggle in South Africa, a role that became a source of inspiration to me and to others activists in the solidarity movement in the US.

The march, numbering up to 20,000, brought women from all over the country from all backgrounds. While the majority was African, the only one of apartheid four designated racial categories to be affected by the pass laws, the protest included a significant number of whites, Coloureds and Indians, a diversity reflected in the leadership. The marchers, resolute and dignified, gathered in front of the Union buildings, the seat of the South African government administration. When the Prime Minister refused to meet with the leaders, they placed a petition with over 100,000 signatures at his office. A particularly moving moment was when the women stood for half an hour in perfect silence.

As successful as the event was at rallying so many South African women it failed to stop the extension of the law to include African women.

After leaving the exhibition in St. George's crypt I am invited to have lunch with the Cathedral's Sub Dean Fr. Terry Lester, Lynette Maart, organizer of the exhibition and Josette Cole, a researcher focusing on the current struggles of the informal settlements. They are committed to educating the next generation about what happened under apartheid and about the role St. George's Cathedral played in supporting the resistance, as Maart states it, "to excavate the social history of the Cathedral, using its role in the struggle against apartheid as a lens through which to view current social justice issues." As I listen I reflect on the words of Amilcar Cabral: "When our revolution is over, that is when our struggle will really begin."

They talk about how Cape Town is being transformed into a city for foreigners, for tourists to enjoy.

They talk about resources being poured into making the centre of Cape Town safe and beautiful, a magnet for the privileged.

They talk about lack of access to resources for those who continue to live in dire conditions on the Cape Flats which apartheid had relegated to the so-called Coloured and African people.

They talk about how those continuing to live in these inhospitable outskirts of the city are trapped there, given Cape Town's exorbitantly high property rates.

They talk about iron shacks, and crowded tiny brick houses, and lack of water and lack of electricity; of inferior education.

They talk with concern about what they see as a lack of political will on the part of the government to forge change, so that for too many what they had marched for, what people by their thousands had died for is still in the realm of dreams.

What I hear too is that what was learned in resisting apartheid continues to fuel protest for real transformation.

I know, and knew, that the South Africa I would return to, would be a complicated and often distressing place. Without living here, without being engaged is specific aspects of working for change, can I, I wonder, regard South Africa as home?

'Home', imbued as it is with emotion and feelings and personal perspective, is a fluid and often mercurial concept. While it can be attached to more than one place and space, for me Cape Town, the city of my birth still resonates as "home." Or as African friends would say, "home home."

Meanwhile, as the days of my visit stretch forward, I continue to be captivated by the history of struggle in South Africa, to be inspired by the tenacity of those who lived through it and won and by those who continue as activists to struggle against continued inequalities, a new form of privilege and a growing injustice. I am moved in a way that seems only possible because I was born there. Being raised and socialized in Cape Town and South Africa became intrinsic to who I would become, as part of me as genetic makeup.

I cannot give it up or give up on it.

# Beyond an epistemology of bread, butter, culture and power: Mapping the African feminist movement

Sinmi Akin-Aina

> For African women, feminism is an act that evokes the dynamism and shifts of a process as opposed to the stability and reification of a construct or framework... Feminism is structured by cultural imperatives and modulated by ever-shifting local and global exigencies.
> — Nnaemeka, 2003; 378

The objective of this study is to identify and frame the elements that make up African feminisms and the African feminist movement. In this task, I borrow Sperling, Ferree and Risman's definition of feminism as, "that in which participants explicitly place value on challenging gender hierarchy and changing women's social status, whether they adopt or reject the feminist label" (2001, p. 1158). As stated in the preceding quote, African feminisms are shaped by a variety of contexts, movements and historical moments; a reading of African feminist movements must be grounded in these elements.

Thus, the African feminist movement is characterized by: an ongoing process of self-definition and re-definition; a broad-based membership; a resistance to the distortions and misrepresentations by Western global feminism; a 'feminism of negotiation'; as well as efforts to reconcile power dynamics on the continent, nationally and within the movement.

Maendeleo Ya Wanawake (MYW), Kenya's oldest and largest women's organization, embodies the tensions and transformations inherent in African feminisms. MYW personifies African feminisms as it enjoys a broadly-based membership. It is also continuously engaging in processes of definition and re-definition; although the organization pursues feminist ideals, it is unwilling to subscribe to the label of 'feminist', as within the Kenyan context this is coded as Western, anti-religious and anti-man. Additionally, MYW has periodically contended with issues of power brokerage within the movement and nationally. Lastly, MYW undertakes a 'feminism of negotiation,' tackling specific cultural issues in a manner which emphasizes and is embedded in the emancipatory elements of Kenyan traditions.

This paper shall map the evolution of the African feminist movement from its genesis in precolonial women's activities and social organizations to its contemporary incarnation in women's organizations. Much of the literature shall draw specifically from examples in Eastern and Western Africa. The majority of early theorizing on African feminisms originates from West African scholars in the Diaspora or on the continent. As such, this study shall draw from historical examples from East and West Africa, and shall be framed by the theories produced mainly by West African scholars.

The African feminist movement, in spite of its internal lack of homogeneity, often posits itself as counter-canonical to certain tendencies of mainstream Western feminism and encompasses various sometimes oppositional strands, which inform each other and create a reflexive internal dialogue (Edwin, 2006). By referring to Western feminisms, the aim is not to essentialize the different strands of feminism stemming from the Global North, but to draw attention to the spatial distinctions between African feminisms and Western feminisms, the relationship between the two, as well as the power asymmetries, distortions and co-optations that have characterized this relationship. In light of these tensions and history, it remains difficult for African feminists to unite in 'true global sisterhood' with feminists of the Global North (Nnaemeka, 2005). Such 'global sisterhood' remains somewhat elusive as the aforementioned distortions, co-optation and silencing persist.

African feminisms cast a critical eye on the processes of colonization and on post-coloniality with regards to writing, activism and theorizing around Africa. African feminisms also point to a diversity of tactics, theories and standpoints, especially in the interplay between scholarship, practice and activism and how these inform each other.

The first section of this essay will look at the concept of social movements and what it means for African feminisms. The second part of the paper then explores a definition of African feminisms. This is followed by a mapping of women's movements in African history and an examination of gender and social organization and the impact of processes of colonization and nationalist struggles thereon. Colonialism transformed traditional modes of social organization, predicated for the most part on status and kinship, rather than gender. Additionally, nationalist struggles created a space for women's organizing within the independence movement. These were largely ghettoized or co-opted into the state machinery of primarily single-party states after independence (Wanyande, 2009). Lastly, the paper looks at the evolution of women's organizations and their contemporary representation as embodied by the Maendeleo Ya Wanawake organization from its origins in the colonial era until the single-party state period of the 1990s.

Maendeleo Ya Wanawake is an interesting example of a home-grown broad-based women's organization that cuts across social class differences. It is led by middle class women but has a large rural base made up of women in trading and agricultural occupations (Nzomo, 1989). Maendeleo Ya Wanawake was allied with the dominant nationalist party but has built an extensive nation-wide independent base of women's groups genuinely involved in large-scale zonal mobilization of women (Nzomo, 1989). Because of its broad-base it is ideologically eclectic and is better defined as an 'umbrella of women's issues that recognize its multi-class, multi-regional and multi-ethnic composition.

A brief statement on methodology is in order. This paper is not a comprehensive study of African feminisms or feminist movements but rather an exploration of how certain strands within the broad movement are defining and asserting themselves in response to certain dominant trends emerging from conventional Western feminism. It is based mainly on content analyses, literature reviews and examination of secondary sources that profess this counter-canonical trend. The aim is to outline the differences and enrich our analysis of the broad range of alternatives that constitute the feminist movement and feminisms.

## African feminisms

The project of circumscribing the parameters of a social movement is a potentially difficult one to undertake. Movements by their very nature evolve and are subject to changing objectives, goals and contexts. Political scientist Cyrus Zirakzadeh defines social movements as:

- A group of people who consciously attempt to build a radically new social order;
- Involve people of a broad range of social backgrounds; and
- Deploy politically confrontational and socially disruptive tactics. (1997, p. 4)

While this paper examines an African feminist movement, it recognizes that African feminisms are multi-faceted, multi-purpose, and reflect the diverse nature of feminist organizing, practice and scholarship on the continent.

In her discussions on African feminism, Nigerian scholar and feminist Obioma Nnaemeka notes:

> It will be more accurate to argue not in the context of a monolith (*African feminism*) but rather in the context of a pluralism (*African feminisms*) that captures the fluidity and dynamism of the different cultural imperatives, historical forces, and localized realities conditioning women's activism/movements in Africa...the inscription of feminisms...underscores the heterogeneity of African feminist thinking and engagement as manifested in strategies and approaches that are sometimes complementary and supportive, and sometimes competing and adversarial. (1998a, p. 5)

As such, African feminisms are in continuous flux; engaging with the context in which they are wrought, they resist elements of Western feminism which do not speak to the African experience. They are in constant negotiation with elements of custom and tradition and the goal of emancipating women. Lastly, they wrestle with the various power dynamics implicit in the movement, as well as those outside of it.

Important variants of African feminisms resist the importation of certain European feminist paradigms into African society because the latter are defined by the struggles and contexts from which they emerge. One such notion is the idea of the social construction of gender. According to Oyewumi (2005), understandings of the social construction of gender as a means by which all women are oppressed universally and across the world does not take into account variations in histories, world-views and social organization across the globe. Indeed, women are not all socialized in the same way. Additionally, the primacy given to gender as the 'primary unit of social analysis' may not be universal according to all cultures and worldviews. The emphasis on gender as a means of delineating social positionality does not occur the same way everywhere. Oyewumi writes:

> From a cross-cultural perspective, the implications of Western biologic are far-reaching when one considers the fact that gender constructs in feminist theory originated in the West, where men and women are conceived oppositionally and projected as embodied, genetically driven social categories... On what basis are Western conceptual categories exportable or transferable to other cultures that have a different cultural logic? This question is raised because despite the wonderful insight about the social construction of gender, the way cross-cultural data have been used by many feminist writers undermines the notion that differing cultures may construct social categories differently. (2005, p. 11)

She further asserts, "In Yoruba society…social relations derive their legitimacy from social facts not from biology. The bare biological facts of pregnancy and parturition count only in regard to procreation, where they must… the nature of one's anatomy did not define one's social position" (2005, p.13).

Nnaemeka (2004) coins the term nego-feminism to speak to the tensions and aspirations of African feminisms. She speaks of this as the feminism of compromise, contending with the multiple aspects of patriarchy on the continent and dealing with this in an African-specific way:

> First nego-feminism is the feminism of negotiation; second nego-feminism stands for "no ego" feminism. In the foundation of shared values in many African cultures are the principles of negotiation, give and take, compromise and balance. African feminism[s] (or feminism as I have seen it practiced in Africa) challenges through negotiations and compromise. It knows when, where, and how to detonate patriarchal land mines; it also knows when, where, and how to go around patriarchal land mines. (2004, p. 22)

Thus, nego-feminism is a guide for dealing with the feminist struggles that occur on the continent; it considers the implications of patriarchal traditions and customs and aims to dismantle and negotiate around these. Nego-feminism also hopes to detach personal gain and pride from the overall goal of achieving equity for women—thus 'no ego'. This is not always the case, as with all ideological constructs, the practice of nego-feminism on the ground is subject to emotionality, personal goals and even ego. However, aspirations for a more complete form of nego-feminism remain a noteworthy goal.

The main point of contention by feminists in the Global South with regards to Western feminism has been in relation to the representation of Third World women and feminists. These distortions have been elaborated upon by Chandra Talpade Mohanty in her seminal 1988 essay "Under Western Eyes". In her work, Mohanty points to the universalization of Third World women in Western feminist writing, alternatively, concurrently and unceasingly as victims of patriarchy, religion, globalization, development, economics, neo-colonialism and colonization. Not only are they described as a homogenous group, the nebulous conflated entity that is 'Third World' woman rarely resists or challenges the multiple forms of oppression she is subject to. Even while challenging and resisting, she never sheds the status of 'victim'. Thus, according to Mohanty:

> … third world women as a group or category are automatically and necessarily

defined as: religious ( read "not progressive"), family-oriented ( read "traditional"), legal minors ( read " they-are-still-not-conscious-of-their-rights"), illiterate ( read "ignorant"), domestic (read "backward") and sometimes revolutionary (read "their-country-is-in-a-state-of-war-they-must-fight!" (1984, p.352)

Both Oyewumi and Nnaemeka seek to challenge the distortions, misrepresentations and silences that occur in history, theorizing and teachings about African women, both in Africa and the West. Nnaemaka notes that African women are either portrayed as a universal, singular entity, or left out of the narrative altogether;

> Distortions in the study and teaching of African concerns stem from imperialism's refusal to historicize and differentiate African space and people. We Africans must realize that our survival depends to a large extent on our ability to reclaim our history. As bell hooks correctly notes, "our struggle is also the struggle of memory against forgetting." (2005, p. 63)

Such distortions construct African women as a homogenous monolith without a diversity of experiences, knowledge and objectives. Additionally, the misrepresentations of African women further reproduce relations of inequality, with the first world and first world feminist writing doing the objectifying and defining of Third World women. Lastly, the stereotyping of African women creates a neocolonial discourse, whereby *knowledgeable* and *enlightened* Western feminists step in to save poor African women.

This distortion and silencing also occurs in the dissemination of African feminist thought for Western (in this specific case, American) study. Nawal El Sadawi, Egyptian feminist and novelist, speaks to her experiences in producing work for consumption in the United States:

> Yes and here is a very subtle form of exploitation practiced unfortunately by feminists.... Gloria Steinem of Ms magazine writes me a letter in Cairo and asks me for an article about clitoridectomy. So I write her an article setting forth the political social and historical analysis as well as comments about my personal experience. She cuts the political, social and historical analysis and publishes only the personal statements... The second example is Beacon Press in Boston. I gave my book, *The Hidden Face of Eve*, to the publisher in London: he published all of the book—the preface, introduction, everything. The preface which is a long preface is crucial and important to the book. Beacon Press cut it without my permission, making me feel that I have been exploited and my ideas distorted. Without the preface, it appears that I am separating the sexual from the political, which I never do. (as quoted in Nnaemeka, 2005, p. 54)

In light of these distortions, misperceptions and silences, it is impossible to reach true global sisterhood, a political goal of Western global feminism. Such global sisterhood is represented by standing in solidarity with women across the globe, acknowledging and recognizing their unique struggles and contexts, as well as by *not* further replicating systems of oppression through the silencing of their voices and potential usurpation of their roles:

> We African women have witnessed repeatedly the activities of our overzealous foreign sisters, mostly feminist who appropriate our wars in the name of fighting the oppression of women in the so-called third world. We watch with chagrin and in painful sisterhood these avatars of the proverbial mourners who wail more than the owners of the corpse. In their enthusiasm, our sisters usurp our wars and fight them badly—very badly. The arrogance that declares African women "problems" objectifies us and undercuts the agency necessary for forging true global sisterhood. African women are not problems to be solved. Like women everywhere, African women have problems. More important, they have provided solutions to these problems. We are the only ones who can set our priorities and agenda. Anyone who wishes to participate in our struggle must do so in the context of our agenda. In the same way, African women who wish to contribute to global struggles (and many do) should do so with a deep respect for the paradigms and strategies that people of those areas have established. In our enthusiasm to liberate others, we must not be blind to our own enslavement. Activities of women globally should be mutually liberating. (Nnaemeka, 2005, p. 57)

Lastly, Oyewumi (2005) points to branches of Western feminism that posit African feminisms as singularly concerned with bread, butter, culture and power—a politics of subsistence and survival as it were, which speak to the conditions and concerns of women on the continent. Oyewumi (2005) challenges this depiction of 'bread and butter politics' as not representing the multiplicity of concerns expressed, and struggles and ideological battles waged, by feminists on the continent. The African movement draws from a wide base of membership that includes: urban women, rural women, scholars, activists, politicians and community workers. Issues of survival and culture are present in the movement, but so too are concerns over political representation, gender and sexual identity, and class.

## Women's movements in African history

In keeping with Zirakzadeh's (1997) definition of social movements, this paper describes the African women's movement as the diversity of activities, engagements and tactics used currently and historically to advance the rights and opportunities of African women in multiple spheres of their lives. As such, this would span a broad-range of multi-class, multi-generational and ideologically—and spatially—differentiated individuals and groups advocating for African women's concerns. Such movements could include premeditated organizing by formal groups such as trade unions, or spontaneous acts of protest that turn into collective political dissent. I will give a few examples from colonial Nigeria and Kenya.

Historian Judith Van Allen (1972) details the collective action of the Igbo women of South-Eastern Nigeria as practiced in the custom of 'sitting on a man', whereby the public censure by the women in the community was a form of discipline. 'Sitting on a man' or 'making war on a man' involved:

> Gathering at his compound, sometimes late at night, dancing, singing scurrilous

songs which detailed the women's grievances against him and often called his manhood into question, banging on his hut with the pestles women used for pounding yams, and perhaps demolishing his hut or plastering it with mud and roughing him up a bit. (Van Allen, 1972, p. 171)

A man could be sanctioned in this manner, if he mistreated his wife, disobeyed the women's market rules, or let his cattle eat their crops (Van Allen, 1972).

The Aba Women's War in South-Eastern Nigeria in 1929 was a seminal display of women's political action in African history (Geiger, 1990). Upon discovering that they were to be taxed by the colonial government, women in the South-Eastern region of Nigeria proceeded to 'sit on' British warrant officers. This became a mass movement involving more than 10,000 women who, with painted faces and fern-covered sticks, set upon the administrative offices of the colonial government. The women destroyed several colonial buildings before intervention by soldiers and police, resulting in the death of 50 women, and 50 more were injured. There were no male casualties, either British or Igbo (Van Allen, 1972).

In the South-Western region of Nigeria, women grouped together to form three different kinds of organizations: the Lagos Market Women's Association, which came to its inception in the mid-1920s, the Nigerian Women's Party and the Abeokuta Women's Union of the 1940s (Hunt, 1989). These groups were distinctly concerned with the organization of women's markets, the mobilization for women's welfare, and anti-taxation protests.

In the 1920s in Kenya, women subversively resisted unfair labour policies by singing scurrilous songs while engaged in work (Hunt, 1989). Additionally, during the anti-colonial Mau Mau rebellion in the 1950s, several women were imprisoned; some participated in secret networks supplying food, weapons and medicines to the fighters. Other women joined the struggles and went into the forest to care for their families and to fight.

## Colonialism and gender (dis)parity

With the advent of colonialism came the practice of 'benign female exclusion' by colonial administrators. During colonial reign there were three main apparatuses for spreading and consolidating Western control in East and West Africa: the colonial administration, the mission/church, and trading establishments. With the use of colonial control as a tool for instituting the mechanics of capitalist economics, and Western Christianity as a means of regulating African social and cultural life, the colonial regime drastically altered the conditions and roles of African women from the late nineteenth century and through to World War II. Colonial governments controlled economic life through law, taxation and the creation of an economic and bureaucratic infrastructure. Western Christianity regulated much of social and cultural life, delimiting the boundaries of what was socially and morally acceptable and right. As such, this process had the unprecedented result of granting power to local imperialist regimes.

Colonial rule led to the decline of various Islamic imperial regimes in the

West African region. One of these was the Sokoto Caliphate, ruled by Usman 'dan fodio from 1802, which encompassed the region of now Northern Nigeria and Niger. Umar Tal also formed a similar empire in Senegal in the 1850s (Hill, 2009). The British and French colonial governments disbanded the political and geographic holdings of the various caliphates and imperial regimes (Hill, 2009). Yet, even while its political structures were eroded, Islam as a religion tended to spread widely under colonial rule, in part as a way to resist the latter. In West Africa the spread of Islam was often accompanied by the institution of Shari'a, according to which the practice of *purdah* required the seclusion of women from the opposite sex, public space, status and office (Bergstrom, 2002). The combined influences of Islam and Christianity further eroded the traditional rights and roles ascribed to women.

Four factors were instrumental in instituting a new form of gender bias that pervaded the African colonized states: Christianity, Western education, the adoption of Western marriage systems and alternative legal systems (Mikell, 1997). Christianity's emphasis on monogamy as well as its imputed message of female subjugation, obedience and domesticity redefined roles for African wives, mothers and daughters (Mikell, 1997). By the same token, Western education privileged the scholarly advancement of men over women (Mikell, 1997). Male education was emphasized as men were expected to later be integrated into the labour market and formal systems of production. Additionally, in a concession to traditional modes of social organization, colonial governments allowed for both Christian and traditional marriage systems (Mikell, 1997). Christian marriage, however, often gave property rights to women, something traditional marriage did not do. Alternative legal systems instituted by the British colonial governments acknowledged women's rights to independence in theory, while substantively treating them as legal minors (Mikell, 1997). These preceding changes affected gender relations, progressively undermining the power, freedoms and positions women had traditionally held, while at the same time limiting their access to new forms of status which were increasingly male-dominated, male-focussed and patriarchal.

In this period, however, European settler women, colonists' wives and missionaries, were instrumental in creating some of the formalized structures of social welfare and activism still in existence in parts of Africa today (Wipper, 1975). They created community groups, charities and services, which although not radical in nature, saw to the needs of women, children, families, the poor, sick and indigent. One such group was Maendeleo Ya Wanawake, as discussed below.

With the introduction of capitalism in the precolonial period came the transformation of gender roles and relations. In economic activity, male-focussed modes of production were emphasized above all else. For example, in West Africa women's production of cotton was taken over by the colonial government who sought to expand and consolidate cotton production and exportation (Mikell, 1997). As such, women were progressively eliminated from the production of cotton, effectively removing the former from an independent source of income and autonomy. The arena of cotton production came to be solely dominated by men who benefitted from its avails. As land became more important for cash cropping, there arose a general confusion over the means by which wives and children were to be compensated as it was difficult for women to inherit property within the traditional system (Mikell, 1997). Traditionally in much of West Africa wives and children farmed the land and received shares of the crops they had cultivated for the running of their respective households. Additionally, modes of colonial governance as well as labour market dynamics resulted in the predominance of men in urban settings and government bureaucracy positions, despite the increased presence and migration of educated women to city centres (Mikell, 1997). According to Mikell, "most African women were restricted from the cities by either statutes, the dynamics of apartheid, or the difficulty of finding housing and employment" (1997, p. 21).

## The promises of independence

With the advent of nationalist struggles and independence, leaders promised gender inclusion and a return to traditional modes of corporatism and social equity, in return for women's support for and engagement with the independence cause (Mikell, 1997). Post-independence, African leaders betrayed their promises of corporatism, claiming that a return to traditional modes of organization would result in tribalism. What emerged were single-party states, meant to symbolize a classless African society devoid of ethnicity, status distinctions, traditional political models, and above all, gender differences (Mikell, 1997). State efforts to ensure social services in health provision, access to education, water, sanitation and roads, were seen as benefitting both men and women, and notable reasons to defer the gender question. Gender bias continued to pervade in governance structures with a marked absence of women, despite increasing female literacy and education (Mikell, 1997). The end of the liberation and nationalist struggles in the 1970s was characterized by the popular injunction for women to retreat from the public sphere, take on the role of caregiver and 'rebuild communities' (Mikell, 1997).

The 1980s saw the continued oppression of women in the labour market as a result of the financial crisis at the time. The implementation of Structural Adjustment Programs designed by the IMF and World Bank resulted in cuts to social programs across the continent, an emphasis on free trade, tax cuts to foreign investors, and the production of goods for export (Rakodi, 1997). This was a process global social policy analysts dubbed 'the race to the bottom,' which further resulted in the excessive downloading of social welfare activities such as childcare, care for the sick, poor, old and indigent to communities, families and ultimately women (Gibson, 2003).

## Women's organizations

Women's organizations in the colonial period were the primary social organizations upon which the formal institutional structure of the African Women's Movement—and subsequently African feminisms—was built. These organizations were legitimately recognized state and civil society institutions that brought women's issues and concerns to the fore. They provided services to a wide range of women, sought to improve the conditions of women's lives, were implicated in the political struggles of the time, and shifted their priorities according to the changing concerns of women.

The arrival of colonialism transformed the roles and status of women, as a result of patriarchal capitalist norms and their collusion with pre-existing patriarchal gender relations (Akin Aina, 1997, p. 2). This instigated the creation of new and different forms of female autonomy that addressed the changing social and material conditions of women, such as women's market associations, farmers' groups and hawkers' associations (Akin Aina, 1997, p. 3). Apart from representation in various municipal structures, and a platform from which to air their concerns, these economically-focussed groups also provided mutual support, personal development and communal aid. In the post-independence era however, women's groups were perceived as having lost their autonomy and as mere puppets of the state machinery (Akin Aina, 1997, p. 4). Ngunyi and Gathaika identify three major factors in the erosion of autonomy of women's groups in Kenya, these include:

> 1. The beginning of gravitation towards a "maximum leader" and the disintegration of the "nationalist coalition".
> 2. The emergence of factional patronage networks.
> 3. The enfeeblement of certain institutions of civil society and actors on the... political stage. (1993, pp. 31-32)

Aili Mari Tripp further details how women's organizations in Tanzania were repressed in efforts to centralize political power:

> The government and party expanded their monopoly control of social relations by gradually centralizing party activities, by abolishing local governments in 1972, and by absorbing, eliminating or curtailing key independent organizations, creating new ones and preventing others from being formed... The crowding out of interest group activity was part of a trend of party and government expansion that saw these institutions increasingly encroach into new political, economic and social spaces. (Tripp, 1992a, 230)

In many postcolonial African nations, the formal women's organization was co-opted by state powers in a bid to further the party agenda. Informal organizations, which were involved in activities such as 'mutual aid', childbirth, local death, and burial organizing, were largely ignored by the state. As a result of the economic crisis of the 1980s, African states were unable to provide services and guarantee protection; people then looked to informal organizations to fill the widening gap left by state abandonment of social welfare.

> Where the state's attempts to exert monopolistic control over society and the economy exceeded state capacity to regulate social relations and allocate resources effectively, people own organizational structures often emerged to fulfil a variety of societal needs. The state's growing inability to guarantee adequate police protection, ensure that wages bore some relation to the cost of living, and provide basic social

and public services led people to form their own organizations to cope with the difficulties they faced. (Tripp, 1992a, 235)

In African city centres, women were a main component of this welfare provision, both as women's groups and with men, responding to the AIDS pandemic, providing health, education and a myriad of other services. The state reaction to this surge of global interest and independent organizing was to integrate these groups into the political infrastructure, in what Amina Mama terms a 'femocracy':

> State-directed feminism operated via the first ladies (wives of African presidents and heads of state). With the dual intention of cornering the increasing international funding for women's organizations and directing efforts away from protests, femocracy emerged in the 1980s as an alternative mode of organizing the relations between the state and women's organizations (1994).

Thus, African states saw the integration of women's organizations and single party politics. On the one hand women's organizations granted the state some of the popularity and mass appeal it enjoyed, while the government provided these organizations with a broad range of resources. This gave women's organizations mainstream and state-sanctioned legitimacy, moving them from the periphery of social movements to a position of relative primacy. However, this was not always in the interest of all women, as women's organizations were often aligned with the power elite and served to keep dissenting female voices in line. This system however was only tenable as long as there were resources to sustain it and only through its connection to a male head of state or first lady (ladies) who controlled it (Akin Aina, 1997, p. 5).

## Maendeleo Ya Wanawake: Ongoing African feminist activism

Maendeleo Ya Wanawake (MYW) was part of this original breed of colonial women's organizations, and it has remained active through the colonial period, the independence struggles of the 1960s, the subsequent single-party government and is still thriving in Kenya's present democratic state. Today, the organization exemplifies the African feminist movement as it embodies the tensions, ideals, struggles and objectives inherent in African feminisms. MYW enjoys a broad-based membership, has and is undergoing a process of self-definition and re-definition, engages in a 'feminism of negotiation', and, lastly, pursues efforts to reconcile power dynamics on the continent, nationally and within the movement.

MYW has long enjoyed membership from a wide range of women, a result of its long history as well as its status as an umbrella organization under which women's groups with a variety of concerns, needs, and contexts can be integrated. MYW is the largest of the women's organizations currently operating in Kenya, both in terms of membership as well as the number of women's groups associated with it (Nzomo, 1989).

The organization was started in 1952 by a small group of European women with the injunction of the colonial government's Department of Community Development and Rehabilitation, to "promote "the advancement of African women" and to "raise African living standards" (Wipper, 1975, p. 99). The name of the group roughly translates to "women's progress" in Kiswahili. In the first ten years of its existence MYW was quite effective in mobilizing and engaging women, especially those who lived in rural areas. During this time, the organization focused on subsidizing skills-based training for women in areas such as hygiene, nutrition, housekeeping and childcare. MYW was also able to offer financial incentives to its members through a number of its subsidized programs (Nyancham-Okemwa, 2000). The organization was also closely linked to and supported by the colonial administration, both socially and financially. Kenyan women joined MYW in large numbers in their search for respite and diversion from the harsh conditions of forced colonial labour (Nzomo, 1989).

MYW was also characterized by moments of definition and re-definition of their objectives, goals and aspirations for women in Kenya. One such period was in the early 1970s following independence. At this time, the role of MYW had decreased significantly to the point where the organization was ineffective at mobilizing a mass group of rural women (Nzomo,1989 ). This was as a result of the overall exclusion of women's organizations in the post-independence political landscape, as women and women's issues were ignored in the nation-building project. Upon realizing that women had been left out of the nation-building process, and were not given the space to speak their concerns or opportunity to provide input and leadership, MYW articulated a clear position on the social and political marginalisation of women in Kenya in their magazine, *Voices of Women*:

> Although women have an important role to play in the development of the nation, yet the role which women have to play in Kenya in the nation building seems as yet undetermined. Open though the opportunities are, the men assume that the women have not as yet reached a level where they can effectively participate in the nation building.
>
> According to the African man's view, a woman is only supposed to be in the house. Her role educated though she might be seems only to look after the home and the entire nursing of the young ones. This view has been taken to such extremes that the men appear to neglect or completely underrate the part which our women folks can play in the nation. (Wipper, 1971, p. 433)

MYW was subject to the power struggles that characterized the Kenyan state from the colonial period to President Moi's post-independence single-party rule. In his 1986 bid to do away with civil society, President Arap Moi gave the directive for MYW to be officially affiliated with KANU, the then only political party in what was a single-party country. By 1987, MYW had officially changed its name to KANU-MYWO (Adar and Munyae, 2001). Thus, with presidential support as well as the internal restructuring that took place earlier in 1975,

MYWO had returned to the privileged status it previously enjoyed under the colonial government. This had an effect on membership and participation; the organization again became the leading NGO with the ability to muster and mobilize a wide range of women, particularly rural women (Nzomo, 1989). By 1985, MYWO had the largest countrywide membership, 300,000 divided into 8,000 women's groups (Nzomo, 1989).

Despite the external power struggles it was subject to, this period marked a shift in the focus of MYW's programmatic activities from one concerned primarily with care work (childcare and domestic activities) to one concerned with women's health, livelihoods and human rights. From the mid 1980s to today, MYW's programmes have centered on reproductive health, maternal health, infant mortality, family planning, female genital cutting, forced child marriages and employment training (http://mywokenya.org, Mazire, 1994). Although some of their programs were firmly located in specific arenas such as healthcare and economic livelihoods, a number of MYW's programs sought to address the intersecting struggles of Kenyan women. One such program was the *jiko* or cookstove program established in 1992. Women and girls were spending a significant amount of time and labour collecting and using firewood for various domestic tasks, and activity which had a significant impact on their health, safety and standards of living (Kammen, 1995). Women in both rural and urban households were continuously exposed to the smoke from the fire, were at potential risk when collecting firewood, and were required to collect firewood in addition to their other domestic duties and possibly after a full day of work (in or outside the home) or school (Kammen, 1995). The *jiko* stove program provided women with cookstoves and training in the repair and upkeep of the *jikos* as an income-generating activity (Kammen, 1995). The *jiko* program was an energy-saving measure, as well as a livelihoods and public education campaign.

As a result of its connection to the ruling party and the previous colonial government, MYW has been seen to benefit and prosper from its close relationship with state machinery. The organization itself was also embedded in power brokerage within the national women's movement and engaged in the *de facto* disciplining and censure of women's group and voices that did not reflect KANU's party line.

For example, MYWO was a vocal critic of Kenyan Nobel laureate Wangari Maathai and her activism around the Green Belt Movement, a grass-roots movement concerned with sustainability and the protection of the environment. Maathai was considered a threat to the single-party leadership as a result of her growing popularity and vociferous campaign against 'land grabbing' by Moi and his cronies (Mathenge, 2011). Maathai protested the co-optation of public forests and lands for private use by the members of Moi's cabinet. Moi engaged in multiple efforts to undermine her legitimacy and leadership, attempting to prevent her from accessing leadership positions and re-directing funds and leadership upon her accession to the role (Mathenge, 2011).

MYW also engages in a 'feminism of negotiation' in their campaign against female genital mutilation (FGM). In 1995, MYW established an Alternative Rites Program, to counter the practice of FGM in Kenya. FGM is highly prevalent among the Kisii, Masaii, Kalenjin, Taita Taveta and Meru/Embu ethnic groups (Chege, Askew & Liku, 2001). MYW sought to address FGM in a culturally appropriate way, pointing to and eliminating the harmful practice of cutting itself, while emphasizing the beneficial components of the ceremony such as inter-generational exchange and education, peer socialization and the public recognition ceremony:

> An alternative rite of passage ritual refers to a structured programme of activities with community-level sensitisation to first gain support and to recruit the girls who will participate, which is followed by a public ritual that includes training for the girls in family life education (FLE), and a public ceremony similar to that in traditional rites of passage. The intention is to simulate the traditional ritual as closely as possible without actually circumcising the girls. (Chege et al, 2001)

As such, MYW engages in a 'feminism of negotiation', dealing with a culturally-specific issue in a way that upholds the rights of women and girls in Kenyan society, while also valuing the positive aspects of the tradition.

Maendeleo Ya Wanawake has always occupied a somewhat paradoxical position, initially as representative of colonists, and later as that of the political elite, while at the same time striving to engage in grassroots organizing. Although this particular women's organization has been subject to many of the dysfunctions that have formerly plagued women's organizations (such as being implicated in power struggles, being a tool of the state machinery, or left out of the governance process altogether), it is still popularly recognized for its ability to effectively mobilize a large number of people and vast amount of support and resources, and subscribes to some of the key values inherent in African feminisms, namely the inclusion of a diversity of women, advocacy for women's rights and strategies of negotiation.

## Conclusion

Although MYW would not describe itself as a feminist organization, this group embodies much of the tensions, struggles and history of African feminisms. MYW is comprised of a broad range of multi-class, multi-generational, multi-regional and multi-ethnic women. It is fully embedded in the institutional history, struggles and successes that characterize the growth and formation of social movements in general and African women's organizations in particular. MYW has always reflected and advocated for a wide range of women's rights and opportunities. This group is the first and longest lasting institution of the women's movement in Kenya, and as such is integral to the definition, contestation, activities and pursuits of African feminisms. Lastly, in keeping with Nnaemeka's definition of ngo-feminism, this group engages in the negotiation of cultural constructs and traditions while also ensuring the protection of Kenyan women's rights.

Much of the political action undertaken by the African feminist movement has been shaped by oppositional historical forces, differing trends, and sometimes competitive ideologies, including: traditional leadership vs. colonialism; colonial governments vs. nationalists; and single-party governments vs. civil society advocating for greater democratic space. The debates within this movement (over topics such as the contested notion of global sisterhood and power dynamics within the movement) have also played a central role in shaping what African feminisms look like, react to and engage in today. However, these debates, differences and oppositions force African feminist theory and activism to respond to the multiplicity of conditions and contexts on the continent, and to engage in real women's lives and the naming of their own conditions. Whether through negotiation and compromise, rejection of hegemonic notions of gender and cultural identity, or working towards the emancipation of women through a variety of tactics, strategies and acts, these are all context-specific and reference the locations in which these struggles are waged.

## References

Adar, K. G., & Munyae, I. M. (n.d.). Human Rights Abuse in Kenya 1978-2001. *Center for African Studies at the University of Florida*. Retrieved March 18, 2011, from http://web.africa.ufl.edu/asq/v5/v5i1a1.htm

Akin Aina, T. (1997). The state and civil society: Politics, government, and social organization in African cities. *The Urban Challenge in Africa: Growth and Management of Its Large Cities (Mega-city)* (pp. 1-6). Tokyo: United Nations University Press.

Allen, J. V. (1972). "Sitting on a Man": Colonialism and the Lost Political Institutions of Igbo Women. *Canadian Journal of African Studies, VI* (ii), 165-181.

Bergstrom, L. (2002). Legacies of Colonialism and Islam for Hausa Women: An Historical Analysis, 1804 to 1960. *GPID/WID Working Papers (2000-Present) Center for Gender in Global Context | Michigan State University*. Retrieved October 29, 2011, from http://gencen.isp.msu.edu/publications/papers.htm

Chege, J. N., Askew, I., & Liku, J. (n.d.). An Assessment of the Alternative Rites Approach for Encouraging Abandonment of Female Genital Mutilation in Kenya. *Population Council | Home*. Retrieved October 29, 2011, from http://www.popcouncil.org/topics/fgmc.asp#/Resources

Edwin, S. (2006). We Belong Here, Too Accommodating African Muslim Feminism in African Feminist Theory via Zaynab Alkali's The Virtuous Woman and The Cobwebs and Other Stories. *Muse, 27*(3), 18.

Geiger, S. (1990). Women and African Nationalism. *Journal of Women's History, 2*, 227-244.

Gibson, I. (2003). The Race to the Bottom: Globalization or Brand Imperialism? *The International Studies Association of Ritsumeikan University: Ritsumeikan Annual Review of International Studies, 2*, pp. 59-73.

Hill, M. (n.d.). The Spread of Islam in West Africa: Containment, Mixing, and Reform from the Eighth to the Twentieth Century – SPICE. *Stanford Program on International and Cross-Cultural Education (SPICE)*. Retrieved October 29, 2011, from http://spice.stanford.edu/docs/the_spread_of_islam_in_west_africa_containment_mixing_and_reform_from_the_eighth_to_the_twentieth_century/

Hunt, N. R. (1989). Placing African Women's History and Locating Gender. *Social History, 14*, pp. 359-379.
Kammen, D. (1995). Cookstoves for the developing world. *Scientific American, 273*, 72-75.
Lewis, D. (2001). Introduction: African Feminisms. *Agenda Empowering Women for Gender Equity, 50*, pp 4-10.
MYW. (n.d.). Research. *Maendeleo Ya Wanawake Organization*. Retrieved October 10, 2011, from mywokenya.org/research.html
Mathege, G. (2011, October 23). Maathai's last wish on Church, leaders. *The standard*. Retrieved October 23, 2011, from http://www.standardmedia.co.ke/commentaries/InsidePage.php?id=2000045387&cid=4&
Mazire, D. (1994). Une organisation de femmes au Kenya: Maendeleo ya Wanawake. *Politique Africaine, 53*, 139-143.
Mikell, G. (1995). African Feminism: Toward a New Politics of Representation. *Agenda Empowering Women for Gender Equity, 21*, pp 404-424.
Mikell, G. (1997). Introduction. *African Feminism: The Politics of Survival in Sub-Saharan Africa* (pp. pp10-26). Philadelphia: University of Pennsylvania Press.
Mohanty, C. Talpade. (1984). Under Western Eyes: Feminist Scholarship and Colonial Discourses. boundary 2, 12-13 (3, 1), 333-358.
Nnaemeka, O. (2004). Nego Feminism: Theorizing, Practicing, and Pruning Africa's Way. *Signs, 29*(2), 357-385.
Nnaemeka, O. (2005). Bringing African Women into the Classroom. *African gender studies: a reader* (pp. 51-65). New York: Palgrave.
Nzomo, M. (1989). The Impact of the Women's Decade on Policies, Programs and Empowerment of Women in Kenya. *Issue: A Journal of Opinion, 17*(2), 9-17.
Oyewumi, O. (2004). *African Women and Feminism: Reflecting on the Politics of Sisterhood*. Trenton, NJ: Africa World Press.
Oyewumi, O. (2005). Visualizing the Body: Western Theories and African Subjects. *African gender studies: a reader* (pp. 3-21). New York: Palgrave.
Palmer, H. (1927). History of Katsina. *African Affairs, XXVI*, 216-236.
Rakodi, C. (1997). Global forces, urban change, and urban management in Africa. *The urban challenge in Africa growth and management of its large cities* (pp. 17-73). Tokyo: United Nations University Press.
Sperling, V., Ferree, M. M., & Risman, B. (2001). Constructing Global Feminism: Transnational Advocacy Networks and Russian Women's Activism. *Signs: Journal of Women in Culture & Society, 26*(4), 1155-1313.
Wanyande, P. (1995). Mass media-state relations in post-colonial Kenya. *Africa Media Review, 9*, 54-75.
Wipper, A. (1971). Equal Rights for Women in Kenya? *The Journal of Modern African Studies, 9*(3), 429-442.
Wipper, A. (1975). The Maendeleo Ya Wanawake Organization: The Co-Optation of Leadership. *African Studies Review, 18*, pp. 99120.
Zeleza, P. T. (2005). Gender Biases in African Historiography. *African Gender Studies: A Reader* (pp. pp207-229). New York: Palgrave Macmillan.
Zirakzadeh, C. (1997). *Social Movements in Politics: A Comparative Study*. Addison. Wesley: Longman.

# Setting the agenda for our leaders from under a tree: The People's Parliament in Nairobi

Wangui Kimari and Jacob Rasmussen

> In Kenya the social movement (Bunge la Mwananchi) concept has grown organically and spread in towns across the country. The oldest gathering being Jeevanjee grounds where members meet every day for more than 15 years now. Amongst the towns that the movement has grown are Mombasa, Kisumu, Eldoret, Nakuru and Kakamega. The unique thing about the movement is that membership is voluntary and one can participate in actions anytime and disengage at will. This has enabled the movement to survive being hijacked by donors or infiltration by state security agents, who apparently are not amused when ordinary citizen s have the audacity to take a matter affecting them into their own hands.— *A Call to Liberation*, Bunge la Mwananchi (2009)

In a park in the heart of Nairobi, members of Bunge la Mwananchi, which means "the people's parliament" in Swahili, meet every day.[1] Four benches placed in the cool shade of bougainvillea trees form the physical base of the parliament, or Bunge, as it is more colloquially known. Each day, heated debates about topical issues concerning Kenyan politics and the occasional scandal take place. The daily gatherings are public debating forums, open to all ethnic groups, genders, occupations, and party affiliations. By virtue of this inclusivity, Bunge la Mwananchi transgresses many of the boundaries that routinely frame Kenyan politics.[2]

Bunge la Mwananchi is one of the most vocal grassroots organizations in Nairobi and defines itself as a social movement. There is no formal membership required and the movement is made up of whoever chooses to be part of it. Nevertheless, there are an increasing number of people whose sustained presence and practice has permitted for them to be regarded as essential members, and it is from these people that a ceremonial "leader"[3] is chosen

---

1. The article is dedicated to the memory of our friend and engaged activist in Bunge la Mwananchi, Jacob Odipo Odhiambo, who passed away on November 4, 2010.
2. Even with this inclusivity and the outreach that has been done to ensure as much diversity as possible, the typical Bunge member is male, between 25 and 45 year of age, and of any possible ethnic affiliation. To our knowledge, there are not many people of different abilit ies/disabled who participate in Bunge. Nevertheless, within the last two years, since the Bunge women's movement (these are women in Bunge and in the Bunges around Nairobi) has begun to gain more ground, there is more and more gender diversity within Bunge.
3. Although the membership of Bunge is in constantly in flux, there is a group of core members (a core that is constantly increasing) who have been attending Bunge the longest. When we refer to Bunge we refer not to just this core group but to the increasing number of people, who although they do not come to the park every day, identify as being part of Bunge. To our knowledge there has never been an attempt

every two years. The majority of the participants in the movement come from the lower socioeconomic strata of Kenyan society, and consequently it would seem that Bunge la Mwananchi is at the margins of Kenyan society and politics. However, the focus of this article is not to discuss whether Bunge la Mwananchi is marginal or not. Rather the aim is to understand the everyday practices and transgressions of political boundaries of Bunge la Mwananchi by looking at the creative processes of alternative politics its members employ in a country where the common person's access to the formal political system is limited. Such an endeavour does not deny the existence of hegemonic political hierarchies and centre-periphery relations that frame Kenyan politics, but instead it highlights the everyday political practices of Bunge la Mwananchi to reveal how members practice a politics without boundaries.

A central assumption in the article is that to be able to claim a politics without boundaries and to focus analytically on the challenges and transgressions of the boundaries, one must recognize the existence of boundaries. Bearing this in mind, it is important to note that, despite our use of the notion of margins when describing Bunge la Mwananchi, our emphasis is on how members deliberately use and reproduce their marginal position to transgress and overcome not only the marginality of the social movement, but political boundaries in general. Essentially, we look at how members of Bunge la Mwananchi continuously struggle for space while concomitantly challenging hegemonic pre-defined perceptions of space in their work, work that endeavours to establish and fortify "infrastructures of resistance" that they recognize as engendering the alternate democracies needed by the Kenyan people. Here, space is understood as both physical and political.

Before we detail the history of Bunge la Mwananchi and engage in an analysis of their political practices, we need to outline the understanding of political engagement and political practice that frames our analysis of Bunge la Mwananchi's actions. The analyses in the sections following the theoretical outline focus primarily on the appropriation of space (physical and political) and the often-non-conformist and counterhegemonic approaches to politics. The article is based on ethnographic material, which stems from Kimari's on-off engagement in Bunge la Mwananchi's activities between 2007 and 2010 and from Rasmussen's cumulative year of fieldwork in Nairobi between 2008 and 2010. Our collaborative effort combines the gazes of two differently positioned anthropologists, who could be conceptualized as an insider and an outsider, but

---

to count all of these people, but a conservative guess is that least 5000 people identify as being part of Bunge in Nairobi. It is important to note that there are also other Bunges across the country with a membership that is growing and each of these Bunges are organised according to community requirements. In addition, Bunge is intentionally de-hierarchical and the aforementioned core group of members hold no formal position in the movement, but their experiences, dedication and contributions are highly valued. It is usually from these members who are consistently present at the park that a ceremonial leader (who can also be called Ambassador, President, Chairman or Speaker) is chosen. The role of this leader is for the most part to present the face of the movement—both for members and for observers—as decisions are never taken by the leader alone. However there are also some members who may be chosen as leaders of a specific activity. The present ceremonial leader of Bunge at Jeevanjee gardens is a young woman called Dinah Awuor.

perhaps are better distinguished as an observing participant and a participant observer.

## Being political

As has already been mentioned in the introduction, our focal concern is how the members of Bunge la Mwananchi are political. Nevertheless, before we can investigate their political practices in more detail we need to outline how we can theoretically understand their ways of being political. In this regard, we have found great inspiration in Isin's (2002; 2005) philosophical approach to ways of being political and are also informed by Gramsci's (1971) discussion on hegemony.

In his work, Isin is concerned with what he terms "the city as a difference machine" and with "investigating citizenship historically as a generalized problem of otherness" (2005, p. 374). A key point in his argument is the distinction between politics and being political (Isin 2002; 2005). Though our concern is not with citizenship and otherness as such, nor with the city, we do investigate Bunge la Mwananchi members' attempts at political inclusion (from a perceived outsider position) through their various everyday practices in the city of Nairobi. Nevertheless, we are principally interested in a specific element of Isin's analysis, namely his perception of everyday ways of being political, which we find particularly helpful in understanding Bunge la Mwananchi and its members' activities.

Isin defines being political as relational and as expressed through people's everyday activities (2005, p. 382). This doesn't mean that any everyday activity qualifies as a way of being political; one only becomes political when one's activities question the virtues of the dominant or when they reveal the arbitrariness of this dominance (Isin, 2002, p. 21). This can be done by making claims of justice either as dissent, affirmation, or resistance (Isin, 2005, p. 382). It is the actions that challenge, expose, and redefine the previous meaning and order of existing political domination that qualify as ways of being political (Isin, 2002, pp. 21– 22). In other words, being and becoming political is dynamic and momentary, temporal and fluid, and is as much about agency as it is about claiming rights and justice.[4]

In his discussion of what constitutes the political, Isin draws on a variety of disparate thinkers such as Heidegger, Foucault, Weber, Elias, and Simmel to name just a few. Though our concern here is with the above outline of how one becomes political, this outline would make little sense if we failed to interrogate how Isin arrives at his definitions. In short, he argues that citizenship is relational; it is about the dominant groups of the city articulating their virtues,

---

4. Isin's argument is more complex than the summary here; for example he suggests that forms (orientations, strategies, and technologies), modes (solidaristic, agonistic, and alienating) and positions (citizen, outsider, stranger, and alien) together form ways of being political (Isin, 2002; 2005). Though we talk of forms in terms of strategies, modes in form of resistance, and positions in forms of marginalization, we are more interested in a practical application of Isin's ideas in the analysis of everyday political processes and practices than in distinguishing specific forms, modes, and positions.

morals, and identities as citizens, thus definingthemselves against others (strangers, outsiders, and aliens). However, Isin argues that these dominant articulations do not constitute politics in itself nor are they examples of ways of being political, as one only becomes political in the moment when hierarchical positions are questioned, redefined, reversed, and re-evaluated. It is this element of being and becoming political that renders imperative the questioning of the arbitrariness of dominance, which we complement with Gramsci's (1971) discussions on hegemony.

Bunge members, in their rejection of the hegemonic "common sense" of politics in Kenya—a common sense that is also shared by the civil society—act in ways that are often counterhegemonic, because they seek to create alternate institutions and a strong and questioning civil society that is not the vanguard of a "passive revolution" but rather resists the hegemony of the dominant class (see Cox and Sinclair, 1996, p. 129). There are exceptions to this, such as when alliances are made with members of the civil society such as NGOs, as seen during the recent 2010 campaign for a new Kenyan constitution in Kenya. Nevertheless, in their day-to-day practices in both political and physical space, seeking to undermine the hegemonic political and social structures that have been put in place, Bunge members more often than not act in ways that are counterhegemonic in their insistence (both in theory and praxis) that what is really required are the negation of the hegemonic "common sense" politic and rather the implementation of alternate forms of democracy. Therefore, we find it fitting to use both Isin's (2002; 2005) discussions on being political that are part of his discussions of historical citizenship as well as Gramsci's (1971) concept of hegemony in order to und erstand political practice at the grassroots level in Kenya.

Though Isin has the historical Western city as the locus of his analysis, his ambition is to challenge the notion that citizenship could have developed only in Western cities, thus refuting the notion that it is only in these spaces where people have struggled to constitute themselves (Drummond & Peake, 2005, 341-342). We therefore find some support for our attempt at applying parts of his argument in an empirically different setting and context than the Western city. We take the risk of not only simplifying Isin's theoretical and philosophical argument but also turning away from his focus on citizenship and instead looking at only one aspect, namely the process-oriented and dynamic political practice. We claim that our exegetic reading of Isin, complemented by Gramsci's discussion of hegemony, provides us with a framework for understanding how Bunge la Mwananchi members practice a politics without boundaries.

## Jeevanjee Gardens and Bunge la Mwananchi: Incarnating democratic participation in the city

The park that hosts Bunge la Mwananchi's very lively daily debates is called Jeevanjee Gardens. The raked paths and well-kept lawns are the result of a recent rejuvenation of the site. With the shade of bougainvillea and jacaranda trees, the park provides a resting place for office workers and students from the nearby Nairobi University, or whoever chooses to pass through from the bustling city centre. In the centre of the park, two small statues guard each side of the common green space. These imperial busts are reminiscent of a different time, portraying Queen Victoria and the original founder of this recreational space, Alibhai Mulla Jeevanjee. Bunge la Mwananchi members have their parliament in the quiet northeastern corner of this location. It has not always been this quiet though, for both Bunge la Mwananchi and the park have over the years been at the centre of struggles over their right to exist.

If Bunge la Mwananchi represents a grassroots alternative to political participation, Jeevanjee Gardens constitutes an alternative political space as it has been a contested site since its creation in 1906 (Patel, 1997, p. 211). Like many other colonial cities, Nairobi was planned as a segregated city, where areas were designated hierarchically for the different "racial" groups: the Europeans, the Indians, and the Africans. The founder of the park, the Indian businessman Jeevanjee, had the ambition of creating a public leisure area for urban residents and not only the Europeans. As an homage that would make it difficult for the imperial government to oppose the park, the statue of the British queen was erected at the centre of Jeevanjee Gardens as an honour to the British royal family. Though Jeevanjee's grandchild Zarina Patel has described it as a sincere respect paid to the royal family, the statue also stands as an example of creative resistance against the otherwise exclusive politics of space in Nairobi at the time.

In the early 1990s, motivated by the *laissez-faire* approach to urban planning in Nairobi, developers planned to build an underground carpark at Jeevanjee Gardens, and the park was threatened with demolition. At that time, Jeevanjee Gardens was considered a no-go area inhabited by street-preachers, homeless families, and criminals. A campaign lead by descendants of A. M. Jeevanjee, and supported by the winner of the 2004 Nobel Peace Prize Wangari Maathai, managed to mobilize people in defence of the park and against the grabbing of public land (Patel, 1997, p. 216). At that time, before the multi-party elections of 1992 when public debate and political gathering were not without risk, the park was protected through the support and protests of a diversity of people. In celebration of this feat, the Jeevanjee family donated a number of benches to the park.

In the latter part of the 1990s, people from various informal forums around the city (bus stages and street walks) took their debates to the park, as the Nairobi City Council launched a crack-down on street hawkers, vendors, preachers, and political agitators in the downtown core of the city. The debates took place on two of the donated benches that faced each other and were initially referred to as simply "a place to sit" but quickly became known as the "people's gatherings." These debates marked the beginning of Bunge la Mwananchi, whose members today meet around four benches. During the early hours of the afternoon, these benches are surrounded by concentric circles of people listening to and engaging in communal discussions. Despite having gathered in Jeevanjee Gardens since the 1990s, Bunge la Mwananchi gained its name in 2003, when the movement held its first elections as a mockery of the parliamentary elections that were held in December 2002. These elections signalled the broadening of a national space that permitted freer public dialogue and debate, but in no way did they hasten the decriminalization of dissent. Until 2002, the associational space in Kenya had been limited, despite the first steps towards free assembly that were taken with the introduction of multi-party democracy in 1992 (Nasong'o, 2007, p. 33). Nevertheless, Bunge la Mwananchi members still find their meetings occasionally interrupted by the police and a significant number of their members under frequent surveillance[5] (see *Sukuma Kenya*, 2009, and Human Rights House, 2010).

The daily meetings in the park have become an institution in Nairobi and have established an alternative political space in the city. They have become a public training ground for both political debate and agitation and a space for creative political practice. In a bid to expand these spaces, Bunge la Mwananchi is in the process of setting up "congresses" all over Kenya and around the different neighbourhoods within Nairobi. Even so, the forum in Jeevanjee Gardens retains a special position within the movement. In Nairobi, Jeevanjee Gardens is often just referred to as "Bunge" (Parliament). Insiders use this colloquial term to refer not only to the park, but also to mark the particular Bunge faction meeting there as the main part of the movement. In many ways the park and the movement have a dialogical relation, as Jeevanjee Gardens historically presents itself as a place that not only encourages political being but also as a place whose existence has relied on people's resistance to dominance—on their being political.

Bunge la Mwananichi members define themselves as part of a social movement, but contrary to members in many other social movements, they accept affiliation to political parties across the spectrum (Bunge la Mwananchi, 2009; cf. Castells, 1983). Bunge la Mwananchi's somewhat organic growth out of the park also sets it apart from many other traditional social movements, in the respect that it has not evolved into a social movement from a fight for a specific localized goal, such as local service provision, housing rights, and local environmental issues (see Castells, 1983). This is the case of many of Bunge la Mwananchi's African allies, such as the South African slum dwellers movement Abahlali baseMjondolo, which grew out of the fight against evictions. What Bunge la Mwanachi shares with these other more traditionally founded social movements is their grassroots orientation, their un-hierarchical organization, their partiality to mass action and activism, and their revocation of class aspects, understood as a conflictual relation to the state (see Castells, 1983; Ferrarotti, 2007; Melucci, 1989).

---

5. It is becoming increasingly frequent for Bunge la Mwananchi meetings to be disrupted by the police and members to be arrested for "idling in the park" or being part of an "illegal one-man assembly" or an "illegal movement," despite the fact that affairs are con ducted in the open (Nyongesa, 2009). Even when not at Jeevanjee Gardens, members have been arrested. One example of this occurred on February 22, 2009 when Gacheke Gachihi, a longterm member of Bunge la Mwananchi, was arrested that Sunday morning while he was drinking tea in a local restaurant in his neighbourhood (Sukuma Kenya, 2009). On the more extreme end of this surveillance and persecution, some members such as Samson Owimba Ojiayo and Godwin Kamau Wangoe have been abducted and harassed and their families have been threatened as a direct result of their political work (Human Rights House, 2010).

## "The Kenya we DO NOT want"

The political actions and everyday practices of Bunge la Mwananchi members relate in one way or the other to their overall aims and objectives as a movement. In order to discuss their political practices and their ways of being political, we need to contextualize the movement, by conveying its historical background, aims, and objectives.

In 2009, Bunge la Mwananchi members arranged an alternative workshop called "The Kenya we DO NOT want" in response to a highly publicized and expensive government conference titled "The Kenya we want." This workshop was motivated by what Bunge members perceived as the government's neglect of salient issues such as poverty, high food prices, corruption, and human rights abuses in its recently published vision for Kenya (Bunge la Mwananchi, 2010). The alternative event and its sarcastic title reveal the arbitrariness of the government's agenda and the contention over who is the "We" that is spoken of, a contention that illustrates the division between the political elite and the ordinary people of Kenya.

The workshop is but one example of the activities of Bunge la Mwananchi members that express dissatisfaction with the government and the present state of things: the "common sense" that prevails in Kenyan politics. In pamphlets are phrases such as "a call for liberation" and "dreaming of another Kenya," as well as "We aspire to mobilize one Kenyan at a time into a strong political force that will transform Kenya's politics" (Bunge la Mwananchi, 2010, p. 8). In their activities and in their written sources, it is apparent that members are working to create "infrastructures of resistance" to engender the societal change needed for political transformation in Kenya. The overlapping desires for political transformation are expressed and employed in the members' daily debates and actions in the park.

Furthermore, Bunge la Mwananchi's mission statement reiterates the same quest for "a Kenya where citizens enjoy unfettered sovereignty to organize so as to free themselves from all forms of oppression and domination; are aware of their socioeconomic and political rights and responsibilities, demand accountability, and have accessible opportunities and resources to realize their full potential" (Bunge la Mwananchi, 2010, p. 10). The very foundation of Bunge la Mwananchi, the quest for change, and the will to fight for transformation by challenging, redefining, and exposing, is consistent with Isin's (2002; 2005) ideas of being political, as it is about questioning the authority of leaders by making claims of freedom, rights, and justice. The goal that is fervently pursued is change, inclusion, and influence, and it is about setting the agenda for the leaders from under a tree.

## A politics without boundaries and bureaucracy

Bunge la Mwananchi is not registered with the Non-Governmental Organisation Co-ordination Board of Kenya as an NGO, nor with the Department of Culture and Social Services or any Provincial Administration as a community-based organization. In addition, the movement is not the project of any organization, business, or politician. Consequently, Bunge la Mwananchi has often been criticized for not having a formal or registered status. It is accused for being a movement that is not expressly anchored in the governmentality of a "liberal democracy",[6] and of merely "doing noise" and being no better than "mobsters",[7] as one observer noted. Despite this, Bunge la Mwananchi members have chosen to remain organic and informal, regardless of the fervent criticism this provokes (Bunge la Mwananchi, 2010).

What are the reasons for this rejection of formality, the disavowal of an institutionalized status that would confer legitimacy and allow for the negation of the "noise makers" title? In this section we analyse in detail the reasons for the aversion to institutionalization. Although Bunge la Mwananchi members are insistent about not registering, they still consent to alliances with many of the formal organizations that constitute the "Euro Dollar Chaser Industry," as the movement members have dubbed the NGOs and other civil society organizations whose intentions they often hold suspect (Bunge la Mwananchi, 2010).

The reluctance of Bunge la Mwananchi members to institutionalization indicates their concern with the stringencies that would result from such a formality. For the purposes of this article, these concerns are captured in three broad and overlapping themes.

First, there is a recognition by members of Bunge la Mwananchi that the registering body that would confer to them an institutional legitimacy is part of the very same governing structure and "historical bloc" (Gramsci, 1971) that contributes to their marginality and the severe human conditions that most Kenyans live in. Therefore, participation in this system would render the task of questioning the arbitrariness of dominance increasingly difficult, a task Isin (2002) asserts as imperative for being and becoming political. This is because registration in any national organization would regulate and restrain Bunge la Mwananchi's activities much more than the periodic disruption of their meetings by the police, thus hindering the counter-hegemonic strategies and technologies that are essential to the movement (cf. Gramsci, 1971). Furthermore, this is coupled with the reality that a large majority of the organizations that are registered often become part of what Shivji (2007) terms the "neocolonial offensive" and what Bunge la Mwananchi members deem the "Euro-Dollar chaser Industry" (Bunge la Mwananchi, 2010). In regard to the latter, the Bunge la Mwananchi secretariat asserts,

> The mainstream civil society has turned itself into "Euro-Dollar" chaser industry focussed on championing Western interests at all costs. This repugnant behaviour has turned civil society into an elite society of academicians writing proposals,

---

6. The assumption that Kenya is any sort of democracy would be sneered at during any Bunge la Mwananchi meeting.
7. On a Kenyan Discussion Platform called Jukwaa, Bunge's call for the resignation of members of the Kenyan cabinet who had voted against the new constitution was being discussed. One contributor to this discussion Kamalet, in the voicing of his discontent against this call by Bunge called them "mobsters." This can be found on the following link from the Jukwa Pro Boards site. http://jukwaa.proboards.com/index.cgi?board=general&action=display&threa d=4 374

papers, holding workshops and press conferences one after the other, without much or anything to show for it in terms of positive change. It is the impatience with this sad state of affairs and an appreciation of a functional civil society as strong pillar in a functional democracy that formed the crucible that crystallised Bunge la Mwananchi as an organic movement. The movement is an initiative to leverage people's individual passions to create collective action and to put a human face on depersonalized policy discussions on complex socioeconomic problems bedevilling a majority of our people (Bunge la Mwananchi Secretariat, Bunge la Mwananchi, 2010).

Nevertheless, it is important to re-emphasize that Bunge la Mwananchi members often create alliances with some of these "Euro–Dollar Chaser" organizations. Isin points out that "while the logics of exclusion would have us believe in zero-sum, discrete and binary groups, the logics of alterity assume overlapping, fluid, contingent, dynamic and reversible boundaries and positions where beings engage in solidaristic strategies" (2002, p. 17). These alliances are forged in accordance with a solidarity strategy, with the ultimate goal of political transformation. Bunge la Mwananchi's mission is defined by the following three enterprises: "organizing citizenry, setting the agenda, transforming lives" (Bunge la Mwananchi, 2010).

Second, as has been discussed earlier, Bunge la Mwananchi is a movement that began through informal and organic embodied practices that were not the impetus of any institution. Akin to many of the historical resistance movements in Kenya, Bunge la Mwananchi was merely continuing "the culture of coming together among Kenyans, formally or informally, in neighbourhoods, at the markets, on the roadside, under a tree etc. to dialogue on pertinent community issues" (Bunge la Mwananchi, 2010). Members assert that it is this type of coming together "that fomented political consciousness among Kenyans for self determination towards democratic rule" and moreover that

> This politics-motivated coming together can be traced to the 80s and 90s, during the agitation for multiparty democracy, when it was difficult to freely organize political meetings in fear of former President Moi's use of the Kenya Police to terrorise dissenting voices. During this period of terror, Kenyans involved in the underground struggle for change would hold secret meetings, especially in the parks such as Jeevanjee Gardens Park in Nairobi to exchange views on Kenya's political problems (Bunge la Mwananchi Secretariat, Bunge la Mwananchi, 2010).

A formalized status would not sustain the informality that is characteristic of this type of grassroots organizing. The formalizing of Bunge la Mwananchi, and the hierarchy that would be imposed by institutionalization, would work to negate the intentional personal-community and inclusive dynamic that prevails, a dynamic that permits for people from all walks of life—"progressive university intellectuals, conscious students, politicians and the disempowered population of workers, peasants and unemployed" (Bunge la Mwananchi, 2009)—to come together. Rather than allowing for "the reality of the social world [where] in the everyday experiences of beings, there are no clear group boundaries and group identifications or affiliations and disassociation or differentiations are multiple, fluid and overlapping" (Isin, 2002, p. 16), the registration of Bunge la Mwananchi would lead to the privileging of such factors as education, professionalism, national identification documents, hierarchical structures, and registration fees. This would create both tacit and visible limitations to participation, engendering ruptures between this organic social movement and the history that provoked its becoming.

In addition, the issues that are interrogated and the "direct political action" employed by Bunge la Mwananchi members (Bunge la Mwananchi, 2010) would not be possible if the movement's actions had to be approved by an overseeing body. As a consequence of their deliberate institutional marginality, members can freely discuss Kenya's "flag independence" and "imperialist allies." And they can support and contextualize comments on their website about being "governed by mostly mentally ill or bankrupt, definitely in all cases stupid selfserving politicians, each aspiring to be the richest lazy fool in the world sitting like an overfed baboon atop the tallest tree in our devastated and rotting vineyard, savouring their exploits amidst squalor, hunger and decaying corpse" (Osahon, 2010). If Bunge la Mwananchi were registered or a project of a civil society group, the explicit and unrelenting opinionation and direct political action employed by members would most likely be vetoed by a governing body or an organization accountable to an international donor or the national government.

Its informal status, which initially appears to emphasize the boundaries to political participation, conversely works to the bene fit of Bunge la Mwananchi. For it is in the role of outsiders within a "passive revolution" that members are able to more efficiently and creatively question the arbitrariness of the municipal and national governments. As we have seen, Bunge la Mwananchi members are able to participate in both formal and informal settings, and they navigate and transgress these boundaries with an immense knowledge of the city, with resourcefulness and determination to carry out their political agenda. Isin argues that "we may owe the existence of politics not to citizens but to [...] outsiders" (Isin, 2002, p. 26), and in this regard we can think of Bunge la Mwananchi members' intentional marginality in relation to Kenyan formal politics as a positional strategy, one that allows them to more insightfully challenge the hegemony of the dominant political class.

## The "Mwananchi Freedom from Hunger Train": Debating the city

When Rasmussen passed by Jeevanjee Gardens on a February day in 2010, there was a heated debate about the constitutional draft that was being assessed by the government. A group of men were concerned about rumours that rights for homosexuals would be introduced in the proposed constitution. In response to this concern, others argued that it was a strategic card played by clever politicians who wanted to divert people's attention from the "real issues" by introducing a controversial theme such as gay rights. On a previous occasion, the debate had been about food shortages in remote areas of Kenya, and another day it had concerned housing and civic rights. On all of these occasions there was consensus that the "real issues" of food shortages and housing policies were grave and required immediate resolution. Despite this consensus, there was disagreement about how best to solve the problems and where to place the responsibility for their persistence. Despite Bunge la Mwananchi's declared openness to all party affiliations and ethnic identities, issues of who to blame sometimes brought about accusations of ethnically motivated politics, which then fueled debates about ethnicity internally in Bunge.

Though the debates in Jeevanjee Gardens are often vibrant, detailed, and well informed, they are more often than not characterized by disagreement, and few decisions and agreements are actually made here. Many people from Jeevanjee Gardens meet in small groups in restaurants and teahouses around the city before or after going to the park. It is often in these small groups of likeminded people that activities are planned, and decisions are taken. After brainstorming beforehand about what activities should take place, these groups then introduce their ideas in Jeevanjee Gardens in order to gain wider support in terms of mobilizing people or raising funds. Nevertheless, regardless of the popularity of proposed ideas, they usually do not remain uncontested.

A number of these different groupings affiliated with Bunge la Mwananchi collaborate with civil society organizations and NGOs, which in turn are intent on making alliances with this increasingly powerful and ubiquitous grassroots movement. Bunge la Mwananchi members have been involved in spearheading a demonstration for a proposed free information bill in parliament. They have been commentators at public debates at cultural institutions such as the Goethe Institute and fierce critics of impunity at debates arranged by Release the Political Prisoners and Kenyans Against Impunity. Furthermore, one evening while Rasmussen watched a public debate on TV, a participant from the audience who had asked critical questions introduced himself as a member of Bunge la Mwananchi. As briefly illustrated by the above examples, the members of Bunge la Mwananchi are negotiating and pushing their way into debates all over the city and they take every opportunity to get their message across.

French philosopher de Certeau (1988) has written about how the ordinary person can change and influence the city space by taking advantage of the opportunities offered by the moment. He defines space as relational, that is, the meaning ascribed to a certain space depends on the people passing through this space and the events that take place there. Therefore, space is not defined only by its immediate functions or by the intentions ascribed to it by planners and lawmakers. Central to de Certeau's theory of man's appropriation of space is that it is temporal. De Certeau argues that the ordinary person influences space through hers or his practices in it, but these actions only redefine the meaning of a certain space for a short time as the space opens itself to other influences and other inscriptions when the person leaves. In other words "what he gains he can't keep", but this does not diminish the power of what has been gained in that moment.

When Bunge la Mwananchi members use events other than their own to make their voice heard, they take advantage of the moment, redefine the space, and make it theirs. When moving within and about Nairobi to attend various events, they take advantage of what the city has to offer in terms of public platforms and in this way they expand their use of space beyond Jeevanjee Gardens. Regardless of whether their appropriations of city space are temporary, they change the meaning of spaces and events by using them as platforms for their political agenda.

It is important to note that Bunge la Mwananchi members are not only using and transforming the city by capitalizing on others' forums, they are above all trying to spread their debate all over the city and the country. The members that come to Jeevanjee Gardens come from every corner of Nairobi and its surrounding estates (neighbourhoods), and it is through these members that the debating forums (so-called congresses) will be set up in the aforementioned locations. Aligned to this pursuit, Bunge la Mwananchi members initiated what they call the "Mwananchi Freedom from Hunger Train."

From various often poor and peripheral locations around the city, a commuter train carries people to work in central Nairobi and the industrial area every morning and back home in the evening. On one occasion, likely familiar with the train's winding journeys and the sheer number of passengers that accompany it on its long sojourn, some members of Bunge la Mwananchi boarded the night commuter train with the intention of engaging the Nairobi workers in political discussion. They carried with them 2,500 leaflets titled "Why are President Kibaki and Prime Minister Railia begging Foreigners to feed Kenyans" (Bunge la Mwananchi, 2010) that highlighted the grave food situation that many Kenyans faced. These leaflets discussed the food crisis in the country and provided salient information to the commuters while also acting as an icebreaker of sorts for these activists. With activities such as these, Bunge la Mwananchi members are taking their political debate out of the park and bringing it to the residents of Nairobi, in this way debating the city. On the one hand, they are debating a specific topic—the city—by discussing issues that affect the majority of Nairobians and Kenyans. At the same time, they are actively carrying out the practice of political debate, that is, debating all over the city while moving through it, while engaging the residents who compose the life that is debated in the city.

Through this political praxis, members of Bunge are mobilizing others to become political. While mobilizing people to participate in political debates and while creating political awareness, they train people to argue and agitate for their political view-points, viewpoints that in their difference from the prevailing "common sense" are themselves counter-hegemonic. Furthermore, in debating the city, Bunge la Mwananchi members are transforming the meaning of city space, as what used to be a commuter train for workers is suddenly turned into a rolling political debate forum. A similar point can be made about the congresses set up in the "slums," for a corner at the marketplace in Mathare slum no longer remains just a trading space but is rapidly converted into a venue for political debate. While navigating through the formal and informal public political spaces of Nairobi, the members of Bunge la Mwananchi are working on the city, democratizing it. They practice a politics without boundaries by challenging, transgressing, and expanding the notions of what a given space means by temporarily turning it into a political space, and these moments of spatial appropriation are simultaneously moments of the political (cf. de Certeau, 1988; Isin, 2002).

Writing on the everyday practices in urban Africa, urban theorist Simone concludes that power in urban Africa "increasingly derives from a capacity to transgress spatial and conceptual boundaries, erasing clear distinctions between private and public, territorial borders, exclusion and inclusion" (2006, p. 357). Through members counter-hegemonic actions that transform both political and physical space, Bunge la Mwananchi, similar to other African organizations such as the aforementioned Abahlali base Mjondolo, is becoming increasingly more powerful as a grassroots organization and conferring knowledge about how to transgress political and spatial boundaries, while above all engendering alternative ways to seek inclusion for those who are put at the most at risk by dominant political interests.

## Ironic practices: Inverting the meaning of arrests

Isin refers to Wirth, the Chicago School sociologist who states that groups who are conscious of their oppression and their rights are a political force to be reckoned with (2002, p. 20). We observe d this dialectic relation between rights awareness and political power in a number of encounters between Bunge la Mwananchi members and the police. Members of the movement articulated the police's interference with the movement's activities and meetings as an example of the state's violation of their civic rights, but also as the state's implicit recognition of them as a politically influential force. Every now and then, the police interfere in the daily debates at the park in order to stop or disturb the planning of coming events, or as some participants of the movement stated, "to scare people" from engaging in the forum (Bunge la Mwananchi, 2010; Human Rights House, 2010). Though the police interferences had the immediate effect of dispersing most attendants, the interferences also provoked creative resistance against this violent manifestation of state control.

However, not all confrontations with the police are about existing rights. They may also be about gaining new rights by challeng ing the legal system. Activists from Bunge la Mwananchi have been arrested at different times and charged with incitement to disobedience, idling, and disorderly behaviour, perfunctory charges often laid when the police respond to resistance to the state's dominance. When such arrests occur, other members of Bunge la Mwananchi contact supportive lawyers and often try to mobilize people to go to court and to rally in support of the arrested outside of the courthouse.

One day in December 2008 outside the Kibera Court, a small crowd of Bunge la Mwananchi supporters awaited the hearing of some of their "comrades" who had been arrested for incitement at a demonstration. As the arrested were released, one of them conveyed that she was not concerned about the arrest. It was her third pending case and she had kept a low profile until recently, while another case reached its conclusion. "I can only afford three cases at the time,"[8] she said in a matter-of-fact tone. It took a short investigation to

---

8. BW, personal communication December 2008.

reveal that some of the more engaged activist members of Bunge la Mwananchi deliberately got themselves arrested at public gatherings and demonstrations in order to put pressure on the judicial system in terms of extra workload and extra costs for running minor cases. These deliberate arrests are aimed at exposing what the activists perceive as the absurdity and unjustness of a legal system that criminalizes dissent. As a consequence, these members of Bunge la Mwananchi seek to invert the outcome of the arrests by turning a means of government repression into a burden for the judiciary. Therefore, what on the surface may appear to be a mechanical arrest by a police officer in order to maintain law and order is in fact the result of a political strategy aimed at change.

In rhetoric and linguistics studies the act of inverting the meaning of a given word in order to reveal an underlying meaning is called irony (Burke, 1969, p. 512). The quality of irony not only makes it an obvious tool for uttering or acting out a critique, it also includes a creative element through its ability to transform the meaning of an utterance or act into a different significance. If this definition of irony is applied to the activists' deliberate arrests, these actions can be seen as enactments of irony or ironic practices that are resourceful ways of challenging existing politics (cf. Isin, 2002, p. 26).

Bunge la Mwananchi members' use of irony is not only expressed in subtle ways such as arrests; the ironic mocking of the political elite is central to the movement's counter-hegemonic foundation and is discernable even in its name. As mentioned in the introduction, the English translation of Bunge la Mwananchi is The People's Parliament. By claiming to be a parliament for the people, the movement critiques the real parliament for not representing the ordinary Kenyan people, a critique that they act out in their daily practices.

Bunge la Mwananchi holds elections every two years, and anybody who signs up in advance can vote. At the August 2009 elections in Jeevanjee Gardens, the ballot boxes were made of transparent plastic, an intentional gesture that highlighted the accusations of rigged ballot boxes during the general Kenyan elections of December 2007 and the overall lack of transparency in Kenyan politics. A rewording of the Kenyan national anthem reveals further ironic commentary. On their website, Bunge la Mwananchi members have reworked the second verse, which is full of calls for patriotism, national service, and sincerity. The national anthem had been written hastily in a bid to replace "God Save the Queen," which had been the anthem of the British Empire. The second verse of Kenya's English national anthem reads:

> Let one and all arise
> With hearts both strong and true
> Service be our earnest endeavour
> And our homeland of Kenya
> Heritage of Splendour
> Firm may we stand to defend.

The Bunge la Mwananchi, version however, evokes a less patriotic fervour:

> Let all politicians arise
> With scams both wily and foolproof
> Eating be our earnest endeavour

And our cake-stand of Kenya
Heritage of Plunder
May we fight forever to perpetuate
   (Bunge la Mwananchi Secretariat, Bunge la Mwananchi, 2010)

A further example of Bunge la Mwananchi's attempts at turning things on their head through the use of irony is the aforementioned workshop, "The Kenya we DO NOT want." In addition, in 2007 when Nairobi hosted the World Social Forum, a global grassroots event, Bunge la Mwananchi members arranged a successful Mock Social Forum for the local civil society and grassroots organizations not included in the official event.

In anthropological studies of political rhetoric and everyday resistance, irony and ironic practices are categorized as a tool for opposition and as a weapon of the weak (de Certeau, 1987; Herzfeld, 1997; Paine, 1981; Scott, 1985). The ambiguous character of irony that permits for a word or an action to mean something other than what it seems to mean implies that irony and ironic actions are best suited as responses to other people's statements and actions, as it is dialectic and therefore depends on existing statements and actions to reveal its dualistic potential (Burke, 1969; Paine, 1981). Most oppressed, subjugated, and opposition groups are in positions where they are not in charge of the overall agenda but are charged to react and respond to the work and actions of a dominant other. The use of irony as a political tool then, requires the ability to take advantage of the moment and the chance openings in creative and spontaneous ways such as when the members of Abahlali baseMjondolo, in response to a declaration that they were criminal and "out of order ," fervently asserted that "when order means the silence of the poor then it is good to be out of order" (Abahlali base Mjondolo, 2010). Similarly, Bunge la Mwananchi's use of irony is political as it transgresses and challenges the boundaries established by a hegemonic politic and thus succeeds in revealing the exclusion, the hidden agendas, and the arbitrariness of the "common sense" means of governance in Kenya.

## Setting the agenda for our leaders from under a tree

In this paper we endeavoured to convey the transgressions of political boundaries that are evident in the everyday political practices of the Kenyan grassroots movement Bunge la Mwananchi. In this pursuit we have highlighted how members' creative and often counter-hegemonic technologies and transgressions are dependent on space in the city (both political and physical) and how they concomitantly work to redefine, transform, and reclaim these spaces. In this regard, the public park Jeevanjee Gardens, which hosts daily debates, has a central position and provides for the otherwise grassroots character of the movement and the relative fluidity of activities. Though the location of Bunge la Mwananchi meetings could be anywhere, Jeevanjee Gardens' particular history of resistance and democratic struggle succeeds in enriching the counter-hegemonic processes of Bunge la Mwananchi, as it is illustrative of the possibilities that can be garnered by a strong inclusive political praxis.

This analysis was anchored in Isin's (2002; 2005) discussion of the political, which defines political being as the result of political actions, meaning the ability to question the arbitrariness of dominant governing and governance. We have attempted to turn specific aspects of Isin's genealogical and philosophical argument into applicable tools for understanding and investigating everyday political practices and processes. As Isin's argument departs into a discussion of the notion of citizenship as rooted in the city, we have related his ideas of becoming political to de Certeau's (1988) notions of everyday urban resistance and strategies of spatial appropriation to understand not only how becoming political is linked to the city as a historical institution, but also to reveal how the city as a physical and political space is informed by people's being and becoming political. In addition, in order to articulate Bunge la Mwananchi's practices more profoundly, illustrating their actions towards revolutionary change while also highlighting the local and international power relations that frame Kenyan politics, we felt it was imperative to include some discussions of hegemony as articulated by Gramsci (1971). It is through these complementary scholarly dialogues that we have endeavoured to illustrate Bunge la Mwananchi's praxis, their actions to piece together structures of resistance, which in the not-too-distant future may finally ensure the alternate forms of democracy that are fought for by members of this grassroots movement.

Bunge la Mwananchi members, as we have discussed, perceive and position the movement as an outsider, but as an outsider in search of inclusive change rather than an outsider in search of inclusion within the state hegemony. The fact that non-registration is a deliberate strategy and not a forced position allows Bunge la Mwananchi to transgress the boundaries between formality and informality and to seek ways of questioning and revealing the arbitrariness of the government by actively playing on the ambiguity of being an outsider working on the inside or vice versa. As we have seen, both the marginality and the contradictions inherent in the physical and political space of the movement contribute to the success in pursuing a politics that is boundless. This is coupled with the members' knowledge of the city, a knowledge that allows for the creative pursuance of a political agenda that above all utilizes the temporal and momentary in order to inscribe their message.

In pursuit of this politics without boundaries, Bunge la Mwananchi is placed in a dialogical relationship with the city and in this process both uses and creates the city. It is in this way that members are able to motivate, mobilize, debate, and navigate the blatant and tacit obstacles that are inherent in any political culture that privileges the narratives of the dominant. As anthropologists Das and Poole (2004) have argued, it is often at the margins of the state that alternative political practices are instituted and where political creativity is visible. It is through such deliberate marginal positioning, located under a tree, that Bunge la Mwananchi members, through their resourceful political practices, seek to set the agenda for the political leaders in Kenya. While evoking images of age-old African authority and elders' councils gathered under a tree, it is from under a tree in a city park Bunge la Mwananchi members perform and engender alternative politics, thus bridging tradition and counter-hegemonic creativity in an inclusive politics without boundaries.

## References

Abahlali baseMjondolo. Official Website. Retrieved October 28, 2010. http://www.abahlali.org/
Bunge la Mwananchi. (2009). *A Call to Liberation*. Pamphlet.
Bunge la Mwananchi Working Committee. (2009). The terrain of Alternative leadership in Kenya. *Pambazuka*, 419. Retrieved May 2010, from http://www.pambazuka.org/en/category/comment/54040
Bunge la Mwananchi. (2010). Bunge la Mwananchi. Social Movement, 10 (004).
Burke, Kenneth. (1969). *A grammar of motives*. Berkeley: University of California Press.
Castells, Manuel. (1983). *The city and the grassroots*. London: Edward Arnold.
Cox, Robert. W. & Timothy J. Sinclair. (1996). *Approaches to World Order*. Cambridge: Cambridge University Press.
Das, Vena & Poole, Deborah. (2004). State and its Margins. Comparative Ethnographies. In Das & Poole (eds.), *Anthropology in the Margins of the state* (pp. 3-34). Oxford: James Curry.
de Certeau, Michell. (1988). *The practice of everyday life*. London & Los Angeles: University of California Press.
Drummond, Lisa & Peake, Lisa. (2005). Introduction to Engin Isin's being political: Genealogies of citizenship. *Political Geography*, 24, 341-343.
Ferrarotti, Franco. (2007). New approaches to social movements in Western Europe. In *Social theory for old and new modernities: Essays on society and culture, 1976-2005* (pp. 107-120). Boulder & New York: Lexington Books.
Herzfeld, Michael. (1997). *Cultural intimacy: Social poetics in the nation-state*. New York & London: Routledge.
Gramsci, Antonio. (1971). *Selections from the Prison Notebooks*. New York: International Publishers.
Isin, Engin. (2002). Ways of being political. *Distinktion – Tidssskrift for samfundsteori*, 4, 7-28.
Isin, Engin. (2005). Engaging, being, political. *Political Geography*, 24, 373-387.
Human Rights House. (2010). Living dangerously: Kenyan human rights defenders increasingly targeted. Retrieved October 27, 2010, from http://humanrightshouse.org/Articles/14767.html
Melucci, Alberto. (1989). New Perspectives on Social Movements. An interview with Alberto Melucci. In Keane & Mier (Eds.) *Nomads of the present. Social movements and individual needs in contemporary society* (pp. 180-233). Philadelphia: Temple University Press.
Nasong'o, Shadrack. (2007). Negotiating new rules of the game: Social movements, civil society and the Kenyan transition. In Murunga & Nasong'o (Eds.) *Kenya: The struggle for democracy*, (pp. 58-89). Dakar: Codesria Books. London & New York: Zed Books.

Nyongesa, George. (2009, February 27). Kenya: Bunge la Mwanachi statement on extrajudicial killings findings. *Pambazuka*, 421. Retrieved October 27, 2010, from http://www.pambazuka.org/en/category/socialmovements/54471

Osahon, Naiwo. (2010). *After Fifty years after Flag Independence.* Retrieved May 15, 2010, from http://naiwuosahon.webs.com/apps/blog/show/3402041-after-fifty-years-of-flag-independence

Paine, Robert. (1981). Politically speaking: Cross-cultural studies of rhetoric. Philadelphia: Institute for the study of human issues.

Patel, Zarina. (1997). *Challenge to Colonialism: The struggle of Alibhai Mulla Jevanjee for equal rights in Kenya*. Nairobi: Publishers Distribution Service.

Scott, James. (1985). *Weapons of the weak: Everyday forms of peasant resistance*. New Haven and London: Yale University Press.

Shivji, Issa. (2007). *Silences in NGO discourse: The role and future of NGO's in Africa*. Oxford: Fahamu Books.

Simone, Abdoumaliq. (2006). Pirate towns: Reworking social and symbolic infrastructures in Johannesburg and Douala. *Urban Studies*, 43, 2. 357-370.

*Sukuma Kenya*. (2009, February 23). 25 Bunge la Mwanachi members arbitrarily arrested and held. Retrieved October 27, 2010, from http://sukumakenya.blogspot.com/2009/02/25-bunge-la-mwananchi-members.html

# Politics across boundaries:
# Pan-Africanism: Seeds for African unity

Gacheke Gachihi

Speaking at a farewell party organized by *Chama cha Mapinduzi*[1] in Tanzania on his behalf, Mwalimu Nyerere challenged African leaders on the question of African unity and the existing colonial boundaries that divide African communities and which have arrested their growth and development in the 21st century. Mwalimu stated that the boundaries that were imposed by colonial forces during the partitioning/portioning of the African continent divided mother against child, as well as brother against brother, and hindered the social development of Africa. He gave the example of the Maasai community in Kenya and Tanzania who were divided between two colonial forces, the British and the Germans. This is why today you will find communities in Africa such as the Maasai who are divided by colonial boundaries although they belong to the same family: they carry different passports and identification cards, but ultimately are tied together by a cultural and historical connection. This example manifests itself from the immigration centres of Kaduna, which connects Rwanda and Uganda, or Namanga, which connects Tanzania and Kenya. It is here that you will find women carrying babies and bananas on their backs as they try to cross borders that are usually fortified by the police. Their crossing is made more difficult as they made more difficult as they attempt to balance immigration paperwork with these babies and bananas, and attempt to navigate the innumerable forms asking for occupation, identity and reason for travelling.

On the 12th and 13th of April 2009, I had the opportunity to attend the Mwalimu Nyerere Intellectual festival as a community organizer with the Bunge la Mwananchi social movement. At this forum, Pan-Africanism was debated. We discussed how Africa can stand on this unified political movement of Pan-Africanism, and organize on the unity of Africa towards political, economic and cultural liberation in 21st century. This intellectual festival injected fresh breath into African politics, which have been dominated by neoliberal policies for two decades since the fall of the Berlin wall and since Francis Fukuyama declared 'the end of history' and the triumph of free markets. Since this period, the political space in Africa has been dominated by neoliberal policies that came with neoliberal model packages of privatization, 'good governance,' multi-partyism, 'human rights,' all in the name of saving Africa from the political despotism that existed in the era of the Cold War and after.

These neoliberal policies demobilized the African masses and the progressive middle class that was organizing resistance under a Pan-African movement. Furthermore, the progressive ide ological politics were attacked and Africa

---

1. *Chama cha Mapinduzi* means Party of the Revolution in Swahili.

was lectured on how to implement World Bank and IMF policies. In contrast, during the leaderships of Kwame Nkrumah, Mwalimu Julius Nyerere, Amilcar Cabral and Agostino Neto, this African leadership harnessed and forged the Pan-African political instrument that gave birth to new leadership in Africa, which spearheaded the struggle for independence.

The Annual Mwalimu Nyerere Intellectual festival, which is organized by the Mwalimu Nyerere Chair of Pan-African studies at Dar es Salaam University,[2] creates a space for reflection and seeks to draw lessons from the past, from the social struggles that were anchored in a Pan African movement. The last Pan African congress—which was the 7th—was held in Uganda in 1994. Unfortunately, we, the younger generation, have not been able to read and improve on the Pan African resolutions that were agreed upon at this congress, which had been organizational instruments for the independence era liberation movements.

As Africa develops a means of transport that will be linking many of its capital cities, the young generation will interact, political relationships will be forged, and new fruitful contradictions will continue to shape daily lives. This will be a great and much needed opportunity for a new generation in Africa to forge a united front in creating an alternative, borderless, Pan-Africanist political leadership.

---

2. The first and current chair is Dr Issa Shivji.

# Afterword: Incorporeal words: The tragic passing of Pius Adesanmi

Blair Rutherford

> *And on the way I would say to myself:*
> *"And above all, my body as well as my soul beware of assuming the sterile attitude of a spectator, for life is not a spectacle, a sea of miseries is not a proscenium, a man screaming is not a dancing bear..."*[1]

Perhaps it would be a conversation with Saint Peter, the late great Nigerian novelist Chinua Achebe, the late great Sénégalese author and feminist Mariama Bâ, and the 157 newly arrived about why there are these barriers to enter the welcomed afterlife. One of those who was unexpected to be on this journey, trying to collect his thoughts about why he was there way before his time, yet still swift enough to find one of his usual incisive questions, posed eloquently and yet tinged with his well-known reticence to grant authority any respect it may not have earned. Why, he asks, can't anyone freely enter this desired afterlife? Be it the Gates to Heaven or the eight doors of Jannah, every soul may not enter, as if paradise was one of the fortified, exclusive gated communities on Banana Island in Lagos! A city in the country of his birth and to which he was inelectably committed, despite everything...The dialogue would be profound, on the edge of being profane, weaving in Yoruba deities, quotidian Nigerian expressions, hip hop poetry, African nationalist and Pan-Africanist dreams, searing indictments of the incompetent, the corrupt, the racist, the patriarchal, and the violent that not only tend to overdetermine postcolonial African governments—like the colonial regimes before them—but also are widely found in the oh-so-comfortable so-called Global North, likely bringing in as a case-in-point the recent coming-to-light of the brazen attempts by the Trudeau Liberal government in Canada—where this newly arrived had lived, taught, and also was a citizen—to interfere in prosecutorial decisions to ensure that the Canadian multinational engineering giant, SNC Lavalin[2] (already found guilty for a slew of other corruption cases, even having many of its subsidiaries being debarred by the World Bank for ten years in 2013) is not prosecuted for allegedly paying millions of dollars in bribes in return for billions of dollars in contracts to the murderous Gaddhafi family when they controlled Libya. It would be literate and literary, cogent and contemplative, allegorical and deeply historical, with the phatic thrust aiming to force the reader to appreciate the depthless complexities of life that marks "Africa" inside and outside the

---

1. Aimé Césaire, "Notebook of a return to the native land," in Aimé Césaire : *The Collected Poetry*, translated by Clayton Eschleman and Annette Smith, Berkeley: University of California Press, p45.
2. https://www.nationalobserver.com/2019/03/08/analysis/hidden-key-snc-lavalin-scandal

continent, to fight against the multitudes of injustices, and to empathize with the human dreams, trials, and tribulations of the living....

But this is but speculation on my part, trying to imagine how Pius Adesanmi would write about the untimely, numbing loss of his passing in the tragic crashing of the Ethiopian Airlines flight from Addis Ababa to Nairobi on March 10th, 2019. His rich and imaginative prose and poetry directed always to the many pressing topics of African Studies were unparalleled in multiple ways, as he drew on an incredible depth of knowledge of literature, literary criticism, history, cinema, politics, philosophy, the humanities writ large, mass-mediated current events, and slivers of everyday life in Nigeria, other parts of Africa, Europe and North America. From his 2002 doctoral thesis in French Studies at the University of British Columbia—*Constructions of Subalternity in African Women's Writing in French*[3]—to his award-winning book, *You're Not a Country, Africa*[4], from his articles over a decade ago in *Pambazuka News* (founded by one of our *Nokoko* board members, Firoze Manji) that provocatively challenged many prejudices and inequalities within African countries and beyond (including the canons of feminist literary criticism in "Disappearing me softly: An Open Letter to Sandra M. Gilbert and Susan Gubar,"[5] (which was one of my favourites) to the brilliant eviscerations of Nigerian politics, economics and sociocultural dynamics as a committed, sympathetic, deeply attached but profoundly disappointed observer in important Nigerian online news outlets like *Sahara Reporters*, *Premium Times*, and long-established papers like the *Nigerian Tribune*, let alone his books published in Nigeria (like his 2001 collection of poetry *The Wayfarer and Other Poems*[6] and his 2015 *Naija No Dey Carry Last*[7] and innumerable social media postings engaging with tens of thousands of followers and beyond, along with endless other examples within a "from/to" rhetorical device, Pius was a public intellectual *par excellence* of African Studies, Nigeria, the world...and one that was viscerally connected to Carleton University's Institute of African Studies and its open-access journal, *Nokoko*.

Professor Pius Adesanmi of Carleton's Department of English and Director of the Institute of African Studies has been, was (as it is too hard at this moment to think of him in the past tense), a founding member of the *Nokoko* editorial board. He not only provided intellectual support, editorial reviews, and boundless energy to our publication but he also is deeply implicated in some of our future endeavours. As we will be discussing shortly on our website, *Nokoko* is building on our revised Mission and Vision Statement[8] with a number of exciting initiatives to broaden our reach and our ability to provide different ways for new and novel voices concerning Africa and its diasporas to be heard. One of these initiatives is to gather some articles published in our first five issues into a book, an idea that Pius came up with as a way to both mark the early, formative

---

3. https://open.library.ubc.ca/cIRcle/collections/ubctheses/831/items/1.0058242
4. https://www.penguinrandomhouse.co.za/book/youre-not-country-africa/9780143527541
5. (https://www.pambazuka.org/governance/disappearing-me-softly-open-letter-sandra-m-gilbert-and-susan-gubar
6. https://www.nwokolo.com/piuswayfarer.htm
7. https://pagebookstore.com/products/naija-no-they-carry-last
8. https://carleton.ca/africanstudies/research/nokoko/

### Afterword: Incorporeal words: The tragic passing of Pius Adesanmi

years of *Nokoko* as well as the tenth-year anniversary of the founding of our Institute of African Studies. While he was busy organizing a conference to mark the anniversary originally scheduled for October 2019[9] (which I strongly suspect may become one of many tributes to Professor Adesanmi), I had been writing part of our Introduction for this book, *Africa Matters: Cultural politics, political economies, & grammars of protest*, to be published by Daraja Press[10]. I sent him my incomplete and quite incoherent draft by email on Thursday, March 7th to have him read, revise, and add his own words and thoughts. He soon emailed me back saying "I leave for Nairobi on Saturday. Plenty of inflight reading and working time!" to which I replied the perfunctory "travel well"; a convention to which I say without thinking and to which I assume would happen automatically, save for this unforetold disastrous trip…

Pius's words in his innumerable writings, the recordings of his talks, some of which are found on the Institute's YouTube channel,[11] and the memories so many of us, from near and far, have of him will continue to inspire, to help us hone our analyses, our writings and our actions within African Studies, *Nokoko* included. But it is unfathomable to think that he will not physically be here in person or behind the keyboard or on his phone to discuss, debate, strategize, plan, commiserate, with his intense focus on the academic, the work, the serious, always leavened with his deep humour, delight, and *joie de vivre*.

Mourning practices are intensely cultural and often highly gendered, with particular bodily, sartorial and linguistic expressions of affect and practices of grief typically marked for women and men, for different family members, friends, dignitaries. Like all things cultural, there is usually a great hybridity, even if (perhaps, especially if) they are said to be defined by particular religious, cultural, national traditions. The grieving is always intense for tragic deaths and for someone with Pius's great stature and regard, it has spread incredibly wide as one has been witnessing in the many digital worlds.

One practice that comes to me during this time of such numbing grief is the ChiShona expression of condolences, *kubata maoko*, to grab the arms. From my interpretation of this phrase and experiencing its use in Zimbabwe, it articulates the giving of physical support to those whose normal control of their bodies has given way in this time of intense shock. It also underscores the solidarity one has with others as we all try to work through the indescribable loss of a loved one, a friend, a colleague, an inspiration, a voice. The physical and virtual arms seeking to support each other now are innumerable, a testament to Pius's brilliance in so many ways. This is but one small expression of such solidarity of what will be many tributes we do in his honour here at *Nokoko*.

**Blair Rutherford**, editor of *Nokoko*
11 March 2019

---

9. now postponed to March 2020
10. https://darajapress.com
11. https://www.youtube.com/channel/UCTuiOo9K4adr5FeyLycW77w

# About the contributors

**Grace Adeniyi Ogunyankin** is an Assistant Professor of Women's and Gender Studies at Carleton University in Ottawa, Canada. She is a feminist scholar who is interested in place-making and subjectivity through the study of African urbanisms and popular culture. In her study of African urbanisms, she is primarily intrigued by how local engagements with the Africa Rising rhetoric and global aspects of the political economy work together to (re)produce spatial and social inequalities and provoke resistance in African cities. Her research focus on popular culture explores the issues of subjectivity and belonging and the use of Afrofuturism and Afropolitan Imagineering in geographic projects that address the colonial politics of difference. Her other research interests include new cities in sub-Saharan Africa, critical race theory, postcolonial and transnational feminisms, postcolonial urbanisms, African postcolonial literature, sexuality and urban space in Africa, and gender, development and NGOs.

**Pius Adesanmi** was Professor of francophone and anglophone African and Black Diasporic literatures, politics and cultures and Director of the Institute of African Studies at Carleton University until his passing in the tragic Ethiopian Airline flight ET302 crash of March 10, 2019. His research fields also spanned Postcolonial writing and social media; Popular Culture, Street Culture in Africa; Postcolonial and cultural theory, and Third World feminist discourses. Adesanmi believed in public intellection and held high hopes for a Pan-African future. His first book, *The Wayfarer and Other Poems,* published in 2001, won the Association of Nigerian Authors prize for poetry. His 2010 book, *You're Not a Country Africa*, won the Penguin Prize for African Literature. The remarkable collection of essays tried to unravel what Africa meant to him as an African and pull apart the enigma that is the continent. A subsequent celebrated book of essays on Nigerian politics and culture, *Naija No Dey Carry Last: Thoughts on a Nation in Progress*, was named to Channels Television Book Club's prestigious list of the best 15 Nigerian books of 2015.

**Sinmi Akin-Aina** holds a Bachelor of Arts in Sociology from McGill University and a Masters of Social Work degree from Carleton University, Ottawa, Canada. Sinmi has done extensive work in research, advocacy, and programming with refugee and immigrant communities and young women, on the African continent and internationally. Her research focus is on urban refugees in Kenya, refugee and immigration policy in Africa and internationally, securitization, 'Acts of Citizenship', and African gender studies. Sinmi is currently pursuing Doctoral Studies at the University of Bielefeld, in Bielefeld, Germany.

**Wallace Chuma** is Associate Professor of Media Studies at the University of Cape Town, South Africa, and a former journalist in Zimbabwe. His research interests include media policy, political economy of the African media, and political communication. He received his PhD at the University of the Witwatersrand, Johannesburg, and has published widely in local and international journals. He also co-edited the book *Media Policy in a Changing Southern Africa* (Unisa Press, 2010).

**Elizabeth Cobbett** is lecturer at the University of East Anglia. Her current research project, *Growth of African Financial Networks*, centres on the political economy of financial flows and emergent financial systems across Africa. Focus is on four countries—South Africa, Kenya, Nigeria and Morocco—for their leading role in shaping Africa's continental financial architecture. Elizabeth was 2012 recipient of the ISA Robert and Jesse Cox Graduate Essay Award, a Social Science and Humanities Research Council of Canada's CGS Doctoral Scholarship, the Senior Women Academic Administrators of Canada: Graduate Student Award of Merit, as well being the winner of the Foreign Affairs and International Trade Canada essay competition: Canada's Experience with NAFTA. 2018 she was visiting fellow at Universidad Autonoma in Madrid and visiting scholar at Carleton's BGInS in 2019. She is currently working on a monograph with Edward Elgar: *The Political Economy of African Financial Centres: The New Realm of Global Finance*.

**W. R. Nadège Compaoré** is a Balsillie School of International Affairs (BSIA) Postdoctoral Fellow. Prior to BSIA, Dr. Compaoré was respectively a Research Analyst at the Canadian Institute for Advanced Research and a SSHRC Postdoctoral Fellow in the Department of Social Science at York University. Her research lies at the intersection of International Relations and Global Political Economy scholarships, which guide her analysis of natural resource governance in Africa, as well as her work on gender, race and politics. Dr. Compaoré's research has been funded by SSHRC, the Centre for International Governance Innovation, and the Canadian International Development Agency. Her work has been published in journals such as *International Studies Review*, *Etudes Internationales*, *Millennium: Journal of International Studies*, and *Contemporary Politics*. Dr. Compaoré is co-editor of *New Approaches to the Governance of Natural Resources: Insights from Africa* (Palgrave, 2015). She holds a PhD in Political Studies from Queen's University.

**Jessica Evans (Ph.D.)** teaches in the areas of sociology and political economy at Ryerson University in Toronto, Canada. Her research examines intersections of race, citizenship, immigration and nationalism in the context of shifting regimes of capital accumulation.

**Gacheke Gachihi** is a Pan-Africanist social justice activist for the last 20 years. He has been involved in community organizing, building grassroots social justice movements in Kenya with Bunge la Mwananchi social movements, Unga Revolution and Struggle for democracy and constitutional reform, striving for a democratic state in Kenya founded on social justice and human rights. He has been involved in struggle for rethinking a Pan- African Movement from a working class perspective and unifying struggle of social movements in Africa against neoliberal globalization. He is Coordinator of Mathare Social Justice centre and Member of the Social Justice Centre Working Group, a collective voice for social justice centers in the informal settlements in Nairobi fighting for social justice and documenting cases of police violence and systematic extra-judicial killings.

**Wangui Kimari** is a postdoctoral researcher at the African Centre for Cities in Cape Town, and the participatory action research coordinator for Mathare Social Justice Centre in Nairobi

**Suvi Lensu** is a PhD candidate in African Studies and Anthropology at the University of Edinburgh and simultaneously part of a research project ANTHUSIA—Anthropology of Human Security in Africa. Previously Suvi has worked for human rights organizations in Latin America and in her native country Finland. As a researcher, Suvi has focused on the subjects of gender, sexuality and identity-politics. In her doctoral studies she examines feminisation of poverty and livelihoods in the East African frontiers. Suvi is also a board member at AntroBlogi, a Finnish language anthropological journal. Enthusiastic about film art, Suvi believes the ways in which identities are written and performed offer an endlessly inspiring field for exploring social change.

**Nduka Otiono** is a writer and an Assistant Professor at the Institute of African Studies, Carleton University. Along with two volumes of poetry and a collection of short stories, he is co-editor of *We-Men: An Anthology of Men Writing on Women* (New Horn & Critical Forum, 1998) and *Camouflage: Best of Contemporary Writing from Nigeria* (Treasure Books, 2006). Prior to turning to academia, he was for many years a journalist in Nigeria. His works have appeared in *Journal of Folklore Research, African Literature Today, Journal of African Cinema, Transfers: Interdisciplinary Journal of Mobility Studies, Wasafiri*, etc. His co-edited volume of essays, *Polyvocal Bob Dylan: Music, Performance, Literature* is forthcoming under the imprint of Palgrave Macmillan Studies in Music and Literature Series. He is winner of a Capital Educator's Award for Excellence in Teaching and a Carleton University Faculty of Arts and Social Sciences Early Career Award for Research Excellence.

**Jacob Rasmussen** is Associate Professor in International Development Studies, Roskilde University. A central part of his research concerns social movements, ranging from grassroots movements, civil and human rights movements, to ethnic groupings and vigilantes. He has undertaken several longer ethnographic research stays in Nairobi and Johannesburg. His work on social movements is informed by a broader research interest in urban politics. https://forskning.ruc.dk/en/persons/jacobra/publications/.

**Blair Rutherford** is professor of Anthropology in the Department of Sociology & Anthropology at Carleton University in Ottawa, Canada. For over 25 years, his ethnographic research in various countries in sub-Saharan Africa has focused on the cultural politics of predominantly rural livelihoods, examining in particular the varied terms, conditions and contestations of labour relations along racialized, gendered, classed and citizenship axes within overlapping (and at times competing) scales of action. He is the author of *Working on the Margins: Black Workers, White Farmers in Postcolonial Zimbabwe* (Zed Books and Weaver Press, 2001), *Farm Labor Struggles in Zimbabwe: The Ground of Politics* (Indiana University Press, 2017), and co-editor of *Sexual Violence in Conflict and Post-Conflict Societies: International Agendas and African Contexts* (Routledge, 2014).

**Wendy Thompson Taiwo** is an Assistant Professor of African American Studies at San José State University. Her writing and research interests include the Second Great Migration, race and wealth, black material and expressive culture, and the Nigerian diaspora. She is currently working on a book that examines black placemaking and displacement in the Bay Area. Her scholarly and creative work has appeared in print in *Meridians: feminism, race, transnationalism* and *Nokoko,* online at *Mn Artists* and *carte blanche*, and in several anthologies including *War Baby/Love Child: Mixed Race Asian American Art*.

**Stephanie J. Urdang** was born in South Africa and lives in the US. Her most recent book is her memoir, *Mapping My Way Home: Activism, Nostalgia, and the Downfall of Apartheid South Africa.* She is a journalist and writer, with a focus on Africa and on gender issues. Her writing on Africa includes *And Still They Dance: Women, War and the Struggle for Change in Mozambique*, as well as articles in magazines, newspapers and academic publications.Her work for the United Nations over three decadesincludedsenior advisor on Gender and HIV/AIDS for UNIFEM, the United Nations women's organization, and as a consultant on gender equality and development. She is currently working on a young adult book with a survivor of the 1994 genocide in Rwanda.

# About the Institute of African Studies

The **Institute of African Studies** builds on Carleton University's long history of expertise on Africa amongst its faculty and graduate students by pulling together the growing number of faculty members and experts in the Ottawa-Gatineau region to provide fresh insight into current and historical dynamics of Africa—from the slave trade that reshaped the continent and the Atlantic world to the richly textured and innovative religious practices and livelihood strategies, from conflicts, refugees, and peace-building efforts to the production and reception of world-renowned and locally-consumed literatures, music and film.

Carleton is the only Canadian university to have a stand-alone Institute of African Studies which also offers degree programs[1]. At the undergraduate level, it provides a Combined Honours and a General program in African Studies in the Bachelor of Arts (BA) degree, an Honours and a General program in Africa and Globalization in the Bachelor of Global and International Studies (BGInS) degree, and a Minor program in African Studies open to all undergraduate students. At the graduate level, it offers a Collaborative Masters in African Studies. It also organizes public events and activities concerning the continent and the African diaspora, and highlights and brings together the ongoing research conducted by its faculty and students.

---

1. https://carleton.ca/africanstudies/?p=2

# Nokoko podcasts

The *Nokoko* journal is committed to a world where people are free from all forms of oppression and exploitation, where respect for individuals' varied differences is maintained, and where everyone can realise their full potentials. *NokokoPod* is a companion to the journal, covering current African issues. It aims to bring forth new perspectives that broaden, trouble, complicate and enrich current discourses. Edited and annotated versions of the conversations will be made available on the journal website. You can find the podcasts and transcripts at https://ojs.library.carleton.ca/index.php/nokoko/issue/view/124.

The Uprising in Algeria – Origins, Current Situation and Future: Hamza Hamouchene
Logan Cochrane, Hamza Hamouchene
Books! Readers, Authors, Publishers and Festivals in Africa: Samira Sawlani
Logan Cochrane, Samira Sawlani
The 2019 Elections in Botswana: Context, History and Future: Chris Brown
Logan Cochrane, Chris Brown
The Conflict in Cameroon: Roland Ngwatung Afungang
Logan Cochrane, Roland Ngwatung Afungang
Reflections on open access from the Global South: Melisew Dejene Lemma
Logan Cochrane, Melisew Dejene Lemma
Protests in Sudan – International Actors and the Future (Part 2): Elfadil Ahmed & Tag Elkhazin
Logan Cochrane, Elfadil Ahmed, Tag Elkhazin
Protests in Sudan – History and Demands (Part 1): Elfadil Ahmed & Tag Elkhazin
Logan Cochrane, Elfadil Ahmed, Tag Elkhazin
The Changing Landscape of Freedoms in Tanzania: Esther Karin Mngodo
Logan Cochrane, Esther Karin Mngodo
Discussing the 2018/19 Changes in Ethiopia: Asnake Kefale
Logan Cochrane, Asnake Kefale
Discussing the 2018/19 Changes in Ethiopia: Hone Mandefro
Logan Cochrane, Hone Mandefro
Discussing the 2018/19 Changes in Ethiopia: Bahru Zewde
Logan Cochrane, Bahru Zewde

www.ingramcontent.com/pod-product-compliance
Lightning Source LLC
Chambersburg PA
CBHW051540020426
42333CB00016B/2019